THE SOAP MAN

THE SOAP MAN

LEWIS, HARRIS AND

LORD LEVERHULME

Roger Hutchinson

Birlinn

First published in the UK in 2003 by
Birlinn Limited
West Newington House
10 Newington Road
Edinburgh
EH9 1QS

www.birlinn.co.uk

ISBN 1 84158 184 4

British Library Cataloguing-in-Publication Data
A catalogue record of this book is available from the British Library

The publisher acknowledges subsidy from the
Scottish
Arts Council
towards the publication of this volume

Typeset by Edderston Book Design, Peebles
Printed and bound by Creative Print and Design, Ebbw Vale, Wales

CONTENTS

LIST OF PLATES

William Hesketh Lever in 1877 at the age of twenty-six

A new kind of packaging: Sunlight Soap aims for the working man's wife

'There's nothing there but slavery': workaday scenes from Port Sunlight

Bringing home the peats in Lewis

The battle of Aignish, 1888

A busy mercantile centre: South Beach Street in Stornoway in the early 1900s

Cottars' cottages on the outskirts of Stornoway, 1900

Members of the Lewis Royal Naval Reserve, winners of the Fleet Rowing Race in 1916

Baron Leverhulme of Bolton-le-Moors in full Masonic costume as Junior Grand Warden of England, 1918

Lews Castle from Stornoway harbour

The windswept lighthouse at the Butt of Lewis

The new laird of Lewis: Leverhulme in 1919

Homes fit for heroes: Leverhulme houses in Stornoway

Machair grazing at Coll, north of Stornoway, following resettlement

Obbe in South Harris shortly before being renamed Leverburgh

Tarbert, the main township in Harris

Sir Harry Lauder, Lord Leverhulme and Provost Roderick Smith at the opening of Stornoway's new bowling green in 1922

The Tarbert Hotel in Harris, with one of the estate's Ford motor cars parked outside

Lord Leverhulme in 1919

A prayer aboard the *Metagama* before her departure for the New World in April 1923

The Hebrideans are coming: Canadian newspapers anticipate the depopulation of the islands

The opening ceremony at the Lady Lever Art Gallery, 16 December 1922

Viscount Leverhulme of the Western Isles

The castle on the hill

PREFACE

The Highlands and Islands of Scotland have seen a greater variety of landowning thugs, philanthropists, oafs and autocrats than any comparable region of the western world. Of them all, William, Viscount Leverhulme must be the most perplexing. He owned the largest single landmass in the Hebridean chain for less than a hundred months, yet in that short period he succeeded in dividing and confusing more intelligent people than seems possible.

To his family and his friends he was a good and simple soul brought low by Highland intransigence. To his acquaintances in Scottish government he became an irritant hardly to be borne. To the Gaelic Society of Inverness he was an English interloper trampling on a fragile heritage. To his fellow businessmen and directors of Lever Brothers he was an old but still formidable widower building castles in the sky. To the people of Lewis and Harris he was all of those things, occasionally at the same time, and ultimately another in a very long line of proprietors who could not bring themselves to understand the attachments and exigencies of their Hebridean lives.

Leverhulme's impact on Lewis and Harris in the first quarter of the twentieth century can still be felt today, and will resonate into the future. The period spent researching and writing this book coincided with the passage of a Land Reform Bill in Scotland. This piece of legislation offers to Highland crofters the right to purchase through their communities the land upon which they live and work.

For most Scottish crofters this represents an historical opportunity: their first chance to take control of their inherited home. Those in Lewis, however, might have enjoyed this privilege for more than eighty years, had their grandparents and their parents accepted an extraordinary offer made by Leverhulme during his brief period as their landlord. Some of them took advantage of this offer, and their democratically accountable landowning trust has subsequently stood for almost a century as a beacon on the bare northern hills. Others, for reasons which have previously been too often misrepresented, were obliged to decline. Only now are their descendants in western Lewis and in Harris able to reconsider the matter.

We may never understand the dead, but we can always try. The story of Lewis and Harris between between 1918 and 1925 was not only the story of a Lancashire industrialist's twilight dream. It was also the legend of the men and women that he encountered at the end of the trail. Many people helped me towards a tentative comprehension of what happened in the northernmost Hebrides in those years, some without knowing it. I am indebted to them all, and especially to Joni Buchanan, Derek Cooper, Torcuil Crichton, James Hunter, Iain MacIver, Cailean Maclean, John MacLeod, Suisaidh MacNeill, Ian McCormack, John Murdo Morrison, Ishbel Murray, and Brian Wilson. All errors of fact and interpretation are, of course, mine.

It is the wish of every author of such a documentary as this to uncover an emblematic tale; one single anecdote as defined as a woodcut, that might stand forever as a metaphor of the whole tangled narrative. No such perfect item here exists, but one comes close. One of the medical officers for Lewis in Leverhulme's time, Dr Harley Williams, dined out for years on legends of the fall. He told a story which - unlike, I hope, most of what follows – has been set in type at least twice before. Apocryphal or not, it bears a third rendering in the fresh light of what we now know of Viscount Leverhulme's character and motivations in the early 1920s, of the company he kept, and of the evidence before our eyes of the proud persistence of community life in the island of Lewis.

Leverhulme (said Williams) was one day visiting a rural village. An elderly woman standing at the door of her house noticed him, and wondered aloud: 'An e sin bodach an t-siabainn?' – 'Is that the old soap-man?'

'She is asking,' explained the proprietor's translator, ' "Is that the Soap King?", my Lord.'

Roger Hutchinson, Isle of Raasay, 2003

SCOTLAND

0   10   20   30   40   50 miles
0 10 20 30 40 50 60 70 80 kilometres

Orkney Islands

Atlantic Ocean

North
Sea

CAITHNESS

SUTHERLAND

Lewis

Harris

North
Uist

The Minch

ROSS-SHIRE   Alness
Dingwall
Strathpeffer

Skye

South
Uist

Applecross

Fraserburgh

Buchan

Inverness

Plockton

Kyle

INVERNESS-SHIRE

Aberdeen

Barra

SCOTLAND

Mull

Edinburgh

Glasgow

IRELAND

ENGLAND

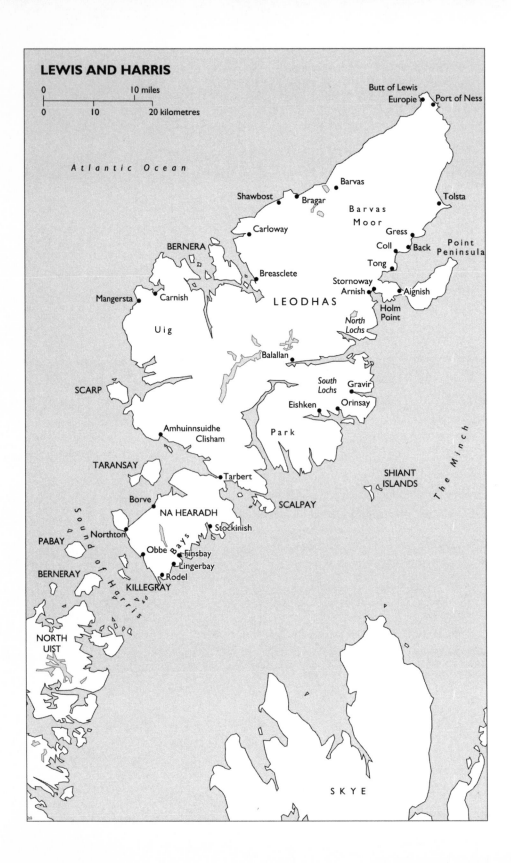

LEWIS AND HARRIS

0 _____ 10 miles
0 ____ 10 ____ 20 kilometres

Atlantic Ocean

Butt of Lewis
Europie
Port of Ness

Barvas
Tolsta

Shawbost
Bragar
B a r v a s
M o o r

Carloway
Gress
Coll   Back   P o i n t
P e n i n s u l a

BERNERA
Tong

Breasclete
Stornoway
Aignish
Arnish

Mangersta
Carnish
L E O D H A S
Holm
Point

*North
Lochs*

U i g
Balallan

SCARP
*South
Lochs*
Gravir

Eishken
Orinsay

Amhuinnsuidhe
Clisham
P a r k

TARANSAY
SHIANT
ISLANDS

T h e   M i n c h

Tarbert

Borve
SCALPAY

Sound
NA HEARADH

PABAY
Northton
Stockinish

of
Obbe *Bays* Finsbay

BERNERAY
Harris
Lingerbay
Rodel

KILLEGRAY

NORTH
UIST

S K Y E

1

THE UNIVERSITY OF LIFE

Port Sunlight was the embodiment in bricks and mortar of the social and industrial philosophy of William Hesketh Lever. In 1887 it was an unpromising windswept area of marshland on the eastern coast of the Wirral peninsula, overlooking Liverpool and the broad Mersey estuary. In search of a new site for his expanding manufactory that year, Lever had boarded stopping trains up and down each bank of the Mersey from Warrington to the sea. He arrived at this reach of sodden fields and clutch of ramshackle shanties named Bromborough, turned to his companion and said: 'Here we are.'[1]

Thirty years later there were those who chuckled at Lever's apparent naivety in buying for development 770 square miles of Hebridean bog and stone. They may not have been familiar with Bromborough in 1887. 'It was mostly,' said one contemporary, 'but a few feet above high water level and liable at any time to be flooded by high tides and thus to become indistinguishable from the muddy foreshores of the Mersey. Moreover, an arm of Bromborough Pool spread in various directions through the village, filling the ravines with ooze and slime . . . it did not, at first sight, seem fitted for human settlement.'[2]

One year later, in 1888, William Lever's wife Elizabeth cut the first wet sod out of the Bromborough turf, the shanties and cabins and the very placename itself were quietly removed, and Port Sunlight – christened in honour of Lever's celebrated brand of household soap – slid optimistically onto the map. There were hard-headed business reasons for this relocation, insisted Lever characteristically at the banquet in Liverpool which followed the turf-cutting ceremony. Bromborough/Port Sunlight was beyond the grasp of Liverpool's harbour dues, saving him four shillings and tenpence on every ton of tallow. The festering mire of Bromborough Pool could be converted to an anchorage with straightforward

1

access to the shoreside soapworks. And that very anchorage in the sheltered waters of the inner Mersey River would release Lever Brothers from their expensive dependence on rail haulage. He could export his cargo by *ship* to the grimy, soap-hungry hordes of late-Victorian London. That might teach the railways to become competitive, and William Lever was ever in favour of teaching others the necessity of competition.

What was more, Bromborough came cheap. Who else in their right mind would bid for such a waterlogged wasteland on the depressed southern outskirts of Birkenhead? He walked straight into a buyer's market; into negotiations with local landowners who were delighted to exchange their unproductive swamp for a handsome handout from the *nouveau riche*. William Lever initially bought 56 acres at Bromborough. By 1906 he had 330 acres of the place. Ninety of those acres were occupied by the Lever Brothers' industrial plant. A further 100 acres were held in reserve. And 140 acres of reclaimed land were devoted to the mock-Tudor houses, gardens, broad avenues lined with spreading chestnut trees and fluting with birdsong, streams and quaint stone footbridges that comprised the model workers' village of Port Sunlight.

William Lever was far from being the first such improver. The notion that capitalism's servants might enjoy longer, healthier and more pro-ductive lives if released from the fearful urban stews had been proposed since the earliest years of the Industrial Revolution. Seventy years before Lever first set eyes on Bromborough Pool the socialist Robert Owen had constructed a workers' mini-state at New Lanark Mills, and had recorded to his great satisfaction improved per capita production. In 1851 the wool-stapling millionaire Titus Salt had built a haven of sanitary terraced housing and schools for his workers beside the River Aire in Yorkshire. Even Queen Victoria's lamented consort Albert had involved himself in the design and construction of new dwellings for the working Londoner.

Sir Titus Salt, Lord Mayor of Bradford, and Prince Albert were, unlike Robert Owen, no proto-communists, and neither was William Hesketh Lever (both Salt and Lever adhered, in fact, to William Gladstone's Liberal Party). They were undoubtedly motivated by some sense of pity for the human flotsam of the nineteenth century. Lever cannot but have been aware of what a paradise a two-up-two-down semi-detached residence in Port Sunlight must have seemed to a worker's family imported from the slums of Birkenhead. But socialist he was not. Trade union officials would repeatedly insist that Lever was the most autocratic and unreasonable employer in their considerable experience of autocratic and unreasonable employers. What agitated the Lancastrian industrialist William Lever was not the Rights of Man. 'There could be no worse friend to labour,' he would pronounce in 1909, 'than the benevolent, philanthropic employer who carries his business on in a loose, lax manner, showing "kindness" to his employees; because, as certain as that man exists, because of his looseness and laxness, and because of his so-called kindness, benevolence, and lack of business principles, sooner or later he will be compelled to close.'[3]

This was not entirely logical. Benevolence and philanthropy and kindness are not automatically anathema – as Lever implied – to efficient 'business principles'. But it was a typically uncompromising statement of intent, and one which would echo down his entrepreneurial years until the end of his life, touching and deeply affecting such distant quarters as West Africa, the Solomon Islands and the Outer Hebrides.

Profits came first. Even Port Sunlight, the young entrepreneur's flagship venture, would have to pay its way before workers could be re-housed. The first twenty-eight 'cottages' (they were actually, by twenty-first as well as late nineteenth-century standards, reasonably-sized houses) would not be built until the soapery workplace was up and running. But once they were built the houses were model dwellings: strong, weatherproof, roomy and warm.

The price demanded of his workforce for such domestic luxury was their acceptance of benevolent dictatorship. The inhabitants of the New Jerusalem by the side of the Mersey would be asked to relinquish virtually all self-determination, and most of their collective rights, in return for a golden security in the young and infinitely promising twentieth century. Their employer, William Hesketh Lever, would become rather more than a dispenser of wage-packets operating in a free market of commodities and labour. He would determine not only the future and conditions of the industry which supported them all, but also the future and conditions of his workers' private lives.

Lever saw no reason to be shamefaced or shy about this presumption. Why should he? 'If I were to follow the usual mode of profit-sharing,' he proclaimed, 'I would send my workmen and work girls to the cash office at the end of the year and say to them: "You are going to receive £8 each; you have earned this money: it belongs to you. Take it and make whatever use you like of your money."

'Instead of that I told them: "£8 is an amount which is soon spent, and it will not do you much good if you send it down your throats in the forms of bottles of whisky, bags of sweets, or fat geese for Christmas. On the other hand, if you leave this money with me, I shall use it to provide for you everything which makes life pleasant – viz. nice houses, comfortable homes, and healthy recreation." Besides, I am disposed to allow profit sharing under no other than that form.'

Eight pounds in 1890 was the equivalent of more than £500 at the start of the twenty-first century. It would have bought a lot of confectionery. The late-Victorian Merseyside proletariat would doubtless have preferred the opportunity to eat goose and drink whisky as well as live in comfortable homes. But it was given only the choice between decent housing and relative destitution. It opted naturally for teetotal Port Sunlight, a model village which had, on the order of its proprietor, no public house. For the late-Victorian Merseyside proletariat had suffered a hundred years of squalor, disease and early, miserable death. Having known nothing else, its priority was to stabilise itself in the face of a future which, however uncertain, could hardly be worse. Trades unionists may have heard Lever's words and grumbled; doctrinaire socialists may have cursed him as a tyrant; but the bulk of his workforce scrambled to accept both his terms and the keys to his cottages.

Thirty years after Elizabeth Lever cut those first turfs at Bromboough, thirty years after William Lever told his employees at an early works outing that they must improve his profits and then trust him to improve their livelihoods, another group of British men and women 400 miles to the north of Port Sunlight would listen to identical sentiments. But the response of the people of the islands of Lewis and Harris would be so unanticipated, so unconquerable, so radically different that it broke the resolve of William Hesketh Lever, and in so doing seemed to break the man himself.

~

William Lever was born in Bolton on 19 September 1851. His father, James Lever, the scion of an old Lancashire family which had turned to trade, was a partner in a wholesale and retail grocery business. The Lever family was Nonconformist. James had met his wife, Eliza Hesketh, at chapel. They made their home in a three-storeyed Georgian terraced house in a comfortable middle-class district of Bolton. And there, in an improving smoke-free atmosphere of abstinence and duty, Eliza gave birth in quick succession to six girls. William was her seventh child and the first boy.

His childhood was unexceptional. Like so many other sons of the northern merchant classes he was thoroughly educated. At the age of six he was sent to a small local private preparatory school run by two maiden ladies. In the day care of the Misses Aspinwall he met two other children: an attractive draper's daughter named Elizabeth Ellen Hulme and a talented boy called Jonathan Simpson. He would marry the former and befriend for life the latter.

William and Jonathan progressed together to a middle school and then, at the age of thirteen, to a Church of England secondary institute. Both boys decided that they wished to study architecture. Eliza Lever wanted her son to become a doctor. William and Eliza were both frustrated. At the age of fifteen William was withdrawn from the Church Institute by his father and put to work in the family grocery concern. Jonathan Simpson remained to study and, finally, to qualify as an architect.

It would not have mattered whether or not the 15-year-old William Hesketh Lever was a bookish child. As it happened he was not: he preferred carpentry to academia; making things to parsing phrases. But as the eldest son of a mid-Victorian north-of-England Nonconformist grocer William was destined for the family company from birth, regardless of his other ambitions and interests. James Lever celebrated the accession of his heir by giving the boy for his sixteenth birthday in 1867 a copy of Samuel Smiles' best-selling manual for character improvement, *Self-help*. Once more, this was not extraordinary. Thousands of teenaged boys had been donated *Self-help* since the book's publication in 1859. The genius of Smiles was not so much to blaze new philosophical trails as perfectly to express the half-formed principles of the Victorian working bourgeoisie. William Lever may have been among the most prominent men to credit Smiles with granting him a template for life, but he was not the only one.

> Laws, wisely administered, will secure men in the enjoyment of the fruits of their labour, whether of mind or body, at a comparatively small personal sacrifice; but no laws, however stringent, can make the idle industrious, the thriftless provident, or the drunken sober. Such reforms can only be effected by means of individual action, economy, and self-denial; by better habits, rather than by greater rights . . .
>
> Daily experience shows that it is energetic individualism which produces the most powerful effects upon the life and action of others, and really constitutes the best practical education. Schools, academies, and colleges give but the merest beginnings of culture in comparison with it. Far more influential is the life-education daily given in our homes, in the streets, behind counters, in workshops, at the loom and the plough, in counting-houses and manufactories, and in the busy haunts of men. This is that finishing instruction as members of society, which Schiller designated 'the education of the human race', consisting in action, conduct, self-culture, self-control – all that tends to discipline a man truly, and fit him for the proper performance of the duties and business of life – a kind of education not to be learnt from books, or acquired by any amount of mere literary training.

William Hesketh Lever digested those sombre sentences and others like them from Smiles' book, along with Dickens and Shakespeare. He never forgot them, for they dignified and justified his young existence. He had been obliged to relinquish 'schools, academies and colleges' in favour of the shop counter and the street. When his tasks at James Lever's warehouse – sweeping the place out before dawn, breaking up wholesale bars and loaves of soap and sugar into retail sizes, stacking delivery carts – seemed an arduous apprenticeship he could fall upon Smiles' wisdom and thank the Lord for delivering him from mere literary training into the infinitely more valuable University of Life.

William naturally progressed more quickly up the business ladder than the other apprentices at his father's warehouse. He started as a dogsbody at a shilling a week. By the age of nineteen in 1870 he was drawing thirty times that amount and working from a pony and trap as a commercial traveller. When he was twenty-one it was judged that he had learned enough about the trade to become a junior partner on £800 a year.

Those were the wages of a prosperous young man. Eight hundred pounds in the 1870s would be worth almost £60,000 today. William Lever paid income tax at only 10 per cent, and the comparative purchase value of the pound sterling was greater than it would be 130 years later. What better to spend his riches on than a wife? He sought out Elizabeth Ellen Hulme and her widowed mother. In April 1874 the childhood friends were married – by the pastor who had baptised them both – at Bolton's Congregational Church.

Having established his bride in a comfortable, newly decorated town house the 23-year-old returned to immersion in the Lancashire grocery trade. He was still working as a traveller for his father, taking orders for butter, eggs, mustard, starch, sugar and soap in the corner stores and village shops of industrial Lancashire. While on the road in 1879 he had noticed a failing grocery concern at Wigan. William bought it out and opened there his own branch of Lever & Co. He then visited Ireland to make contact with dairy farmers and began to receive eggs and butter directly from their source. Having established a cheap, wholesome and plentiful supply William Lever wrapped weighed chunks of butter in greaseproof paper, labelled them 'Ulster Fresh Lumps', distributed them to grocery outlets throughout Lancashire . . . and, daringly, advertised his product extensively in the local press.

Groceries before the 1870s were largely unpackaged, unprocessed and unadvertised. Produce was bought in bulk, marked up and sold off. Eggs were eggs and butter was butter; sugar and salt came in loaves and cakes, and soap in large rectangular bars. Brand names were rare. William Lever would make his astonishing fortune by seizing on one particular essential product, adding extra value to it at source, and transforming it through packaging and advertising from an unremarkable everyday item into an elixir of life, a symbol of leisure and luxury.

He was not the first to do so. As we have seen, in 1867 his first job involved breaking up loaves of sugar for retail. Five years later, in 1872, another former grocery assistant from Lancashire named Henry Tate patented a sugar-cubing machine which suddenly enabled him to package this commodity in standard sizes and allowed his customers to exercise product control. 'Tate's Cube Sugar' lumps very quickly made their 54-year-old inventor very rich – so rich that within twenty years he had assembled the greatest single collection of British contemporary art. They also helped to revolutionise the world of grocery marketing, launching its speedy transit away from the traditional generics of the street-stall into the Modern Age of pre-packaged and branded goods. Tate had not invented a product: sugar had been widely available for centuries. He had invented a new way of selling that product for a greater profit margin. His rapidly escalating business was unlikely to escape the attention of an ambitious young grocer from Bolton.

But William Lever would be unable to reproduce Tate's trademark success with 'Ulster Fresh Lumps' butter. There were important differences between dairy produce and sugar. Butter was quickly degradable, had a limited storage- and shelf-life, was virtually impossible to transport over any great distance, and was therefore disturbingly dependent upon an efficient ratio between supply and demand. No amount of trips across the Irish Sea would invent refrigeration or inject urgency into the Hibernian herdsman. So William Lever remained, for the time being, a wholesale and retail general grocer rather than a manufacturer of consumer goods.

It would have been a satisfactory life for most. Lever & Co thrived and William was able to nurse his own outlet, commissioning his old schoolfriend Jonathan Simpson to design new premises for the Wigan store. By 1884 Lever & Co in Wigan was the biggest wholesale grocer in the north-west of England outside Liverpool and Manchester. William and Elizabeth Lever need never have worked again. To celebrate the tenth anniversary of their wedding, in the summer of that year the couple took off on a cruise of the Scottish Highlands and Islands. They took ship from

Liverpool, called at Oban, and on a fine August day their vessel put in to Stornoway, the main town of the island of Lewis. There they met a waiting Jonathan Simpson, who would accompany them for part of the rest of the voyage. And there, for five or six hours, they saw for the first time the land and the people who were to provide the coronach to William Hesketh Lever's lonely final years.

2

A LAND APART

William Lever saw at Stornoway in 1884 a place of 'natural beauty and variety of scenery' inhabited by people of 'charm and attraction'. There is far more significance in what he did not see.

Lewis was another land, entire unto itself. The largest and most heavily populated of all the Hebrides, it encompassed the placid and picturesque lochside villages in the shadow of the mountains which separated them from Harris, the urban centre of Stornoway and the northerly windswept fishing parish of Ness. It ran from fertile machair soil on the north-eastern seaboard to rocky, cliffbound inlets on its distant south-western shore. A vast, brooding, uninhabited moor of peatbog and low hills dominated its northern inlands, and to the south a kaleidoscope of miniature lochs shone under a flat and shifting sky. These no-man's-lands were deceptive in scale and proportion. While entirely visible from north to south and – mostly – negotiable on foot in a day, they were hostile, uncharted territory to any stranger. From the beginning of recorded time the stern heart of his island had offered refuge to the Lewisman, sanctuary from the incursions of violent invaders or officers of lowland law.

It was and would remain a proud and foreign place. Its size and variety of landscape had meant that, almost uniquely within the Hebrides, Lewis was largely self-supporting. It had been able to survive, if not to prosper, far from and free from the compromises of the British mainland. Its Gaelic language was, in 1884, intact. Its faith was unitary. Its sons and daughters were far-flung, but their belief in themselves as Leodhasaich was strong. Even their accent, in Gaelic and English, was starkly different from that of any other Hebridean island. It was an intelligent, curious, obstinate voice, fully aware of and wholly indifferent to its insistent inflection.

The very size and variety which lent strength to Lewis also divided the place. Men and women would be raised on the eastern peninsula of Point or the northern village of Tolsta who had never seen, nor had any intention of seeing, the western tidal island of Bernera or the southern townships of Uig. They knew of each other, of course, and frequently they knew each other, but Barvas Moor lay like an ocean – or like a mainland mountain range – between them. From Carloway to Mealista there stood whole settlements of black houses: low, thatched, stone dwellings for beast and man that had changed little since the Iron Age. But Stornoway was a modern Victorian port and market town. Since earlier in the nineteenth century its neat rows of dwelling places and commercial and administrative premises had almost all been roofed with slate. In the late 1840s the new proprietor – Sir James Matheson of the Hong Kong opium-dealers Jardine Matheson & Company – had built high above the town a Gothic revival of Stornoway's fortified mansion house which he named, in anachronistic homage to the island's ancestral English name, Lews Castle. Matheson died in 1878, leaving his widow as chatelaine of the building and proprietress of the island.

In 1884 the island of Lewis, without Harris, held some 25,500 people. Ten thousand of them were listed as belonging to the parish of Stornoway, but as Stornoway parish included several densely-populated outlying crofting communities, it is possible that the township itself contained just 3,000 souls. Town and country were important divisions in Lewis. The minority of townspeople exercised a disproportionate influence on the island's life. Outside Stornoway the vast majority of the 20,000 rural dwellers – small-scale agriculturalists and fishing families – were mainly or solely Gaelic-speakers (more than 65 per cent of people over the age of twenty-five in the whole of Lewis in the 1880s spoke only Gaelic). Inside Stornoway, English – an accented, biblical, precise and colloquial English – was virtually universal among the shopkeepers, harbour staff, soldiers and sailors, inn-keepers and ministers, school-teachers and pupils.

Stornoway, one authority had written thirty years before the Levers set foot on Lewis soil,

> . . . is well and regularly built, and its streets are lighted with gas. Most prominent of its buildings are the Parish Church, Free Church and

Episcopal Church, several schools, jail and the Masonic Lodge. On an eminence overlooking the town is the magnificent mansion of the proprietor, recently erected in the castellated Tudor style. The castle grounds are extensive, and laid out with great taste . . .

The masonic lodge contains elegant assembly rooms, reading rooms and a public library. Stornoway has a branch office of the National Bank of Scotland, customs house, a savings bank, sailors' home, hospital and a gas and water works. There are also commodious piers and a building dock . . . fitted to haul up ships of 800 tons burden.

To the north, south, east and west of this tidy and prosperous little burgh perhaps 15,000 people lived and worked on crofts: the small acreage of arable and grazing land which, it had been estimated in the nineteenth century, could support them at subsistence level for only half of the year. And yet Lewis exported, through the commercial hands of Stornoway, a million-and-a-half eggs a year from those crofts; 90 tons of wool; 400 sheep and lambs and almost 2,000 cattle. The island's fishermen, most of whom worked in small sailing boats in hazardous Atlantic seas out of such ramshackle jetty complexes as were to be found at Port of Ness, sent to the mainland through Stornoway as many as 40,000 barrels of herring a year. At 30 shillings a barrel this haul earned for Lewis some £60,000 per annum (which would be worth £4 million today). Substantial quantities of cod, ling, salmon and lobster were also carted to Stornoway, boxed and shipped to the mainland.

On that hot day in August 1884 William Lever observed not only charm and scenic beauty, but also a busy and affluent little port. The 33-year-old may have been surprised to find such respectable mercantile prosperity perched so precariously at the edge of Europe. A short, trim, athletic figure with a mop of dark, well-tended hair, mutton-chop whiskers, an incisive edge to his clean-shaven mouth and chin and deep, fearless, penetrating eyes, he looked out over a calm and sheltered harbour, at the ships lying at anchor and boats drawn up on the shore, at the sturdy stone facings on the front, at the union flag fluttering from the highest turret of Lady Matheson's castle, at the blue-brown hills which lowered in the distance. Like any other tourist, he could never have sensed (had he five or six days, five or six weeks, let alone five or six hours) the rumbles of discontent and expressions of insecurity which disturbed the peaceful tenor of rural Lewis. Nobody in Stornoway, certainly no mason, no banker, no customs officer or harbourmaster was likely to draw those unfortunate phenomena to the visitor's attention. Yet what he failed to see or hear was more important than the tiled roofs, street lights and commodious piers.

A land war was simmering in this island where the sense of land and place was absolute. Leodhasaich shared with their fellow Gaels an attachment to their country which the disinherited Sasuinn would regard as almost mystical. By the late nineteenth century they and their forebears had occupied the same rough patch of land for longer than any other group, indigenous or otherwise, in the United Kingdom. Their millennial unbroken tenure of the Highlands and Islands had resulted in a deep familiarity with and respect for its earth and sand. Every hillside, every lochan, every erratic rock told a story and had a name. They moved from such gnosis only under duress, and they took it with them like a charm.

In an island, any island, such Gaelic sentiment was if anything intensified. The indisputable boundary of the hostile sea limited the homeland as no stone dyke or mountain range could do. Lewis had been created as strictly finite. Its people might settle to the west of Timsgarry, east of Portnaguran or south of the Clisham, but corporeal Lewis would remain behind them, no more and no less than 770 square miles of precious heath.

Every fraction of those square miles was consequently dear. It was in fact beyond price. It had been held in trust by the generations who gifted their patronyms to every Leodhasach. In return it had presented them with house-sites and fuel and crops and grazing land. The men and women who had emerged following the dissolution of the clan system at the end of the eighteenth century, men and women who seemed somehow to believe that they could buy and sell the earth and rock like trinkets, were regarded at best with suspicion and at worst with dull, uncomprehending hostility. The private 'landowner' would be tolerated on Lewis by its proud people for only as long as his or her blasphemous presumptions did not impact severely upon the life and faith of the Leodhasaich.

The certainties of religion replaced the securities of the old order. Throughout the nineteenth century Lewis was intermittently swept by bush-fires of evangelism. In 1843 one-third of the ministers of the established Church of Scotland walked out of the General Assembly to form the Free Church of Scotland, taking with them 50 per cent of the lay membership. The Great Disruption – 'probably the most important event in the history of nineteenth-century Scotland' according to one ecclesiastical historian – was hugely pervasive in the Highlands and Islands. It was a social as well as a denominational revolt. A major touchstone of division between the Moderates (who stayed) and the Evangelicals (who walked) was the patronage of the landowner. The men who followed Thomas Chalmers into the Free Church of Scotland did not believe that the proprietor of an estate should have the right to nominate a parish minister regardless of the wishes of his congregation.

This principle may not have lit many fires in the bourgeois burghs of the south, but it blazed through the industrial cities and through the Gaidhealtachd, whose citizenry had by 1843 a greater appreciation than most of the damage done by unfettered landowning power. Here was one area – a person's communion with their God – into which no factor's interfering hand should stray. Lewis walked, almost to a man and a woman, into the Free Church of Scotland. In 1874 the local presbytery itself estimated that, from a population of 23,479, only 460 Lewis souls were not adherents of the Free Church. Others suggested that non-communicants were slightly, only slightly more numerous: perhaps as many as 1,000 (the figure of nineteen out of twenty Victorian Leodhasaich belonging to the Free Church is commonplace).

But few would dispute the overwhelming appeal of the radical democratic Presbyterian Church on the island. In 1882, two years before William and Elizabeth Lever first visited Stornoway, Reverend Alexander Lee of Nairn told a Lewis joke to the General Assembly of the Free Church. It concerned an elderly woman on the island who was asked by her catechist:

'Can you tell me now what we are to understand by the term: the invisible church?' To which, after due consideration, and with all that air of respect that our Highland people ever manifest towards their spiritual overseers, she gravely replied: 'Well, no, unless it be the Established Church.'

'And . . .' continued Reverend Lee as the laughter subsided, 'and, verily, as far as spiritual work and moral power is concerned, that answer most truly describes the condition of the State church not only in Lewis but also throughout the Highlands generally.'[4]

Throughout the Highlands generally, perhaps . . . but it was Lewis, that large and self-contained world apart, which became the acme of a Free Church society – the home of the largest congregations outside a Scottish city, and the only substantial, clearly defined community in Britain over which a Presbyterian church held virtually unchallenged dominion. It would be difficult to overstate the powerful and enduring relationship between the Free Church and the Leodhasaich. One hundred and fifty years after Reverend Lee's creed had first been welcomed by the thankful islanders, another theologian would write movingly of his grandparents in Lewis, of men and woman who walked with their God, free and proud, belonging to a church which 'lived by the principle that the strong should help the weak'.

The Nonconformist Englishman William Lever may have briefly thought that he understood the Free Church in Lewis. He shared many of its precepts: its respect for the Sabbath; its distaste for alcoholic excess; its belief in social responsibility; its knowledge – and frequent practical appliance – of the chapters of the Old Testament. But he would have been deceiving himself, for this was a sterner, more demanding, more integral faith than ever had sunk roots in the respectable terraces of Bolton. Lever's was a comparatively softer, southern religion; one which allowed for his disbelief in the afterlife, for example, and which could be mollified by the occasional act of worship and address to the village Sunday School.

Most crucially, he would never have encompassed the Free Church's lack of regard, verging on contempt, for landownership. When, in the 1880s, land agitation and land hunger became important social issues in the Hebrides barely a voice would be raised from behind a Lewis pulpit in support of the proprietorial interest. How could the Free Church support that interest, when in the years following 1843, well within living memory, its ministers and its congregations had been locked by landowners out of their places of worship, had been forced to meet and pray on rainswept open ground, to conduct services from the relative immunity of boats anchored offshore?

How could the Free Church, which owed its existence to the principle that the landed classes should not impose their choice of spiritual advisor upon the people, accept that the same landowners should be allowed to dictate in secular matters? It could not and usually it did not. When the war between Lewis crofter and Lewis factor erupted, the man of most respect and influence in any Lewis community – the Free Church minister – may not have helped to man the barricades, and may have preferred to talk down 'wild talk and wild plans among the younger men', but he significantly failed to speak up for the big house. This often entailed remaining silently aloof, which irritated more than one agitator. But there is little reason to doubt the judgement of the historian of the Disruption, James Lachlan MacLeod, that there was 'a depth of feeling within the Free Church in support of the crofters which has been underestimated'.[5]

Just one year before William Lever looked out upon the enchanting prospect of Stornoway momentous and highly divisive issues had been discussed in the town. In March 1883 Sir William Harcourt, the Liberal Government's Home Secretary, had announced a Royal Commission of Inquiry 'into the conditions of the crofters and cottars in the Highlands and Islands of Scotland'. It would become known as the Napier Commission after its chairman, a 63-year-old lowland landowner and career diplomat who had recently been ennobled as the Baron Napier and Ettrick, and its findings and influence would be epochal.

The seven-strong commission (one chairman, one secretary and five members) wasted little time in bending to their task. Their hearings opened in May at a schoolhouse in Braes on Skye, and for the next six months the Napier roadshow performed at venue after venue, night after night, throughout the Highlands and Islands. The voluminous testimony that Lord Napier and his colleagues recorded would stand for ever as a political and social history of the nineteenth-century Gaidhealtachd. Its clarion-call was identifiably similar from island to island, parish to parish – 'Give us land out of the plenty that there is about for cultivation. Give us land at a suitable rent' – but under cross-examination the witnesses' infinite variations on a theme held their hearers, and their subsequent readers, in thrall. The spectre of injustice and land hunger haunted the Highlands and Islands, and it was a spectre with many forms.

The principle which informed so much of the Highland and Hebridean land campaign of the late nineteenth century was one not so much of crofting expansion, as of restitution. Traditional Gaelic attachment to the land meant that any form of private charter which removed it from the communal, clannish township and placed it into the assets column of an individual's accounts was regarded as being as illegitimate as common theft. Throughout the nineteenth century this simmering grievance was exacerbated by a good deal of actual common theft.

Estate sheep farms were built and expanded upon what had previously been common grazing or arable land. Whole vast areas of moor and heath were enclosed and turned into game parks: playgrounds for the shooting of grouse and deer, where a common native of Lewis dared to set foot only in the very real danger of being captured and arraigned as a poacher of 'private' wildlife. Between 1818 and 1886 almost 50,000 acres of the peninsula of Park in south-eastern Lewis had been methodically fenced off, firstly for sheep-farming and latterly as a deer-run. Age-old villages were emptied; their names – Valamus, Ceann Chrionaig, Ceannmore – would henceforth be heard only in legend or in song, and their ruined walls would turn to ridges in the bracken. Many of the dispossessed emigrated to Canada or to Scotland. Those that stayed huddled together on tiny plots of bad land in the vestigial coastal communities: by 1881 an estimated 1,700 people were crowded into nine villages in Park. Those nine villages had between them just 181 crofts. The Matheson Estate itself would grudgingly admit in 1883 that it had spent £100,000 on 'improving' its land – of which huge sum only the pitiful fraction of 1.5 per cent had been newly invested in crofting townships.

On 8 June 1883 the Napier Commission arrived in Stornoway. Precisely one week earlier, on Friday 1 June, the town had been the setting of a large political demonstration. Between 2,000 and 4,000 people (the lower figure is the estimation of the conservative national press; the higher the guess of the organisers) marched through its streets. They were led by pipers and carried red banners inscribed in white and black with such phrases as 'Land To The People'. They came from most parts of rural Lewis; many of them had walked thirty or more miles to attend the rally, and many had sacrificed a valuable day's fishing at the height of the season. They were addressed by Alexander Morrison and other officials from the Stornoway branch of the Lewis Land Law Reform Association, who urged them to testify with the utmost frankness to the Napier Commission.

There would be people in later years eager to testify that land hunger was a minority concern in Lewis, and that land reform was the clarion of a few unrepresentative malcontents. The June demonstration in Stornoway would be in itself sufficient to dispel that illusion. At least one-tenth and possibly one-fifth of the island's rural population marched on that day from Bayhead to the Marybank market stance. As they were almost all men, it is arguable that barely any of the extended family households of Lewis was unrepresented beneath the banners and flags.

This was far from being the only such mass protest. Three months earlier, immediately after the Napier Commission had been announced, more than 2,000 people had trekked from as far afield as Uig in the south-west to Perceval Square in Stornoway (which had been named in tribute to Lady Matheson's family) where, following a prayer led by the Church of Scotland minister Reverend Angus MacIver, twenty speakers were heard and signatures were collected for a petition to William Gladstone at 10 Downing Street. And a few months later the rural forces came once more to town to emphasise their need for land reform.

The burghers of Stornoway did not all smile upon their country cousins. Throughout the Highlands and Islands there existed a sharp divide between the landed and merchant classes and the folk who worked the soil and sea. Until the Third Reform Act of 1884 barely any crofters, who comprised the great majority of the population, had the vote. Even then only those who paid more than £10 in annual rental were enfranchised – which is part of the reason why when crofting rents came to be assessed and fixed, so many of them were fixed at the (relatively substantial) rate of £10 or more per annum.

A gulf between town and country, between the landed and the

landless, between the enfranchised and the unrepresented yawned in Lewis as clearly as in mainland Ross-shire and Inverness. Within the sealed world of the Hebrides it was complicated by social, familial and religious factors. Many an affluent Stornoway tradesman had his roots in the hungry villages of Lochs; many a rural minister considered the campaign for land reform to be a satanic distraction from the work of God. But it would be futile to deny the difference between terrace and thatch. The one, living and bartering beneath Sir James Matheson's towering turrets, either had little concern about the distribution of land on the other side of Barvas Moor, or thought the land campaigners to be arrant socialists, misled by mainland ne'er-do-wells and set to steer Lewis on a course towards anarchy and fiscal despair. The other, reaping meagre harvests from a patch of overworked earth, could see no future without land redistribution and therefore no point at all to a public polity which did not cater for land hunger. 'It is well known,' another islander would remark at a later date, 'that Stornoway seldom, or never, represents Lewis opinion'.

These were the two teams which debated before the Napier Commission in the June of 1883. And the crofting, land reform interest won the verbal contest at a canter. The Commission was faced on the one hand with the shifty plea-bargaining of estate factors, and on the other with tales of distress and injustice eloquently voiced by lay elders and communicants of the Free Church of Scotland. History judges their two starkly contrasted versions of the same era with little difficulty: one is pallid semantics; the other is infused with authentic grievance. More importantly, the gentlemen of the Napier Commission found it relatively easy at the time to recognise where justice lay.

The chamberlain of the Matheson Estate, and therefore effectively the administrator of rural Lewis, William MacKay, appeared to believe that the Commission would be satisfied by a litany of expenses incurred in small-scale industrial investment and road construction. His cause was unlikely to be helped by his assertion that a Lewis crofter could not be expected to know the extent of an acre of land (even Baron Francis Napier was by June of that year aware that if there was one measurement with which Gaelic-speaking crofters were fully conversant it was the measurement of land), and that he himself had only 'a sort of' Gaelic. He was ably countered by the same Alexander Morrison who had helped to organise the previous week's march, and by Donald Martin of Back, an extensive and comparatively fertile crofting region on the flatlands between the moor and the dunes to the north of Stornoway. There is a danger that the younger men, said Martin with commendable prescience, might rise 'as the clans of old rose, if they do not get a hold over the land of which they were deprived for the sake of sheep, deer and grouse.'

Another Donald Martin from north of Stornoway, a sixty-one-year-old mason from the isolated hamlet of Tolsta, had earlier addressed the Commission in the unmistakable voice of the largest sovereign land in the Hebridean archipelago. His is not the only testimony to ring down the centuries from the transcripts of the Napier Commission, but this Donald Martin's statement is possibly the most emblematic and identifiable witness to the conditions and the mood of rural Lewis in 1883.

'I do not,' he commenced, 'intend to say much.' Donald Martin then proceeded to say just enough.

> I have seen the people reduced to such poverty that they were obliged to feed upon dulse from the shore. I see them now reduced to such a hard condition that I can compare them to nothing but the lepers at the gates of Samaria – death before them and death behind them.
>
> I see no prospect of improvement in their condition. If one tack is set free, another tacksman comes into it to confront the people as the Philistines did who came out to battle with the people of Israel. The old people cannot be sent away without the young people. It is only the young people who can go, and it is only they who can support the old people.
>
> If the young people go, the old people will die; and it is hard for them to see the sheep and the deer enjoying the price of their father's blood. I have not much more to say.

What William Lever did not see one year later, as he walked among the charming and attractive citizenry of Stornoway, was a proud, God-fearing and independent agricultural population which was on the fragile cusp between despair and rebellion.

William and Elizabeth Lever and Jonathan Simpson sailed on to the Orkney islands that summer. It became apparent to Simpson that his old schoolfriend was at a crossroads in his life. As they toured the northern isles Lever mused openly about the possibility of buying one of the smaller of the Orkneys. He had never, he said, felt more disinclined to return to the drudgery of wholesale grocery. He could drop out at the age of thirty-three, transfer his business interests to a limited liability company and live contentedly ever after, raising his family on the breezy meadows of Ultima Thule. Instead he returned to Lancashire and made a fortune from soap.

In 1874 his father's company had experimented briefly with distributing an in-house soap labelled 'Lever's Pure Honey'. It did not thrive. One year later the Trade Marks Act refused to license brand names which 'describe the product or make implications about its quality'. 'Pure' and 'Honey' were regarded as falling into those categories. Other businesses were consequently free to steal the last two words of the name, and William Lever learned a lesson in brand identity and registered trade marks.

But he did not forget about soap. One of his lieutenants, the Tynesider Angus Watson, would later recall his chief's own version of the revelation which changed British industry:

> One day when on one of his local journeys, he called at the shop of a small general dealer named Ann Radcliffe, who, when ordering her usual weekly requirements, asked him whether he stocked a brand of what she described as 'stinking soap'.
>
> Not unnaturally he inquired why she wished to buy a soap having such an offensive reputation. She told him that in spite of its objectionable odour it was selling freely in the district because of its generous lathering properties. At once he became interested . . .

Lever himself told variations on the same theme – he had Ms Radcliffe enter the Wigan HQ in person to request her 'stinking soap', and he insisted that the soap had only been rancid on its oxidised outer surface. Once used the smelly layer was washed away – but the moral was the same: soap with a character, soap with an identifiable personality, would be recognised and requested above the common herd.

An admixture of caustic soda or potash or resin and animal tallow or olive oil to make soap had been commonplace in Britain for at least 300 years. Although some commercial soap boilers had operated in London from the beginning of the seventeenth century, it remained largely a domestic industry until the nineteenth century – and an industry chiefly patronised by the affluent.

The industrial revolution altered the soap market. It created a huge new class of people who lived and worked in grimy, soot-encrusted cities, and who were consequently more concerned with personal hygiene than before, and who increasingly earned a household wage which might stretch to buying off-cuts of soap from the grocer's slab with which to wash their clothes and linen and bodies.

The frothy 'stinking soap' which Ann Radcliffe encountered had been given its lathering qualities by the addition of vegetable oils instead of tallow. Vegetable oil was also cheaper than the alternatives and had from the manufacturer's point of view the added quality of a speedier built-in obsolescence: vegetable oil soap was softer and therefore more quickly used. Its unfortunate side-effect was that 'the blending of the vegetable oil with the caustic soda left the soap with a searching and unpleasant smell that permeated everything washed with it.'

Because cheap stinking cleanliness was by the 1880s widely considered preferable to unwashed clothes and skin, this was not an insuperable problem. But it would be better for all concerned if the smell could be eliminated. Lever learned of a similar product in the USA named 'citronella' which masked the odour with a cheap lemon-rind perfume.

He needed a brand name which carried none of the loaded implications of 'Pure Honey' and which had not already been registered. Immediately upon disembarking from his tour of Lewis and the Orkneys William Lever visited a patent agent in Liverpool named W.P. Thompson. Thompson heard his new client's requirements, tore off half a sheet of notepaper and wrote down half-a-dozen possibilities.

Lever rejected them all. He recounted:

> At first blush none of those names appealed to me. I had big ideas of some
> sort of name – I did not know what, but it was going to be such a marvel,
> and when I saw it written down in cold ink – the names that were

possible – names that you could register and fight for, names that did not describe the article, that were neither geographical nor descriptive, did not refer to quality, and got over all the obstacles that the Trade Marks Law has very properly put in front of us – none of them appealed to me.

He put the piece of paper in his pocket and left for home a disappointed man. Some days later he realised that W.P. Thompson had actually delivered the goods. Examining the list once more Lever found himself captivated by a single written word. He panicked and left post-haste for Liverpool to ask Thompson immediately to patent the brand-name 'Sunlight' – 'I was all in a tremble to have it registered, for fear somebody else had got it.'

Nobody else had got it, in Britain or elsewhere in the patented world. In 'Sunlight' Lever had stumbled upon a product name which would be internationally applicable.

It was a good time to enter the soap business. Prices of soap tallow and oils were, in the words of the London manufacturers, 'lower . . . than we had ever previously known', and consumer demand was rising dramatically. Lever initially bought soap in bulk from a factory, wrapped it in imitation parchment which preserved its appearance and delayed gangrenous oxidisation, labelled it as a Sunlight product, advertised it in the trade and local press, and wholesaled it to stores. In 1885 he took the logical step of buying out a failed chemical works at Warrington on the River Mersey, 18 miles east of Liverpool, and began boiling down his own tallow, oil and resin.

William Lever's talent, then and always, was not so much to invent a product as to increase its value and market-share by sophisticated packaging and inventive advertising. He was aware of this – 'He was not a creator,' commented an associate. 'He admitted himself that a great deal that he did in connection with his vast business was not original in creation – but he had a genius for adaptation, and could seize on the possibility of an idea that contained no suggestion for the less adventurous mind.'

A certain uniqueness would be expected of Sunlight soap, a neutrally-scented frothiness which, in homage to Ann Radcliffe, was diligently cultivated in the early months of the Warrington works. But soap was soap, whether it smelled of lemons, of pine oil or of industrial waste. It was a simple and easily duplicated item, and Lever was hypersensitive to the fact that his brand image was crucial.

He quickly established two marketing essentials. He identified the biggest, most neglected and most rapidly expanding consumer sector as being the households of the industrial working class – and so when Sunlight Soap was first sent out to the shelves every part of its promotion 'was brought down to the level of a working man's needs'. And he recognised that the working man himself would not go shopping for his soap. That task would be undertaken by his wife. So the packaging and advertising were aimed at women, which led to much emphasis on the sweetness of Sunlight, on its facility for removing stains and for washing fabrics as well as men's grimy necks, and to some extraordinary copy and illustrations. Oil paintings of pretty little girls in new frocks and lines such as

> 'Twill make your brow as snowy white
> As free from grief and care,
> As when with youth your eyes were bright
> And cheeks beyond compare . . .

were not designed to appeal to the purchasing instincts of Liverpool dockers or engineers on the London and North Western Railway, but to their mothers, their wives and their daughters.

It worked with astonishing speed. Within two years the demand for Sunlight Soap in the north of England alone was such that he had expanded the output of his Warrington works 22-fold. Within three years he was at the Bear's Paw Restaurant in Liverpool to toast the removal of the first sod of land at Bromborough on the Wirral to make way for Port Sunlight. By 1890, just five years after his Warrington factory had begun to churn out 3,000 tons of soap a year, the Port Sunlight factory was producing almost 16,000 tons. William Lever had identified and successfully breached an effectively infinite market. It had all appeared so quick and easy that he was unusually sensitive to allegations of extreme good fortune and felt obliged to repudiate 'those who think we have just held our mouths open and success has dropped in. I do not know whether you have heard the story about Mahomet. When he was told to trust in God and leave the camels free, he replied: "Tie them up and trust in God . . .""

His army of travelling salesmen – or 'district agents' – was vitally important to such an industrialist. A decade after removing to Port Sunlight Lever interviewed and employed in that capacity a young Geordie named Angus Watson, who would remember for the rest of his life the atmosphere of the citadel on the west bank of the Mersey: 'The whole village was dominated by the spirit of Soap. All of its occupants were employed in the industry; not only were they engaged in it all day, but it was a constant source of conversation at night. You could no more escape from its influence than from the odour (not at all an unpleasant one) permeating it from the great factory plant . . .'

Watson, who had personal experience of urban destitution in the north-east of England, arrived for the first time at Port Sunlight directly from 'the grey city' of Liverpool by way of the Mersey Tunnel. It appeared in contrast a kind of Shangri-La.

> The sun was shining, and the trees were breaking into the bright-green leafage of early spring . . . I seemed to have been suddenly transported into another world.
>
> The pleasant little semi-detached red-brick houses each had before them a small garden plot of flowers; trees lined the spacious streets on both sides; the various public buildings were tastefully designed, and the church in the centre of the village was a beautiful building. Even the great factory and suite of offices dominating the whole were attractively laid out. There was an air of freshness and prosperity about the whole place.
>
> After a short walk down the main thoroughfare I found my way into the great offices in which, I was told, there worked some 3,000 employees. I felt that at last here was Industry carried on under ideal circumstances.

Watson discovered Lever at his command post, a glass-walled office at the centre of the works from which he could survey the whole of his staff. Significantly, the twenty-five-year-old applicant considered 'the Chief' to be 'about forty years of age'. The year was 1898: William Lever was almost fifty. Not many people forgot their first encounter with the 'short and thickset' Napoleon of this utopian industrial empire, and Angus Watson would recall his introduction – amplified by four succeeding years of business association – vividly four decades later.

At this time, 'his physical and mental zenith', Lever had

> a sturdy body set on short legs and a massive head covered with thick, upstanding hair, he radiated force and energy. He had piercing, blue-grey, humorous eyes, which, however, flashed with challenge when he was angry. A strong, thin-lipped mouth, set above a slightly receding chin, and the short neck and closely set ears of a prize-fighter.
>
> He possessed great physical strength, and a gift of sleep which was always available at his command. His dress was almost always the same. A grey tweed suit, a Victorian-fashioned collar, with a carelessly-worn made-up tie, and a tall grey hat. A white silk shirt, and black shoes on his small, shapely feet. Hands carefully attended to, which were also small. An expression always alert, but rather strained because of the slight deafness, which increased as he grew older . . .

This stern and strangely dainty man had become a committed member of William Gladstone's Liberal Party; a party which in government had exceeded the general expectations of the Napier Commission and passed in 1886 reforms which greatly benefited the crofters of the Scottish High-lands. There is no evidence that William Lever either knew of or cared about such Gaelic intricacies at the time. His mission then was firmly based in the industrial south of Britain: he stood unsuccessfully in 1892 and 1895 for the parliamentary seat of Birkenhead. The double rejection by his Wirral electorate reduced neither his political ambitions nor his growing conviction that he could change the world as effectively from outside Westminster as within it. He was, said Angus Watson, 'not one man, but three or four . . .'.

> First, there was the business man, brisk and keen. He could seize the heart of a business proposal almost instantly, and before the problem was fully presented to him he had arrived at his decision upon it. His restlessly active mind was constantly turning over some new enterprise; no sooner had he reached one goal, but another and a greater appealed to him.
>
> Money for its own sake had little attraction for him, but acquisitiveness in its deeper sense was a passion. He had a genius for organisation, and would take infinite pains with tireless patience to achieve his object. He loved to think on a big scale, and would not readily accept defeat when he had decided on his course of action.
>
> He had a keen sense of humour, so much so that he carried in his pocket a little note-book in which he recorded any amusing story or circumstance

that presented itself to him. He used this to his own advantage when the opportunity offered. If he was not making progress with a business negotiation he would suddenly break off to tell a story which had tickled him, and this he did so humorously that in the hearty laugh which followed this recital he seized upon the situation and gained his point.[6]

Sharp and pugnacious, William Lever was shot through with sentiment and insecurity. As he perceived those delicacies to weaken his personality (and weakness was not to be tolerated) he masked them. Humour clearly did not come to him naturally, so he armed himself with a stand-up storyboard. Recreation – even sober recreation – was a foreign concept, so he forced himself to exercise each morning with dumb-bells and skipping ropes, and when time and the weather permitted by walking or riding before breakfast. He had a self-made man's profligacy with large sums of 'private' money and parsimony with the business pennies – 'I have watched him for a quarter of an hour while he re-worked a cable so as to save two shillings in its transmission, and I have also seen him spend five thousand dollars on a fur coat for a friend in financial embarrassment whom he knew would not accept money from him.'

He was always aware of the 'somewhat narrow' secondary education of the Victorian middle classes that he had received. The answer was to become an auto-didact. His reading as an adult progressed along 'definitely limited lines', but progressed nonetheless. He had always been interested in architecture, and his eye for building design – domestic, commercial and civic, all of which were required at Port Sunlight – was probably the most advanced of his cultural sensitivities.

No sooner were the profits pouring into his account than he began to collect art. His taste was commonplace: moderate and patriotic. The pre-Raphaelites were by the 1890s a safe enough choice, as was Wedgwood pottery and Regency needlework. Much of his representative art was bought with an eye on the advertising of soap. Canvasses of winsome children in need of a bath were especially favoured. (Although on at least one occasion his gauge of public taste betrayed him. Lever acquired an oil portrait of a reclining nude by the immigrant Dutchman Lawrence Alma-Tadema, presumably on the grounds that it was titled 'The Tepidarium' and depicted the lady languorously cleaning herself. His colleagues appear to have pointed out that Alma-Tadema's lubricious realisation of the fully naked adult female form, while slightly qualified by the strategic presence of an ostrich feather, was too explicit even for a fin de siècle poster campaign.)

As his later political comments and actions would illustrate, he was a supporter more of the indomitable person of William Gladstone than of the 'modern' Liberal Party. The Grand Old Man of British politics was invited – while leader of the opposition at the age of eighty-three – to open Gladstone Hall in Port Sunlight, a men's recreation centre and (teetotal) dining room. Gladstone was charmed both by the compliment and by the industrialist's brusque affection.

Lever was markedly uxorious. He would often comment that he could never remember life without Elizabeth, and 'in his domestic circle he was deeply affectionate. Those who were bound to him by ties of blood were never forgotten, and remembered with generosity and tenderness.'

Behind the piercing eyes and beneath the ruthless negotiator there lay a sentimental soul. Angus Watson's job interview on that day in 1898 almost foundered on the matter of wages. Lever was disinclined to pay the bright young Geordie his required rate, until he learned that Watson's father had recently died and there was a widowed mother and two sisters to support, whereupon 'he immediately agreed to give me what I asked'.

'By temperament he was a sentimentalist,' concluded Watson. 'It was easy to appeal to his emotions, and he was readily stirred by any story of distress or misfortune.'

One more thing was readily apparent. As the nineteenth century turned into the twentieth, William Hesketh Lever was possibly the wealthiest sentimentalist in Britain.

3

ORGANISE, DEPUTISE, CRITICISE

The last two decades of Queen Victoria's reign saw an unquiet peace in the Highlands and Islands of Scotland. William Gladstone's well-founded fear that the peasant Gaels of the far north-west might follow the Gaels of Ireland into riot and uprising had led him to do for one what he could not do for the other.

The failure of Gladstone's ambition to give Ireland Home Rule sundered parliament and the nation, and fatally divided his party. Few people in Scotland were at that time requesting anything like Home Rule. The people of the north and west were undeniably a part of Scotland, and what they wanted was land reform – from whichever source it may arrive. So before retiring finally from political office William Gladstone intervened and outflanked the recommendations of Baron Napier's Commission.

This was especially remarkable from a prime minister who personally owned large tracts of private land on the Celtic fringes, and who in common with much of the rest of his class took occasional holidays in the Highlands as a guest of the nawabs of recreational estates. It is a tribute, perhaps, to his famous incorruptibility that William Gladstone was able to ignore the familiar tones of the drawing room and the shooting lodge and hear instead the foreign language of the Highland rural labourer.

Or perhaps it was the echo of history to which this other sentimental Liberal listened. His appointed investigator, Baron Napier, had delivered his report at the end of 1883. The baron recommended that larger crofting tenants should be given a form of secure tenure, but that poorer tenants should be helped to emigrate; and that the subsequent future of crofting should be formalised around a township system which administered common grazings. In offering these solutions Napier put clear blue water between himself and the Land League's demand for the 'Three Fs' – fixity of tenure, free sale and fair rent for all. This would still not be enough to mollify the Highland landowning community. The two members of the northern acreocracy who sat on the commission, Sir Kenneth Mackenzie of Gairloch and the Inverness-shire Tory MP Donald Cameron of Lochiel, both insisted on publishing abstentions from the recommendations, with Lochiel accusing Napier of falling for the romantic fable of a prelapsarian Highland golden age before the dawn of private capital.

Napier, therefore, pleased no single party to the dispute. Worse, neither did his advice win the affections of Home Secretary William Harcourt or of William Gladstone. 1884 and 1885 were not easy years for their Liberal government either at home or abroad – the arduous months would climax in its collapse – and it is therefore instructive to note that while Harcourt appeared to be limiting his interest in the affairs of the Scottish Gaidhealtachd to persuading Highland proprietors to formulate their own plans, Gladstone found time to write a memorandum almost of rebuke to his Home Secretary.

In January 1885 William Harcourt received a letter from his seventy-five-year-old Prime Minister which asserted the astonishingly radical principle that the indigenous inhabitants of places such as the island of Lewis had a historic title to their land, which had been usurped by privateers like Sir James Matheson (a former Liberal MP as well as owner of Lewis) and – by logical extension – Cameron of Lochiel and Mackenzie of Gairloch.

It was this 'historical fact', wrote Gladstone, 'that constitutes the crofters' title to demand the interference of parliament. It is not because they are poor, or because there are too many of them, or because they want more land to support their families, but because those whom they represent had rights of which they have been surreptitiously deprived to the injury of the community.'

Having accepted, complete and undiluted, the historical analysis of the Highland Land League, it was but a short step for this Prime Minister to embrace the same solutions. A Crofting Bill was drafted. It was just as quickly shelved. In June 1885 the wider history of Gaelic discontent, in the form of the Irish Question, stepped in and through a vote of no confidence forced Gladstone and Harcourt to resign.

It was certainly never their intention, but the Irish Gaels did their Highland cousins a favour. Lord Salisbury's Conservatives were obliged to enter a period of minority caretaker government and to call a General Election at the end of 1885. It would be the first national poll following the Third Reform Act, and therefore the first one in which some crofters – those paying more than £10 per annum in rent – would be entitled to vote.

'Crofter candidates' supported by the Land League were put up in every one of the crofting constituencies. Four of them were immediately returned to parliament. The four were returned from Inverness-shire, Argyll, Caithness and Ross and Cromarty. (A fifth county, Sutherland, would fall to the crofters' cause in the following year.) The most densely populated part of the parliamentary seat of Ross and Cromarty in 1885 was the island of Lewis.

Ross and Cromarty had since 1847 been held in the Liberal interest, almost without challenge, firstly by the proprietor of Lewis, Sir James Matheson, and then by his nephew Sir Alexander Matheson of Lochalsh. In 1884 Sir Alexander had been replaced by another landowning Liberal, the twenty-four-year-old Ronald Crauford Munro-Ferguson of Novar.

The Third Reform Act had increased by 500 per cent the Ross and Cromarty electorate. In such an area as rural Lewis the enlarged franchise was yet more dramatic, rising from a mere handful of property-owners to thousands of crofting tenants. Despite being obliged to register themselves as new voters at the Ross-shire county seat of Dingwall, more than 100 miles and at least a day's journey away on the east coast of the mainland, a huge number of freshly enfranchised Leodhasaich were qualified to enter a polling station in the November and December General Election of 1885. Alive to the origins and aspirations of most of his county's additional 7,000 voters, Munro-Ferguson of Novar – who previous to the passing of the Third Reform Act had been a fervid opponent of the crofters' cause – promptly changed his mind and became in public an ardent supporter of the Land League and its Three Fs.

The electorate was unconvinced. Prior to their sitting MP's visit to Lewis in October 1885 the Park branch of the Land League was assured by its secretary that: 'Novar is a landlord, and that is sufficient reason why we should do all in our power to oust him at the general election. Whatever landlords say, we cannot place any confidence in their promises, when we consider how they have acted towards us during the last eighty years.' Novar arrived in Stornoway to a violent reception: the police had to escort him from the steamer to the Royal Hotel.

And when the last vote had been lodged in mainland and insular Ross-shire in December 1885 the Matheson/Novar era was over. (So too was that, immediately to the south in Inverness-shire, of Cameron of Lochiel, who was defeated by his fellow tribune on the Napier Commission, the reformer Charles Fraser-Macintosh.) The new Member of Parliament for Lewis and for the rest of Ross and Cromarty would be the crofters' candidate Dr Roderick MacDonald, a forty-five-year-old physician, surgeon and coroner who had been born in Skye but whose successful career in London caused him to be labelled a 'carpet-bagger' by his foes. In the event MacDonald's radical track record was held by the electors to count for more than his place of work – he had been treasurer to the London Crofters' Aid and Defence Fund and supported reform of the House of Lords – and he polled 4,942 votes to Novar's 2,925.

Previous to 1885 the total electorate in Ross and Cromarty had numbered no more than 1,720. *The Scotsman* newspaper, lamenting the defeat of the landlord, described the 2,000 people who represented Roderick MacDonald's clear majority as 'illiterates' who were unable to read English and consequently 'knew nothing of politics'.

If they knew nothing of politics they had exercised their new powers with remarkable unity and purpose. Dr MacDonald's views, according to the *Invergordon Times*, 'especially on the land question, were in entire harmony with the vast majority of the electors, who were sickened of landlord rule, and who were determined that they would have a member who thoroughly understood their wants and wishes to represent them. The victory was hailed with great delight throughout the counties by the crofters, and bonfires blazed and general rejoicings took place . . .'

Roderick MacDonald would represent Ross and Cromarty and the island of Lewis at Westminster until his retirement in 1891, when the seat was inherited by another crofters' candidate. Throughout most of his parliamentary career MacDonald was, however, conspicuously silent on the issues which he had been elected to raise. Raids came and raids went, crofters demonstrated, were arrested, were tried and were imprisoned, and Dr Roderick kept his counsel. His reticence may have been due to ill-health or to a previously unsuspected native shyness. But it seems most likely that he found himself compromised by love.

For in January 1890 the campaigning Skye surgeon made a late and politically astonishing marriage to Frances Maryon Perceval. His new wife was the grand-daughter of the only British prime minister ever to have been assassinated, the Tory Spencer Perceval, who in 1812 was shot dead in the lobby of the House of Commons by a bankrupt bearing a grudge.

Such a Trollopian liaison would have been entirely digestible by his electors. His wife's other family connections were the problem. Frances Maryon was also related to Lady Jane Matheson, the widowed pro-prietress of the island of Lewis, whose mother and family had become familiar faces on the island (their name was, as we have seen, left on Stornoway's Perceval Square). Roderick MacDonald found himself not only sleeping with the enemy as a guest in her citadel; this middle-aged Romeo had also, as a crofters' champion, married into the Capulet household. He retired from the seat in the following year. MacDonald died at the age of fifty-four in 1894, having travelled a long way from his father's Waternish croft.

None of this star-crossed canoodling was foreseeable in the dizzy year of 1885. In common with other leading Liberals Ronald Munro-Ferguson of Novar was advised by the Land League never again to oppose a crofting candidate. He took the advice and disappeared to rep-resent Leith Burghs, closer to the comforting embrace of *The Scotsman*'s editorial arm. A career in the diplomatic service took Munro-Ferguson later to the Governor's chair in Australia, to the title of Viscount Novar in 1920, and to yet another bizarre re-engagement with this present narrative in 1922 when Ronald Crauford Munro-Ferguson, Viscount Novar and once, however briefly and however long ago, the Member of Parliament for the island of Lewis, became at the age of sixty-two the Secretary of State for Scotland in the Conservative government which was elected at the end of 1922.

At not one election after 1885 was a person who opposed land reform returned to parliament to represent the island of Lewis. At most general and by-elections such candidates did not even bother to court the Hebridean vote.

Gladstone regained office once more as the national results rolled painstakingly in, and recording officers grew weary of their suddenly onerous responsibility to a majority of the male population, and 1885 turned into 1886. But he returned to Downing Street with the additional spectre at his shoulder of Liberal hegemony in north-western Scotland being wiped out by newly enfranchised local militancy.

If a spur were needed to force a Crofters Holdings (Scotland) Act into life, that was it. A Bill which had largely been formulated to salve the weeping sores of rural Ireland, but which would never be applied by a British government to Donegal and Cork, was whittled into the mould of the Highland littoral and the Hebrides and became law in the summer of 1886. It was largely unopposed by the official Conservative opposition. Late-nineteenth-century Tories, who had been educated by Disraeli in the virtues of One Nation politics, recognised the need for some kind of amelioration to the crofting community, if only to stave off more civil unrest. And they found it ideologically difficult to protest too loudly against the creation of a new class of hardy, self-sufficient tenant agriculturalists, even while the Tories deplored those agriculturalists' baffling but evident affinity for the militant politicking of the urban proletariat. A century of sweet and sour relations between the Conservative Party and the Scottish crofter was born in 1886.

As the years passed, the 1886 Act would achieve mythological status in the Highlands and Islands (and would, not coincidentally, help to re-establish that belt of Liberal representation around the north-western seaboard). It dawned on people slowly, but dawn on them it did, that following 25 June 1886 each and every one of Scotland's crofters suddenly possessed virtually unassailable security of tenure at a fair, independently assessed rent. To other, later citizens of Britain such benefits might appear nugatory. To Scottish Gaels in the 1880s they were transforming. After so many lifetimes of loss and grievance they must adjust to a new freedom from fear. They could plough, breed and build without the oppressive threat of eviction. It was only a successful battle, but to many of the people of Lochs, Uig, Tolsta and Ness it was a battle which indicated that the war was there for the winning.

All they needed – and they still needed it badly – was the land. Once the land was won, the moment it had been retrieved acre by petty acre from shooting and sheep and brought under crofting legislation, it would be theirs by law for good. This is largely why the Park deer forest and Galson and Aignish farms in Lewis were the objects of raids and demonstrations in the winter of 1887/8. These actions, in common with other post-1886 land seizures, were represented by the landowning classes as being mere anarchy unleashed by Gladstone's leniency. Having been given an inch, they argued, the irresponsible crofters were now grabbing miles of private land under the impression that they would receive unlimited government support.

The truth was more complex. It may be viewed from either side of the political spectrum. For the Right the continuance of unrest in the Gaidhealtachd was evidence of one of the major landowning nostrums: that the Highlands and Islands were suffering not from bad policy, but from a great historical imperative which had created a kind of territorial inflation. Too many people were chasing too little land. The solution, as even Baron Napier had seemed to realise, was not more redistribution but depopulation by way of assisted emigration.

To the Left the problem appeared in a different light. Nobody had ever claimed that 'fixity of tenure and fair rent' would alone deliver Paradise. They were an essential halfway house, but they would not solve the land problem. Unlike Irish peasants with their backyard pigs and allotments of potato-patch arable land, unlike the kailyard agriculturalists of the Scottish lowlands and east coast, Highlanders depended chiefly upon grazing animals. On the thin soil of the far north-west sheep and cattle required to forage across large tracts of hillside and glen. Without access to all the traditional 'common grazings' of heather-covered moor and grassy bog the crofter could not maintain adequate flocks and herds.

In an island such as Lewis, where the amount of available grazing was strictly limited, the exclusive devotion of tens of thousands of acres to game-birds and deer was most keenly felt. It was proposed by one agitator in the years before the 1886 Act that if all the surface of Lewis was available for crofting pasture, the island would be able to support 80,000 rather than 24,000 people. That is doubtful – almost as doubtful as the claims of William Hesketh Lever for an even more explosive Hebridean revival some forty years later. But what cannot be disputed now, and could not seriously be denied then, is that if the 50,000 acres of Park were free once again to be grazed by their cattle and sheep rather than enclosed for the landowner's grouse and venison, the existing population of south-eastern Lewis – where in the late 1880s perhaps 1,000 people were landless squatters – would have enjoyed a more stable and comfortable life. And if they could not run their beasts on Park they could run them nowhere, for over the hill lay not another county, not another glen. At the other side of the heights of Beinn Mhor, Gormol and Uisenis and the cliffs of Kebock Head lay nothing but the open sea.

They had attempted to operate within the new property market. When the section of Park which had been enclosed as a sheep farm was put out to let, people from the cramped remaining villages duly applied and petitioned not for the whole of it, but for a few smallholdings in the lonely hills beneath Ben Eishken. They knew that land – 'We remember the men that left it. They were old men when we were boys, and to the day of their death they used to mourn their removal from Park, and wished to go back to it.' Their applications were ignored.

The township of Balallan was always the first settlement of any size to be met by the traveller entering Lewis from Harris. It sprawls lengthily along the great north road between the needling inlet of Loch Erisort and the low hills of southern Lewis. With the sea to its south and the moor to its north, there was never anywhere for Balallan to go but east and west along both sides of the winding thoroughfare, so east and west it went, until traversing the settlement from one extremity to the other amounted to almost an hour's hike from Ceann Loch Erisort to the city line with Laxay.

Balallan and neighbouring Laxay were unlikely refuges, but so they had become to the people of Park and South Lochs when their villages were emptied in the nineteenth century. A sixty-three-year-old told the Napier Commission in 1883 that he had arrived there in 1828, 'along with my father and another ten crofters, who were driven away with all their belongings from their thriving and agreeable holdings at Aline and Park, in which they knew nothing beyond prosperity and happiness'. The blue remembered hills of Aline, ten miles away, are almost always visible from Balallan and Laxay. The huddled, thatched shoreline villages of South Lochs and Park sat just across the thin neck of Loch Erisort, as alive as a memory, as tantalising as a dream and as untouchable as a mirage.

Balallan's slender resources of a sheltered anchorage and good inshore fishery supplemented by rough grazings were stretched to capacity by the immigrant population from the eastern peninsula. And like most harbours of the dispossessed, in any country at any time, Balallan became a melting pot of grievance. Its branch of the Land League was strong and active; its schoolteacher Donald MacRae – a Gaelic-speaking incomer from Plockton in Wester Ross – was a celebrated radical; it was from Balallan that the call had been made during the 1885 election to mistrust the sitting MP Munro-Ferguson of Novar simply because he was a Highland landowner.

On Friday 11 November 1887, it would later be reported in the Scottish press, people from all over south-eastern Lewis gathered at Balallan and resolved that 'groups of crofters and cottars . . . should leave the various townships and meet at a place half-way between Balallan and Eishken, then to proceed into the forests of Park, in one body, and shoot all the deer they might come across or drive them into the sea.'

This incursion, half-uprising and half-demonstration, was scheduled for Tuesday 22 November. Far from any attempt being made to conceal the plans, they were broadcast as widely as possible. The national and local press was informed. The proprietress Lady Jane Matheson, the lessees of the Park game forest (an English manufacturer named Joseph Platt and his wife Jessie) and Sheriff Alexander Fraser in Stornoway were all not only told of the impending action; they were invited to the district to observe for themselves its immediate cause: the poverty and land-starvation of the people of South Lochs and Park. They declined.

Day broke at 8.30 on the morning of Tuesday 22 November to the sound of horns in the villages of South Lochs, horns blown into the winter air from Balallan and Laxay to Gravir and Calbost. Men then began to walk eastward across the marshy head of Loch Erisort from Balallan and westward down the neat defile of Glen Gravir, each group of forty or more carrying supplies, sail-cloth and rifles. Pipers were in their van, and red flags waved, and women and children cheered them as they passed.

The contingents met at the head of Loch Seaforth, 'half-way between Balallan and Eishken'. Their destination was not the estate house and control centre at Eishken, as some had apparently feared, for as they marched westward along the narrow shore from Seaforth Head they encountered the redoubtable Mrs Jessie Platt (who had been telegraphing the Scottish Office with alarmed requests for government help in quelling the insurrection) and her head gamekeeper Murdo MacRae. There followed one of the memorable exchanges of the Lewis land struggle. Urged in English by Mrs Platt to stop and go home the men replied, in English, 'We have no English, my Lady.'

Murdo MacRae then intervened in Gaelic with the question: 'An ann as ur ciall a tha sibh?' ('Are you out of your minds?')

There was no answer. MacRae pressed on with an idiomatic phrase of slight ambiguity: 'Co tha air ur ceann?' ('Who is on your head? / Who is your leader?') A man from Cromore replied: 'Tha ar bonaidean.' ('Our bonnets.')

They marched on by the dark waters of upper Loch Seaforth to an expanse of low ground at the north-western edge of the Park deer forest. They pitched camp, using the sail-cloth as canvas, opposite the village of Airidh a Bhruaich, whose dim house lights were visible a mile away across the kyle as evening fell. They drove and shot deer, cooking some carcasses and ferrying the remainder over to the inhabited shore, where familiar hands lugged them to land and hid them away in the moonlight. (Those carcasses transported for later use were in the event the only Park deer to be 'driven into the sea'.) Fishing boats carrying meal and peats arrived from South Lochs and journalists – filling their notebooks with atmospherics – disembarked, squelched through the shallows towards the sparks from the camp-fires and the gun-toting shadows, and roamed wide-eyed and wondering about the encampment.

They were, on that fine November night, the matinee critics at a melodrama. The Park raid was a staged event. The men with sail-cloth tents and rifles had no more intention of staying there than of burning down Eishken Lodge or guillotining Mrs Platt. They were dramatising their simple requirements and their elementary rights for an audience which had failed to understand them when they spoke plain English. If this meant recreating that same prelapsarian illusion which had been invoked against them by the likes of Cameron of Lochiel, the dreamworld of a free and happy people roaming and thriving on the fruits of their own land, then recreate it they would.

And recreate it they did. The weather favoured them that late November night. The visiting press could easily have been drenched and frozen, or drowned in a squall in Loch Seaforth while being rowed over from Airidh a Bhruaich. But it was calm and mild and dry, and the man from *The Scotsman* was escorted by schoolteacher Donald MacRae (his appointed 'interpreter') into a sylvan idyll. The definitive account of that soiree in Park was assembled later by a contemporary Highland writer and historian, James Cameron, who had the good fortune to be present and was thereby able to combine his own experience with the surprisingly unanimous press reports and summon up . . .

a camp, 100 yards long, illuminated with five peat fires, each as large as a haystack [a stook, or Highland hay-rick, being about the size and shape of a small bonfire].

Over the one in the centre was suspended a magnificent specimen of a Royal Stag. Within yards of this fire there was another of equal size above which there was the carcass of a deer broiling, and there was an immense cauldron with Irish stew.

Behind these fires there were raiders sitting in couches of heather and stone, pretty much in the fashion of their forefathers when they roamed the ancient forests of old Caledonia. Some were eating, others attending the fires, others chanting songs . . . On the approach of strangers no attempt was made to stop them; on the contrary they were asked to listen to the cause which induced them to resort to such methods of hunting for food, and to invite them to partake of a share of what was going.

Then there was the dramatic effect of the white-headed patriarch from Marvig. Alastair Tharmoid, Alastair MacFarlane, standing bare-headed with his back to the blazing peat fire, with uplifted swarthy hands invoking a blessing in rich sonorous Gaelic upon the venison festival.

This marriage of a verse of the Old Testament and a scene from *Les Brigands* was certainly impressive to southern eyes. It had the additional virtue of being not too far removed from actual Victorian life in the Hebrides, whose pastoralists and hunter-herders had much in them of Moses, Ruth and Joshua, with an occasional necessary streak of banditti. And if this was indeed drama, it was drama with the incidental benefit of supplying meat to hungry homes. Of the 500 or 600 deer in Park on the morning of 22 November, it was later estimated that several score had been culled and surreptitiously exported by the evening of the following day.

The Park raid ended on that day, 23 November 1887, when Sheriff Fraser caught up with a group of men and read them the Riot Act, complete with explanatory Gaelic sub-titles. They went home peacefully. Their job was done. In the words of Joni Buchanan, a chronicler of the Lewis land struggle, 'the people of Lochs had, in a superbly effective manner, put their case to the nation – a fact reflected in the massive media coverage and subsequent parliamentary attention given to the raid.'

The effect of their *coup de theatre* would be quickly indicated by incidents elsewhere in Lewis and by the response of the arms of the law. The sympathetic William Gladstone had been removed from Downing Street and replaced by a Conservative administration. Substantial detachments of the military sailed from the mainland to Stornoway in the company of police reinforcements, and four fighting ships of the Royal Navy augmented by a mailboat and a Fishery Board cruiser were ordered to make their presence known in the Minch. This sub-colonial gunboat diplomacy was not new to the Highlands and Islands, where armed police and the military and men-of-war had been deployed to face down land-grabs on previous occasions. But the scale of the response to the Park raids indicated that the authorities were anxious to preserve rather more than Mr Joseph Platt's shooting rights.

In the event all that manpower effected the charging and arraigning before the High Court in Edinburgh of just six men. An original list of sixteen was trimmed down on the advice of the Lord Advocate, who wished to see only the 'instigators' brought before the full majesty of the law. The six – who included schoolteacher Donald MacRae despite his not having marched or hunted on the raid, but because the authorities (with perfect accuracy) suspected him of planning and supporting it – surrendered willingly.

The affair was not closed. It could never be closed on such terms. To the Scottish Gael the issue was a moral one, more black-and-white than any legal formulation, and considerably more easy to comprehend. As the eye-witness James Cameron suggested: 'Does any man in his senses suppose that this country will stand by and see a whole parish simply starve to death, merely because a few Highland lairds are determined to turn fertile lands into deer runs and sheep walks?'

In the middle of December, just four weeks after the incident at Park and shortly after Donald MacRae and his five colleagues had consented to a jury trial in Edinburgh, several hundred men from Borve, Shader and Barvas on the broad north-western fringe – just about as far away from South Lochs and Park as they could be while remaining on Lewis – marched up their cliff-top machair to the farm at Galson. They demanded that the tenant there depart once his lease had expired, and that the pasture land should be turned over to crofting. Their efforts would be rewarded by an interview with Lady Matheson in Stornoway Castle. The proprietress advised them 'to emigrate to new countries, where you can get lands cheap, and send your sons to the army and navy . . . The land under sheep and deer is my property and I can do with it what I like.' Similar demonstrations took place elsewhere in the west-coast parishes of Ness and Uig.

Following a march on two east-coast farms on Christmas Eve 1887, Stornoway constabulary was in receipt of disturbing rumours. On New Year's Day 1888, it was whispered, there would be raids on the enclosed sheep-runs of Aignish and Melbost at either side of the Point causeway.

Point, or the Eye Peninsula, protruded like an affirmative thumb from the body of Stornoway itself, jutting out and up into the Minch to form the sea walls of the sheltered inlets to the north and south of the metropolis. The thumb was almost severed: only a thin, short, tide-swept artery of land connected the bulk of agricultural Point to the paved streets of Stornoway. These parts of the town and the country were close enough to shout at one another, albeit in different languages. A raid on a deer run in Park and a march on a sheep farm at Galson constituted to most citizens of Stornoway scintillae of trouble in faraway countries of which they knew little. A raid on Aignish and Melbost farms, those neat patches of green overlooking the Point causeway, would be like a riot on the front lawn.

And raided they were. Not on 1 January, when a handful of men contented themselves with seeing in 1888 by destroying 300 yards of dyke and fencing at Aignish in the first dark hours of the new year, but eight days later, when the pitched battle which had been seen by both sides as inevitable finally occurred.

Sheriff Fraser was authorised to use his Marines and Royal Scots at Aignish on 9 January. With his regular constabulary this afforded him 100 uniformed men to face the grassy knolls of Point and deny its people access to Aignish Farm. They were not enough. The crofters started coming over the hill from Knock and Swordale in the late morning. By midday there were between 700 and 1,000 men, women and children busily clearing livestock from the pastures and driving them across the isthmus towards Stornoway. There was a stand-off between the military and the police and the demonstrators, the Riot Act was read (with, once again, helpful expositions in Gaelic), scuffles broke out and thirteen men were arrested and locked up in Stornoway jail. It became a part of the town's legend that schoolboys in class at their Francis Street school 'heard the tramp of the soldiers marching past with their prisoners towards the jail, they all rushed to the windows, and there saw . . . the fiscal, riding in front on a horse, hatless and with a bleeding bandage round his forehead . . .'[7]

There was undoubtedly violence at Aignish. Whether it was more disturbing or threatening a scene than any other nineteenth-century workers' demonstration is less certain. Faced with policemen who attempted to arrest their fellows and with fixed lines of soldiers backing up the policemen, many of the young men of Point reacted comprehensibly, by trying to free their friends and by hurling clods of earth at the uniforms. But despite that dramatic sighting of the Procurator Fiscal no policeman and no soldier required medical treatment, and no Leodhasach was badly hurt. Had the demonstrators not attempted, as they certainly did attempt, to curb each other's fury at being confronted by armed British troops on their own soil, and had even the prisoners not warned their friends to leave them to their fate and not agitate the nervous trigger finger of an imported Marine, there could have been a butcher's bill to pay. Aignish was as much of a dramatisation as Park. The difference was that the Park performance had been allowed gracefully to play itself out, whereas the curtain had no sooner lifted on the Aignish show than the stage was invaded by armed men waving warrants.

Three days later, on 12 January 1888, those thirteen prisoners were transferred for security reasons – it was feared that attempts might be made to spring them from captivity in Lewis – to Dingwall. They were incarcerated there until being put on the southbound train to await trial in Edinburgh.

On 13 January 1888 the six Park defendants left Lewis for the mainland railhead at Strome on the same mailboat as various witnesses for and against their side of the case. At the end of their trial an Edinburgh jury took thirty minutes to decide that Donald MacRae and his colleagues were 'not guilty as libelled' on all charges of mobbing, rioting and breaking the Trespass Act.

On 30 January the thirteen Aignish defendants traced their footsteps into the High Court. They would suffer a different fate. Their offence was deemed to be greater, in part because of their proximity to Stornoway, which geographical detail had led them into open confrontation with seconded military squadrons and with a number of the town police. Despite the fact that a number of privately-owned animals had been killed and eaten at Park, and despite the widespread press coverage of the raid from Balallan and Lochs, the massively supported demonstration at Aignish had to official eyes far more of the trappings of an ugly urban brawl. The acquittal of the Park defendants had also led to squawks of anxiety from the Northern Police, the Scottish Office, the landed fraternity and the press (one journalist who had enjoyed the hospitality of the raiders on that November night had agreed to offer evidence for their prosecution).

The Aignish charges were modified to include the more pliable accusation of 'forming part of a riotous mob', a sterner judge was given the reins, and all thirteen men were pronounced guilty. In Victorian Britain any such verdict on a working person, even one with so impeccable a private life and so previously unblemished a record as the average devout Hebridean crofter, meant jail. One man got six months, three men got nine months, seven were sent away for a year and two older fishermen from Aird at the furthest easterly tip of the Point peninsula were imprisoned for fifteen months.

Imprisonment was no solution, of course, and the court authorities knew it. They had heard Samuel Newhall, the Aignish farm lessee, testify that on the previous Christmas Eve he had been approached by some 300 men carrying red flags and asking him politely but firmly to evacuate. They had heard that at least 700 people had attended the 9 January fracas on Newhall's ovine meadows. They knew the size of the population of this district, and the authorities could do their sums. They were clearly faced with the long-term logic of becoming obliged to imprison every man, woman and child on the Point peninsula to quell the unrest, to say nothing of the thousands from Ness, Uig and South Lochs . . .

Seventeen years later, in 1905, the farm at Aignish was removed from private tack, divided into crofts and let to thirty-two different tenants, all from the district of Point. No such happy fate was immediately scheduled for Park. Twice more it was raided before the turn of the old century, and twice more it was emptied again – on the second occasion in 1891 costing twelve men two weeks in Porterfield Prison, Inverness. When that martyred dozen resurfaced they attended a Land League gathering in the Highland capital and heard the Reverend Charles MacEachern demand rhetorically of the Mathesons and Platts and Newhalls and tacksmen of Galson and Melbost and Dell – 'Why displace those who would make [the land] valuable? And why persecute and imprison those who would make it valuable? What we say is what Cromwell said to a like-minded class: "Give place to honester men."'

Somewhere in the north of England, William Hesketh Lever was eagerly plotting his model village on the useless bog of Bromborough marsh.

In the 1920s a man named Harley Williams, who gained national celebrity later in life as an author of popular medical books, was appointed Medical Officer in Lewis. As chance would have it, this posting offered Williams the opportunity to observe at close quarters not only the island and its people, but also William Lever. Twenty years later, in 1947, Dr Williams published a quasi-psychological study of eminent persons which he titled *Men Of Stress*. His fourth subject, in a 35,000-word essay, was the late William Hesketh Lever.

The man was, judged Williams, a human dynamo. His unforgiving daily routine was almost Spartan. He slept in a bedroom with only three walls; the other being open to the Cheshire elements. He rose as early as 4.30 a.m., exercised with dumb-bells and horses, and then dictated business matters – more loudly as the years passed and his deafness grew – to a relay team of secretaries and executives.

He balanced the management of a multinational company interested in both hemispheres and four continents with a spell as a Liberal Member of Parliament, several political campaigns, housing developments, collecting art, satisfying a thirst for the operettas of Gilbert and Sullivan, global travelling and a million other diversions. Such a life was only partially attributable, as Williams suggested, to the fact that Lever did not drink. '. . . The obsession of [his] daily schedule,' pronounced the doctor, 'suggests some deep conflict, something he was trying to forget . . .'

Lever attempted to analyse his own drive, and deduced that its primary motivation was fear. 'What has caused me,' he would ask, 'to begin work at 4.30 in the morning for the last two or three years and to work laborious hours, and to have only one absorbing thought, namely my own efficiency and the maintenance of the task I have to perform; I am bound to confess it has not been the attraction of dividends, but fear, cowardly fear – the growing fear that I have placed myself in the position of accepting money from . . . widows, spinsters, clergymen and others who might possibly have to forego their dividends which would mean the probable curtailment of what they depended on for their day-to-day food, clothing, rent . . .'

Those were the words of a slightly deluded politician. Dr Harley Williams treated with proper disdain the self-analysis of such an obsessive, competitive, controlling personality.

To say that he feared Lever Brothers might have to pass dividends on their preference shares tells us much less than half the truth. Men do not work at such diabolical intensity merely so that spinsters, widows and clergymen may pay their rent.

Fear by itself is paralysing. Any prudent business man could have shown Lever dozens of ways of reducing the risks to his preference shareholders. The average director of the average company would have advised him to stop philanthropy, and to give up such pastimes as the Congo enterprise, and extending his garden village. If Lever had ever in his life suffered from fear of worldly consequences he would never have broken away from his father's excellent business . . .[8]

William Lever worked those days, subjected himself to an athlete's training regime, devoted his lengthy waking hours to improvement of business and character because the process – rather than the result – thrilled and enlivened him. He could never lose control; never be seen by himself or anybody else to relax his authority. He genuinely believed that the late-Victorian and Edwardian working classes deserved a fuller and more rewarding life (and that they would actually make better employees if healthy and happy), but he could never admit the role of their own trade unions, or even of the state, in providing such benefits. 'No man of an independent turn of mind,' the secretary of the Bolton branch of the Engineers' Union would tell him in 1919, 'can breathe for long the atmosphere of Port Sunlight. That might be news to your Lordship, but we have tried it.'[9]

Improvement had to come from him and from him alone: the benevolent, sagacious patron. His commercial mantra of 'Organise, Deputise, Criticise' was only two-thirds revealing. He organised and criticised with assiduity; he deputised reluctantly and never in full. 'I have always viewed you,' he wrote (at telling length and with revealing force) to an ambitious underling who had presumed to offer advice about an imminent meeting, 'as thoroughly alive to what is correct and proper for a Secretary to take upon himself. I am always glad to have your free expression of opinion on all matters that I may discuss with you. But until I do discuss a matter with you, I think you will agree with me that it is not within your province to lay your views before me. I hope that this will be the last time on which you will venture an expression of opinion as to what course I should take at a Meeting unless in response to a request from myself that you should do so.'

It is unoriginal but valuable to describe the man as Napoleonic, chiefly because Lever – perhaps because he felt he ought to be in sympathy with another short, stocky, pop-eyed autocrat – made the parallel himself. When the pretentious Lady Lever Art Gallery was built at Port Sunlight he insisted on a special Napoleon room, based on the Empress Josephine's bedroom, with First Empire palmettes, swags and a frieze of urns. (Two of the eminent architects on the project, who survived long enough to write their employer's obituary, could not resist suggesting in two different published essays that their experience of being contracted to William Lever was comparable to that of junior staff officers under Bonaparte.) It is more interesting to note that he considered there to be similarities between himself and the emperor, than that many similarities actually existed. They were both driven men, both incapable of delegation, both fully alive only when immersed in their vocation. But it is unlikely that William Lever had it in him to slaughter the civilian populations of cities or invade Russia. At a certain crucial point his autocracy stopped short of absolute tyranny. A wry levity rarely deserted him. The sentimentality which informed so many of his activities, from buying art to building workers' homes and fighting for his family firm, subverted the ruthless dictatorial impulse. Once Lever had become one of the richest, best-regarded and most influential businessmen in the world, he would still enter – with a self-conscious humility that was anything but Napoleonic – on the decennial census form his 'profession or occupation' as 'soap maker'.

But if and when his administration was so much as questioned, let alone threatened, Lever felt obliged to retaliate openly and with quite unsentimental force. When the *Daily Mail* and the *Daily Mirror* ran a legitimate investigation into the business ethics of the soap barons, Lever – against the orthodox advice of most legal and public relations experts – sued their publishing company, Lord Northcliffe's Associated Newspapers. He won a very personal victory. His formidable leading counsel, the former solicitor-general Sir Edward Carson, made a point of placing his client in the witness stand for cross-examination, knowing that the steely little Lancastrian would never crack – and then invited the opposition to put Lord Northcliffe through the same ordeal. Northcliffe threw in his hand. His representatives conceded the case on the following morning.

When the disreputable financier Ernest Terah Hooley visited Port Sunlight and made an impertinent offer to buy Lever Brothers, William greeted the Irishman with disarming hospitality. In the course of their conversation Hooley – who drove through his deals more often than not, until he was arrested by the law – confessed to being tempted to buy the Bovril Company. Lever excused himself briefly from the room, and returned to announce that Lever Brothers was not for sale. When Hooley shortly afterwards examined the Bovril portfolio he discovered that a large block of its inflated shares had recently been snapped up cheaply by William Lever. (Who would have been doubly delighted to discover, many decades later, the whole of the Bovril concern nestling comfortably in the embrace of the multinational company named Unilever.)

The chase was the thing. What William Lever misdiagnosed in his aubade as the chill fear of letting others down, was actually an adrenaline rush. It was the fear not of impoverishing spinsters, but of failing to win with the poker hand he dealt himself at dawn each day.

He rarely did fail, if only because few of his competitors at the green baize table could outlast his pace or outbid his stake. His fortune and that of his firm and family growed like Topsy. When he celebrated his fiftieth birthday at the beginning of the twentieth century William Lever was one of the richest individuals and most celebrated entrepreneurs in the Western world. He would mock the suggestion that he had never known a setback, but could hardly deny that while small skirmishes may occasionally have slipped away from him, the major battles had inexorably fallen to his will. Even the setbacks had a way of righting themselves, if diligently pursued. In 1906 he was elected – after three unsuccessful local campaigns – as Liberal Member of Parliament for the Wirral. He would have a conscientious, if brief (he stepped down in 1909) and undistinguished career in the House of Commons, where his workmates were less obedient than in Port Sunlight.

More auspiciously, in 1906 Lever Brothers began seriously to farm coconuts in the Solomon Islands.

In common with all his overseas adventures, the South Pacific experiment was undertaken in the name of commercial realism. In order to make soap William Lever needed plentiful quantities of smooth and sweetly scented vegetable oil. The Polynesian colonies were admirably suited to the growth of the coconut palm, whose dried kernels, or copra, could then conveniently be diverted to his oil mill at Sydney, Australia.

A mode of operation was established in the Solomon Islands which would be repeated, local conditions permitting, in other distant Lever interests. He would bring investment and employment to an apparently needy district, in his name and on his terms. Lever Pacific Plantations Limited expanded mightily, from producing 100 tons on 51,000 acres in 1906 to turning 1,000 tons out of 300,000 acres in 1913. The benevolent nawab of the concern went so far as to announce his plans to build a new model South Seas capital and port. It would be called Ladylever (a name which, as we shall see, he must have chosen with some emotion) and its orderly bungalows would extend up the side of a mountain to the cool and healthy conditions which pertained at 3,000 feet.

There were problems in the Solomon Islands, partly with the bureaucrats of the Colonial Office, but also with the incomprehensible attitude of the locals to work, money and the ethos of Lever Pacific Plantations Limited. During what would turn out to be a valedictory visit to the Solomons at the end of 1913 William visited a chief's hut and was dismayed to find certain Western consumer goods – a gramophone, a thermos flask, three sewing machines – littered inconsequentially 'amid general dirt and disorder'.

'Mr Woodford states,' he mused, 'that the natives are making so much money out of copra at present that they have no idea what to do with their earnings or profits, and either waste them on useless purchases or hoard them in some hole in the ground. He said he had no doubt this old chief could produce hundreds of pounds hidden away somewhere. 'They won't bank their cash, and really, they don't know what to do with it.'[10]

Such wilful fecklessness made the indigent people of the Solomon Islands quite unsuitable as managers, or even as dependable day-labourers. Positions of responsibility at Lever Pacific Plantations were almost always occupied by imported Australian bushmen, but Lever's efforts to introduce 'Hindoos from the teeming millions of India' to work his crops were thwarted by the Colonial Office.

The model township of Ladylever never appeared in the Solomon Islands and after 1913 Lever Brothers reduced their Pacific activities. Another patch of the earth beckoned, wherein the coconut palm thrived but not the British Colonial Office. Lever leased land in the Belgian Congo.

His interest in Africa fermented over many years. There were not many places in the world amenable to the coconut palm with which William Lever was not familiar. Those parts of West Africa which lay within the British fiefdom did not immediately recommend themselves because – as in the Solomon Islands – the British Colonial Office stood there between Lever Brothers and the land. The Colonial Office's policy in West Africa was, if anything, even more obstructive to the outside entrepreneur than in the South Seas. It was settled policy that 'the native populations of West Africa under British rule should have secured to them rights to hold their ancestral soil without disturbance, to cultivate it as they would, and to do with its produce what they thought fit'. That was not much good to a man looking to service the world with soap from boundless palmeries.

No such niceties applied to those parts of the region which languished under the suzerainty of King Leopold II of Belgium. Leopold's hideous human rights record in Africa rendered it impolitic, however, for a British businessman – especially a Liberal British businessman – fully to exploit the old brute's territory until after Leopold's death in 1909, when the Belgian government introduced a reformed colonial regime.

After considering the reports of several scouts, in April 1911 William Lever signed with the Belgian authorities a convention which brought into being La Société Anonyme des Huileries de Congo Belge. This company would lease almost two million acres of Africa in five separate districts of the Belgian Congo (which is now mostly Zaire), and grow upon it the crops needed to service at least five oil mills situated in the regional centres.

Those would be his palmeries, his coconut ranches. It was a scheme of stunning ambition. It has rightly been suggested that in signing the 1911 convention William Lever moved out of the world of business and into the realm of international politics. Lever himself would neither have spurned that suggestion nor thought it impertinent. If his few years in parliament had confirmed him in anything, it was the belief that commerce and not democracy oiled the wheels and fed the boiler of the developing world. He knew that in accepting responsibility for the economic well-being of most of the north-western half of an enormous foreign territory he was effectively placing himself *in loco regis*. He knew, but did not much care. He had assumed for over twenty years a similar position in a small but blessed quarter of north-western England. (The Belgian socialists also knew but did not care. Their leader announced in Brussels that he would have opposed such concessions being offered to any other firm, but his knowledge of the working conditions at Port Sunlight allowed him to bless the intervention in Belgian Africa of Lever Brothers.)

Port Sunlight had not, however, been christened Leverville. That would be the name of the new centre of operations in the southern section of his Congolese principality, 200 miles from the former colonial capital of Leopoldville. In June 1911 the British government – perhaps acting quickly to forestall their most incorrigible industrialist accepting the crown, sceptre, throne and imperial toga of some distant principality – made him Sir William Lever, Baronet.

In November 1912 Baronet and Lady Lever paid a personal visit to their African interests. He had of course already been aware of the liabilities of the region. The provinces surrounding Leverville in the south and Alberta and Elisabetha in the north were separated by 600 miles of jungle and malarial swamp. There were no roads, just one railway which failed to connect any of his five isolated territories, and a single precarious telegraph and telephone line strung by the Belgian government up the course of the Congo River. A visiting European baronet and his lady wife were therefore obliged to traverse the country by river steamer.

It had been written into the 1911 Convention that a part of the appointed task of the Huileries de Congo Belge was to introduce the natives to the joys of capitalism. The Congolese were to be weaned away from their fondness for barter and exchange, delivered from the limi-tations of self-sufficiency and introduced to a cash economy. To facilitate this the company was committed to delivering a minimum daily wage to people who held a franc in less regard than a fruit tree. This money was to be paid on top of their company board and rations. The purpose was clearly to create a cash-in-hand surplus on the banks of the Kasai and the Kwilu, which would in due course lead to the formation of a consumer economy.

It was not an easy task. Baronet Lever was an endlessly optimistic man. The African, he pronounced liberally, was not lazy. 'He is a child and a willing child, but he wants training and handling with patience.' The notion would never occur to him that the Africans, like the Solomon Islanders and like those elsewhere who lived in a mature, proud and well-established culture, might prefer to retain their familiar way of life than trade it all in for a bag of copper coins.

The evidence of their reluctance to deal was clear to William Lever. 'The problem of labour,' he wrote in the Congo at the very end of 1913, 'has grown as an ominous dark cloud.' It stemmed mainly from the difficulty of trying to persuade with wages people who did not particularly value money.

> The fact is, the native has few wants, a little salt and a little cloth are his indispensables.
>
> After this, beads, brass rods and other luxuries. Chief Womba at Leverville can be taken as an example. Twelve months ago he and his people were poor and few in number, and were keen to bring [coconut] fruit. After twelve months or less of selling fruit he is rich and lazy, has ten wives, and his village is about four times what it was, but he gathers little or no fruit . . . The Palm tree is in these parts the Banking account of the native and he no more thinks of going to the Bank for fruit for money when his wants and ambitions are supplied than a civilised man would. His bank is always open when he wants to draw on it.

The lifestyle, wants and ambitions of Chief Womba were as mysterious as those of any South Seas headman to the liberal imperialist. Despite his earlier judgement, in private moments William Lever clearly did consider his African workforce to be 'lazy'. This niggling contradiction was his creed at war with his commercial instincts. He had built a massive business concern on the principle that workers performed better if well treated and amply rewarded. In the Congo and the Solomon Islands that principle hit the buffers. Presented with the evidence that not all human

beings would respond with grateful obedience to his benevolent management, Lever tussled for an explanation. He never found it, partly
because he never really listened to the best advice. Cemented firmly in
the conviction that his own aspirations and those of any other urban
Lancastrian – for health, lifelong security and home comforts – must be
the ultimate goal of all mankind, he was unable to sympathise with or
even properly to imagine a society with older, more deeply rooted totems
of contentment. Thirty years later his acquaintance, Dr Harley Williams,
wondered:

> Did he know what it meant to substitute for that innocence of native life
> his own idea of ordered effort and exploitation? He was exorcising a dark
> spirit, he was curbing the cruel majesty of a life which had existed ever
> since humans appeared on the earth, and he was doing it all in the way of
> business. His practical mind wished to bring order and civilisation, and
> though he sympathised with those colonising Jesuit Fathers, he felt
> inwardly that his own economic gospel could make those black faces
> respond even more readily . . .

It was an almost inevitable failing. Without his bull-headed obstinacy, his
refusal to court alternative strategies, Lever would never have taken his
company to such peaks. Had he remained within the tidy purlieu of
western industrial society he may never have faced frustration or defeat.
But he was drawn outside his natural bounds and into the forest, where
his compass no longer worked.

He could not give up on Africa. There were contractual reasons for
persisting. The 1911 Convention had committed Lever Brothers to over
two decades' involvement in the Belgian Congo, and the business
imperatives which had led Baronet Lever to sign that document were
unlikely to go away. Port Sunlight and every other soapery needed oil in
ever vaster quantities as the western washing population soared. Less
mule-headed men would nonetheless have cashed in their chips. It was
one thing to agree, as he had, to devote twenty years to building every
necessary road and railway track and throwing essential telegraph lines
across 350,000 square miles of tropical rain forest. It was surely quite
another if, at the end of that massive investment, the workforce could
only be persuaded to deliver coconuts when in need of another wife.

But his vaunting, iron-clad pride alone would have denied him an easy exit from Leverville; his contract with the Belgian Government and the long-term hunger of his company for palm oil offered the rationale to stay.

So, as ever, when in doubt he built. The street layouts at Leverville were pegged and repegged under his personal inspection. On the February day in 1913 that he and Elizabeth sailed for home he wrote of his renewed confidence in 'our great undertaking'. He foresaw with something approaching glee a full quarter-century of gainful and rewarding enterprise in Africa: '. . . I set to work at once in the afternoon on a plan for the plantation villages . . .'

And then his life, which had previously run a gruelling but painless course, was rocked by irreparable loss. It would never afterwards be the same.

In the summer of 1913 Lever went on a business trip to continental Europe. In Marseilles he was told by telegram that his wife Elizabeth was severely ill with pneumonia. He raced northwards and reached her bedside a few hours before she died on 24 July. She was sixty-two and he was sixty-one years old.

This was the woman without whom, he said, he could neither remember nor imagine life. They had known childhood and youth, marriage and middle age together. Every day that he had woken up at home for the past thirty-nine years, be it never so early in the morning, Elizabeth had personally superintended the correct preparation of his breakfast. They had borne a son, had christened him William Hulme Lever to employ both of their names, had seen him come into his majority and seen him marry. She had been a lively, cheerful daughter of Lancashire, with a ready laugh and an easy smile, vivaciously prepared to accompany her husband to the heart of Africa and beyond. Every fraction of his public success, he said, 'came because of the confidence she inspired in me'.

In the month before Elizabeth's death William had asked a local architectural firm to draw up plans for a new art gallery (including a library and Masonic Lodge) in Port Sunlight. This building was clearly destined to be her monument, her Taj Mahal. The couple's eclectic collection of high and low art was bursting out of their Cheshire manor house. The Lady Lever Gallery would become its ideal home.

And so on 25 March 1914 Baronet Lever and his monarch, King George V, enacted a peculiar ritual. They stood together in Hulme Hall, the dining room for day workers at the soap plant, a quarter of a mile south of the village of Port Sunlight. Before them stood a large and detailed to-scale reproduction of the settlement. In the empty space reserved for the Lady Lever Gallery stood a small electric button-switch. At the appointed hour King George pressed the button . . . and 500 yards away on site a large foundation stone was automatically lowered into the ground, while within Hulme Hall a toy crane deposited a small counterfeit stone on the appropriate part of the model town. Everybody who was anybody in Cheshire and beyond broke into delighted applause, and signs on the base of the construction flashed out in electric light the words: 'Stone well and truly laid'. Even on the most solemn of occasions William Lever displayed his beguiling devotion to technological wizardry and the charms of twentieth-century progress. (Progress Lodge No. 4584 would be the name of the Masonic group patronised by William, founded in the completed Lady Lever Gallery some ten years later, before moving to spend the remainder of the twentieth century, appropriately enough, in Hulme Hall.)

Five months later the world went to war. The 26-year-old William Hulme Lever, a vice-chairman of the family company, was somehow exempted from service, but 500 of Lever Brothers' other staff were among the first to be sent to the Western Front in August 1914. Baronet Lever topped up their husbands' service pay to the wives of the Wirral Battalion and sent the men themselves cutlery and utensils from the kitchens at Port Sunlight. He himself became at the age of sixty-three a private in the Birkenhead and District Volunteer Training Corps.

And he looked after business, which thrived throughout the Great War. He could hardly have done otherwise. An unanticipated benefit of the soap trade was the by-product glycerine, which formed as a colourless liquid during the saponification of oils and fats. The more soap, therefore, the more glycerine. Glycerine was essential for high explosives, and so the government developed a keen interest in the welfare of the soap industry. The total employed capital of Lever Brothers doubled between 1914 and 1919, from £13 million to £26 million. The amount of soap produced annually by the group rose from 120,000 tons to 170,000 tons. He lost certain hostile and occupied continental markets, but expanded in a newly affluent America.

He also accelerated his company's previously incidental interest in margarine (which had 'a close connection with oils and fats for the soap kettle') when it became clear that making margarine in wartime was tantamount to minting money – 'we could sell all that we could make at our own terms', he informed his directors. The move into margarine would have huge historical implications for his company and for the twentieth-century food industry. Once the war was over it took Lever Brothers into direct competition with the Dutch butter-substitute pioneers Van Den Burghs and Jurgens, who had been sharing since the 1870s a comfortable European margarine monopoly from the small Friesian dairy town of Gaast. The Dutch companies had at first rendered margarine from animal fats, turning only later to imported vegetable oils. In 1927 Jurgens and Van Den Burghs decided to defend themselves against the assault from the Wirral by amalgamating into Margerine Unie. Two years later Margerine Unie and Lever Brothers combined to form Unilever, which before the end of the century had become the biggest food conglomerate in the world.

But that was beyond the founder's time. His laying of the immense foundation stones of Unilever was all so effortless, so simple. His Midas touch worked its alchemy almost without prompting and even while the rest of Europe haemorrhaged human blood, earthly rewards continued to visit him without invitation. In June 1917 he was made a full British baron, a member of the House of Lords. He decided to unite formally and forever his own memory and that of his wife by merging their surnames into the title Lord Leverhulme of Bolton-le-Moors. His adopted heraldic motto was equally personal: it read, 'I scorn to change or fear'.

The war depressed him; being a widower depressed him; his hearing had deteriorated badly since the death of Elizabeth (although he unscientifically attributed his deafness to the quinine taken in Africa); but he could not stop making money and reaping recognition. What to do with it all, and with the energy that still burned him out of bed before dawn on each and every breezy day? He needed as much as ever some project to adopt, some huge distraction, some gigantic scheme, some means of changing a section of the face of the earth, some gambler's hand to play.

One day towards the end of 1917 he picked up a copy of *The Times* and noticed that the island of Lewis was for sale. It was advertised as a sporting estate complete with castle: a whole island devoted to salmon, grouse and deer. He collected his land agent Frank Clarke, drove north in a motor car and took a ferry across the Minch to Stornoway. Nobody there remembered him.

❦

A small but steady trickle of land in Lewis continued to be redistributed throughout the early years of the twentieth century. As we have noted, Aignish Farm was returned to the common weal in 1905. Mangersta Farm on the far west coast in Uig was turned over to crofting in 1909, and the old military training ground at Stornoway's Battery Park was converted into fishermen's holdings.

These and other minor transfers, which were gestures of goodwill rather than a panacea for the Lewis land fever, were carried out by the new regime of Lieutenant-Colonel Duncan Matheson. Colonel Matheson had taken over the estate from his father, Donald Matheson, in 1899, Donald Matheson having inherited the island from his aunt, Lady Jane, upon her death three years earlier.

Despite his small acts of charity Duncan Matheson was not a supporter of the crofters' case. On the contrary, he confessed in private to having swallowed wholesale the landowning lobby's most recent position paper, which was that crofts were no good for crofters, being too small, and that by opposing the creation of new crofts and the extension of the crofting system landowners such as himself were therefore actually doing crofters a favour, would they only recognise it.[11]

Such concessions as those at Aignish and Mangersta (and it should be recalled that Matheson had not given away the land: he had simply switched his rental income from one farmer to several dozen crofters) were also recognised as a sop, an attempt to buy time. Duncan Matheson had inherited from his father and his aunt the recommendations of the

1892 Deer Forest Commission. That report had scheduled not only Aignish and Mangersta for new crofting land, but also great swathes of the rest of rural Lewis. More than 3,000 acres of South Lochs should be assigned to crofting tenure, considered the Deer Forest Commission, and the entire 50,000 acreage of game shootings at Park and Aline combined should be redeployed for the 'extension' of crofting. Both of the west side farms at Galson and Dalbeg should be returned to crofters, as should the Gress, Tong, Coll and North Tolsta grazings north of Stornoway. For good measure, the Commission advised that the 13,000 acres of Morsgail Deer Forest in Uig might well be better served if used as crofting pasture land.

In voluntarily conceding 2,750 acres of rough pasture and arable at Mangersta and Aignish, Colonel Matheson was getting off lightly. The sops were taken hungrily, of course. But they were not enough.

The Small Landowners (Scotland) Bill of 1911 gave to the Board of Agriculture and the Scottish Land Court both the power to create crofting holdings and some of the compensation money needed to transfer private Highland farms into public property. The Board (which replaced the Conservative Government's Congested Districts Board, whose principle answer to the Highland land question had been to encourage emigration) promptly found itself in receipt of 5,352 applications from throughout Scotland for smallholdings. Of those, no fewer than 1,300 came from the Western Isles, and most of those were from Lewis.[12]

It is a measure of the fortitude and community discipline of the land-starved Leodhasaich that they had been prepared to wait so long in such good faith to fill out a thousand application forms. The 1911 Act had taken fully five years to get through parliament; it became law in diluted form; but in the years of its difficult gestation there had been only minor disruptions on the island. (Where there were explosions, as at Dalbeg Farm on the west side in 1909, it was the result of a grievance long pent up by Shawbost crofters whose families had been cleared from the land less than sixty years earlier, who had petitioned and demonstrated for its return since the 1880s and who were running out of patience.[13]) Lewis was feared by capital and by government alike as a powder keg, an island which might blow into open revolt at any time. It did not do so partly because its people were more sober, more law-abiding, more reluctant to cause social unrest than the authorities credited, and partly because Herbert Asquith's reforming Liberal administrations of the Edwardian period – to which Ross-shire and Lewis duly returned their supportive MPs – promised that constitutional action was in hand.

That action appeared in 1913 to be imminent. After arduous consultations and agonised deliberations the Board of Agriculture decided that it would use its new powers to apply to the Land Court for conversion to crofting tenure of the whole of the farms at Gress to the north of Stornoway, Galson in the west, Carnish and Ardroil in Uig, and Orinsay and Steimreway in South Lochs. That total of 22,000 acres would accommodate 128 new crofts. It would not answer the polite applications of 900 others, but it would be a start.

A certain widespread mythology has it that the First World War then intervened, in August 1914, to put this long-awaited initiative on hold. In fact it was scuppered by the proprietor. Colonel Matheson's Edinburgh solicitors fought a long, dogged, ingenious and doubtless hugely expensive rearguard action in the Land Court against the Board's proposals. They employed every piece of ordnance in the landowning arsenal. They argued that crofters made bad tenants. They claimed that crofting land lost value. They alleged, person by person, that the individual applicants were unsuitable people to be given the tenancy of a smallholding. They suggested that the rateable value and therefore the social infrastructure of Lewis would be harmed. They said that Lewis's roads were not capable of servicing new crofting townships. They refused to hand over documents and delayed replying to letters.

They did all of this in the landowner's name, while – as they and he knew full well – thousands of Lewis men and women were absent from the island, voluntarily staking and too often losing their lives on land and at sea in defence of the United Kingdom. They took advantage of the fact that among those thousands bogged down in Flanders or navigating the North Sea was a majority of the applicants for crofts at Galson, Gress, Ardroil and Steimreway. Duncan Matheson's solicitors began this tawdry campaign in 1913; they were still engaged in it when Germany invaded Belgium; and by March 1916 – when their own conflict had been underway for three years and the world war for eighteen months – they had ground the Board of Agriculture and the Land Court into submission. The Secretary of State for Scotland decided that consideration of the transfer of the four Lewis farms into crofting tenure should be suspended until the end of the war. The filibuster had been successful. It had also spotlit the yawning gulf in class sympathy between landlord and tenant, for both Colonel Matheson and his son – whose life would be preserved by a supreme act of heroism by a ranker in the Cameron Highlanders – were also in France. They may have been composed of the same vulnerable flesh as their troops, but their aspirations lived in another world.

At least one of the Board's sub-commissioners recorded his dismay on paper. Neil MacLean wrote to his employers immediately following the suspension, pointing out that while the high level of recruitment from Lewis might temporarily have assisted the landowner's tactics, a day of reckoning was due when the men returned to Lochs and Ness. They had sown the seeds of ill-will, implied MacLean, and they might yet reap the whirlwind: 'the Lewis people, having had these farms dangled before them for some years, will break the peace if the thing is postponed more or less indefinitely.'[14]

Chronic land hunger notwithstanding, the 1900s were neither especially good nor particularly bad years in the Hebrides. Island long-line fishermen in their traditional home-made lug-sailed sgoths (skiffs) suffered competition from new motor-powered trawlers steaming into the Minches from the south and east coasts of the Scottish mainland. The local commercial fishery went into decline and, lacking the capital to invest in new craft and equipment (a deficiency which was not helped in 1902 when the Fishery Board withheld further grant aid to the island), Lewis fishermen slowly withdrew from the deep-sea export industry. They did not stop fishing, but concentrated instead on catches from their inshore waters for home consumption. The Stornoway fish-curing barons became increasingly serviced by fleets from Aberdeen and Buckie. Of the 237 sailing boats registered at Port of Ness between 1868 and 1901, 205 were over 30 feet in length and therefore equipped for deep-sea work. Of the thirty-four fishing boats registered at Ness between 1903 and 1910, only seven were larger than 20 feet in length. As late as 1939 – when almost all of the rest of the Scottish fleet was motorised – the islands of Lewis and Harris contained between them 34 per cent of the working sailing boats left in the country.

Lewis itself won a new ironclad steam connection with Strome in Wester Ross in 1904, when the *Sheila* first sailed the route which she would ply for twenty-two years. The *Sheila* carried the celebrated notice: 'This deck is available for passengers when not occupied by cattle' – an admonition which was more of a reflection of the comparative priorities of the islanders than an insult by David MacBrayne's ferry company (passengers in a later age would be similarly barred from the occupied car-deck). The fact that it was humorously noted and not forgotten is interesting in itself, as a further indication of the Leodhasaich's proud, almost hyper-sensitive awareness of their independent humanity.

Post offices which could receive telegrams sprang up in virtually every village. The security of tenure granted by the 1886 Crofting Act had encouraged people to improve their properties. Visitors could still be surprised and depressed by the thatched blackhouses of rural Lewis and Harris, but they had stood the test of time in the far north-west and would not easily be relinquished. Despite their hugger-mugger modesty they were not – as a sympathetic tourist could perceive – homes to any underclass, 'for the Lewis people as a whole are well-conditioned physically, mentally and morally, and there is certainly much more intelligence, culture, happiness and virtue in these black houses than in the comparatively well and skilfully built houses of the Canongate and Cowgate in Edinburgh. The people living in these black houses are not the dregs of the community, they *are* the community'.

The infant mortality rate in those houses was high. Inside walls would be covered with clay and whitewashed to guard against cholera, newsprint might insulate the cladding, wallpaper might even be hung, but this was a stern environment and the children continued to die. When Calum Smith was born in Shawbost in 1912 he arrived as the fourth child of 28-year-old parents. Only one of his siblings was there to greet him: the other two had survived for just two or three weeks. Calum himself almost died within days of his birth, and while a toddler contracted firstly pneumonia and then jaundice. Having conquered those he survived – not untypically – for a further eight decades.[15]

Young Calum enjoyed a commonplace childhood in rural Lewis. His mother had spent the day of his birth gathering seaweed for fertiliser. He spent his boyhood in an environment where Gaelic lore cohabited with a Presbyterianism so firmly applied that no water could be collected from the well on the Sabbath day; he was raised on potatoes and barley bread and salted peat-smoked fish. When he was two years old his father went off to war with the Royal Naval Reserve. And when he was eight his entire family was uprooted from the west coast and moved to the ramshackle suburbs of Stornoway because their borrowed croft was reclaimed by its tenant and there was no other land for them at Shawbost – or, mysteriously, anywhere else in the boundless world of a schoolboy's native Lewis.

The North Tolsta historian Donald Macdonald recorded Tuesday, 4 August 1914 – when Macdonald himself was ten years old – as the unforgettable day 'when the postman delivered the buff-coloured envelopes to the Militia and Naval Reservists'.[16] Because of the islanders' abilities at sea and consequent long tradition of naval service, Lewis lost a disproportionate number of its sons to the First World War. Their sacrifice would be made the harsher, had they but known it, by an unprecedented tragedy after the Armistice was signed. But in 1914 they knew only that their country called upon them once again and they rallied to her, walking across Barvas Moor or sailing to Stornoway from Ness, the Naval Reservists then rattling south by train to the Channel ports, the Militia men to France, 'and before long, the postmen were delivering their grim messages of death:'

> First to fall were the regular soldiers fighting at Mons, the Marne and the Aisne, followed all too quickly by the young Militia lads, some under eighteen years of age. French names like Loos, Cambrai, Ypres, Hill 60 and Passchendaele became familiar, all associated with the death of the young islanders.

Calum Smith remembered for the rest of his life the west side funeral processions of those few whose bodies were returned – the black-clad non-combatants, the old men who formed all of the cortège with one exception: a soldier from faraway Park on leave whose khaki-clothed figure loomed over the company.

He remembered another man in khaki 'who made his way down to the shore, and looking out over the Atlantic fired shot after shot from his rifle. I . . . couldn't see or understand what he was firing at. When I spoke about it after I got home I was told that it was the last evening of his leave and that he was setting off for France the following day . . .'

Lewis men fought in France, Italy, Russia, Egypt, Mesopotamia, Palestine, Greece, Bulgaria and the Dardanelles – many youngsters who had joined up straight from the Nicolson Institute secondary school in Stornoway distinguished themselves at Gallipoli. Lewis sailors died at the Battle of the Falklands, at Jutland and on the Dover Patrol. Their regular Ross-shire regiment, the Seaforth Highlanders, won seventy decorations, including five Military Crosses and four DSOs. Stonemasons commissioned at the end of the war to engrave memorials developed a terrible familiarity with the curlicues of such names as MacLeod and Morrison.

In the opening week of January 1917 Lewis was given its first local weekly newspaper. The *Stornoway Gazette* was the brainchild of an Inverness journalist named William Grant, who had been despatched to the island in the early 1900s by the *Highland News*. Grant settled in Lewis, marrying in 1906 a Nicolson Institute teacher named Jane Morrison. When his brother Duncan became a partner in a Dingwall printing concern the opportunity arose to throw one stone at two birds: to launch a newspaper which would tap the virgin advertising and cover sales markets of Lewis and Harris, and which in doing so would put Duncan Grant's new printing presses to profitable use. For the next thirty-one years the *Stornoway Gazette* (and *West Coast Advertiser*) was composed and edited in Lewis, but printed on the east coast of the Highlands. The strategic problems of this dislocation would many times be evident – even without bad weather, the distances over land and sea between the editorial office, the printing depot and the retail outlets were so formidable that the columns of the *Gazette* would often not be read until three or four days after they had been finalised. But William Grant was a diligent correspondent, his journal had no competition, and it quickly established itself as a feature of Lewis society.

On Friday 8 February 1918, readers of the *Stornoway Gazette* found themselves poring avidly over the week's main stories – a tribute to 'our most distinguished soldier', the fallen Colonel David MacLeod, DSO, of the Gordon Highlanders; a letter from some Bernera lads serving in Holland; a petition to the Scottish Secretary requesting that Gaelic be taught in all Highland schools – when the more discerning among them spotted an auspicious five-line item at the very bottom of page three. Clearly inserted late in the day, at the expense of the line-spaces and leading in the Gaelic report which preceded it and which was consequently concertinaed up the page, this short, six-point paragraph read:

REPORTED SALE OF THE ISLAND OF LEWIS

A report comes from Edinburgh that the Island of Lewis has been purchased from Major Matheson by Messrs Lever Bros., the world-known soap firm of Port Sunlight, near Liverpool.

It was almost true.

4

SIGNS OF COMING DAWN

By 1917, when Lord Leverhulme noticed that the island of Lewis was in their portfolio, John Knight, Howard Frank and William Rutley had been in business for only twenty-one years. Property was not their first interest; they were auctioneers and retailers of jewellery and fine art with whom Lever – when he had been just William the collector – had done more routine business.

Knight, Frank and Rutley progressed as a matter of natural course from valuing and selling the contents of country houses to selling off the edifices themselves. When Lieutenant-Colonel Duncan Matheson decided to put his Hebridean estate on the market they presented themselves as the obvious agency. Colonel Duncan was resigned to making a loss. In 1844 his great-uncle Sir James Matheson had paid the widow of Mr Stewart MacKenzie £190,000 for the island. Sir James had since added to the apparent value of the estate by raising the Gothic magnificence of Lews Castle (which cost an estimated £100,000) on the site of an old lodge, by the creation of quays, utilities and fish-curing plants in Stornoway, and by the transfer of land from community use to shooting estates and private farms. As well as the purchase price Sir James Matheson and his widow may have spent on Lewis another million pounds of their opium fortune. Their descendant sold it for £143,000, with a few thousand pounds on top for improvements and accessories. But it was a paper loss rather than a personal deficit. Colonel Matheson, who was commanding his battalion of the Seaforth Regiment in France in 1917 and whose son was also a serving officer, was liquidating an inherited asset in a buyer's market, rather than writing off his own investments. In short, he was suddenly £150,000 more wealthy, with no more castles to maintain or crofters to mollify. He had been anxious to offload the island for many years: in 1913 Duncan Matheson had almost succeeded in persuading the Chancellor of the Exchequer and future Prime Minister David Lloyd George to buy it.

Lewis was not bought – *contra* the *Stornoway Gazette* – by Lever Brothers, whose directors and shareholders (as they would demonstrate in the early summer of 1925) would have baulked at such an investment, but by Lord Leverhulme himself, underwritten by his immense personal holdings in Lever Brothers. The *Gazette* managed both to anticipate the transaction, which was not actually finalised until May 1918, and to run behind its readers, for the purpose of Leverhulme's visit the previous October had been widely noised around Lewis.

But the deal was done early in 1918. From that February onwards Leverhulme spoke of Lewis as if he already owned the place. He wanted it, he had the money and he was not accustomed to failure. He was merely using the interval mercilessly – and almost automatically – to beat down by a full 25 per cent Duncan Matheson's asking price. It was a buyer's market. Over the previous thirty years the value of British estates had plummeted. The grip of titled families on their ancestral (and not-so-ancestral) lands had been relaxed by death duties and other despised taxations, and loosened further by the wholesale importation of cheaper food from abroad. British latifundia, the agricultural properties which had been a measure of wealth and prestige since William the Conqueror, seemed suddenly a shaky investment.

Why then did he want it? He himself may not fully have known the answer. His explanations were uncharacteristically coy and contradictory. He had memories, certainly, of that blissful summer holiday with Elizabeth in 1884, in the last carefree months of their lives, before Sunlight Soap, before Lever Brothers, before parliament, baronetcy, untold riches, old age and death. He spoke publicly and privately about the limits of his ambition. His devoted niece, Emily Paul, who was present for much of his Hebridean adventure, would later insist that her uncle had been unforgettably 'charmed' by Lewis in 1884, and had become 'sympathetic with the difficulties under which he soon discovered the Islanders laboured'.

> Being always on the lookout for some person or community to whom he could bring help and happiness, and some place he could improve, he reflected that if ever the Island of Lewis should come onto the market and

he should be rich enough to buy it, buy it he would, and do his utmost to make it a happy and prosperous Island. Philanthropic gifts he was ready and willing to make as occasion arose, but well-paid work amid congenial surroundings was his goal when planning to give prosperity to a place.'[17]

Emily Paul's observations are not to be dismissed, but they have the advantage of recollections in tranquillity (her words were not written until 1939). It was not exactly an impulse buy, but it is unlikely that William Hesketh Lever had coveted and nursed plans for Lewis over thirty-three unrequited years, as Emily suggested, until he spotted that it was for sale in 1917. (If he had been so inclined he would presumably have instructed his representatives to put out feelers, and they could have reported to him many years earlier that the island estate was available.) He had then, he said himself, no object other than to spend a peaceful last few years in a healthy and beautiful place with friendly neighbours. The fact that a villa in Tuscany or Torquay would have filled most, if not all, of those requirements at a hundredth of the cost was apparently irrelevant.

The judgement of his son would be more pragmatic. For his father, wrote William Hulme Lever,

> recreation meant a change of occupation and, next to the development of a business, he found his greatest pleasure in the development of an estate.
>
> It was in search of an estate, therefore, that he went, not with feverish haste, but quietly and with deliberation. As a matter of fact, he gave serious consideration to and nearly decided to buy an important estate in the Midlands which was then for sale, but its development had already been begun, and he preferred to find one which he could mould to his own ideas from the start.

'One which he could mould to his own ideas from the start . . .' The pretence that he had bought the entire island of Lewis on an old man's fancy as nothing more than a gigantic pre-inhabited retirement garden would not be sustained for many months. He did not believe that Lewis could be an especially profitable speculation, despite the low purchase price. Rather, he considered that the place had too many unexploited resources and underused assets for its own good – and certainly too many for an improving businessman to ignore.

He consulted; he sought advice. That spinner of Hebridean whimsy Alastair Alpin MacGregor later recalled in a moment of lucidity that 'I well remember his discussing with my father in Edinburgh the projects he had in mind'. The latter assured him that the people of the Western Isles, 'though they always voted Radical [were] the most stubborn conservatives on Scotland'. It was doubtful, opined MacGregor Senior, whether Leverhulme would ever live to take a penny out of Lewis, but 'he would find in its peat-mosses ample scope for sinking a million or two. However, Leverhulme was not to be discouraged by such frank talk, for he was a visionary as well as a man who had been highly successful in the world of business.'[18]

It was not as though the Hebrides had palm-oil reserves. Leverhulme in later, more stressful times would unconvincingly attempt to persuade his banks and his associates of the potential worth of Scottish fish-oils, but he gave in 1917 and 1918 no evidence of the slightest interest in such by-products. The London correspondent of *The Scotsman* (following, no doubt, a great deal of editorial head-scratching) came up with the obvious alternative answer: those peat-mosses! As old Mr MacGregor had drily jested (with some authority, as he had been born in the island and was a Gaelic writer), Lewis was literally covered with peat. A sodden, unfathomable mattress of peat lay over large parts of the island. There was not much of anything else in abundance on Lewis, but there was certainly a lot of peat – which once harvested and dried could be deployed as a fuel or a bedding soil. Could his Lordship be intending to diversify out of global soap production and into the industrial exploitation of peat? 'If I wanted peat,' replied Leverhulme drily, 'an island would not be the most attractive investment. It would be much better to keep to the mainland, where the railway service could be made available and where there is plenty of peat.'

He did not want peat. At least, peat was not the first thing on his mind. William Grant in the *Stornoway Gazette* was happy to conclude, two weeks after his announcement of the imminent purchase, that 'Lord Leverhulme had no business intentions with regard to his purchase, his desire being to acquire Lewis solely as a residential retreat . . . In this respect Lord Leverhulme is one of the now considerable number of notable Englishmen who in recent years have been attracted by the notable beauties of our Highland North and West, and, one by one, have been acquiring, in whole or in part, the ancient patrimonies of the old Clan families.' To batten down its point the paper then printed a roll of honour of the seven peers of the realm who owned in 1918 'a portion of the Shire of Ross' – the Marquises of Northampton and Zetland (Lochluichart and Letterewe), the Earl of Lovelace (Ben Damph), Lords Middleton and Wimborne (Applecross and Achnashellach), the Countess of Cromartie (Castle Leod and Coigach), and now, with 400,000 acres and 30,000 people, the majority of whose breadwinners were crofters or cottars, Lord Leverhulme (Lewis). A small amount of inquiry would have corrected the *Gazette*'s misapprehensions about the last name on the list. Unlike the other six, Lord Leverhulme – a son of the new industrial bourgeosie – had little or no time for deer-stalking and salmon fishing. 'We are sure it will be found,' miscalculated William Grant, 'in the case of the new proprietor, that as the years go by the relations between proprietor and people will go on in ever-increasing cordiality.'

The answer lay in the very question. Leverhulme did not want Lewis in spite of its 30,000 people and vast, undeveloped acreage. He wanted the island because of them. The fact that Lewis was, in the words of *The Scotsman*, 'the largest territorial property in the United Kingdom', the fact that its proprietor held dominion, constrained though he was by crofting and criminal law, over a little land entire unto itself was to Leverhulme the salient selling point. While anxious at the outset not to startle the women and children, he hinted as much. In between all that boilerplate about friendly neighbours and pretty scenery and a healthy climate (a gale had blown and it had poured with freezing rain throughout his tour of inspection in October 1917), his inchoate plans were emerging from their invisible ink: 'I feel that I can take a great interest in the life of the isle,' he said. 'If there are any economic problems I shall be glad to work with the people for their solution.'

If there are any economic problems . . . his first sighting of a black-house had provoked the exclamation: 'Not fit for kaffirs'. These were British citizens who lived – in the eyes of William Lever – in more poverty and squalor than South Sea islanders or Congolese tribesmen. He had never been a passive landlord or employer and he was not about to break that habit in a neglected portion of the United Kingdom. This student and admirer of Napoleon Bonaparte was perhaps aware of the Corsican's short shift a hundred years earlier as Emperor of the island of Elba. In the ten months of his administration roads were built and olive groves organised; farms were planned and public buildings were erected; the few thousand people of Elba were hauled blinking into the nineteenth century. Napoleon had been a young man then and Elba was ultimately unsatisfying. He had left them for a larger destiny. Lord Leverhulme was sixty-seven years old and rather less Napoleonic. An Elba would perhaps suffice.

There was another motivation, which was acknowledged more at the time than it would be later. Following a celebrated revolution in November 1917 (which was still October in the old Russian Julian calendar) Vladimir Ilyich Lenin's Bolshevik Party had assumed power in Moscow, with the avowed intention of establishing the world's first Communist workers' republic. The international effect of this accession would dominate the rest of the twentieth century. In the short term it presented the politicians and the plutocrats of the rest of western Europe with a challenge for which most of them were quite unprepared: how to demonstrate that the dispossessed masses and the working poor could improve their lot without overthrowing the established order and putting the royal family in front of a firing squad?

William, Lord Leverhulme believed he knew the answer, but he had never previously had to frame it in such a context. Beforehand his 'improvements' in living and working conditions had been proven only when set beside the hideous alternatives elsewhere in Britain. After 1917 they would inevitably also be judged by comparison with the achievements of a colossal socialist nation.

His philosophy, like that of any thinking person, instantly reflected the change of circumstances. His political and economic thoughts after 1917 occasionally (and unworthily) adopted the blustering tone of an apoplectic Blimp or Baron. 'Talk to the man who would carry the "Red flag" through the land,' wrote Leverhulme unconvincingly in 1918, 'talk to the Socialist or Anarchist of increasing production, or of volume of output and its relation to the costs of production and you receive a vacant stare from out his bloodshot eyes and a scornful reference to "Capitalism" and "Wage Slavery".' But capitalism was good and wage slavery was actually liberty: 'Any attempt at limiting the powers of the individual to acquire Wealth is like endeavouring to lower someone's standard of health because it was higher than the average. The healthy members of a community are a source of strength to others, and so are the wealthy. What we require to do is not to weaken the strong or impoverish the wealthy, but to show to the weak and the poor the way to become healthy and wealthy.'

Such valiant late-in-the-day defences of an economic system which until very recently had appeared to require no defending at all were echoed by the 'Stornoway Merchant' who wrote in his local newspaper in September 1918 that Lord Leverhulme (and not, by implication, the vacant, bloodshot anarchist) was 'a true socialist'. He did not feel the need to flatter himself with the description, but by his deeds ye shall know him. Leverhulme's whole life – unlike that of most self-styled 'socialists' – had been devoted to the improvement of the lot of working people.

'His employees are not mere "hands" and "machines",' continued this Lewis disciple, 'but men and brothers and are treated as such . . . all the world knows that he has built at Port Sunlight a garden city which remains to this hour one of the best object-lessons in the Science and Art of industrial housing.' The Baron Leverhulme was kind to children and devoted to the betterment of humanity. If all the world were Port Sunlight, 'Capital and Labour would not be antagonistic to one another, but would work hand in hand for the common good. Then we would hear less about labour unrest, and "strikes" would be few and far between . . .'

All the world could not be Port Sunlight, but perhaps all of Lewis could. Leverhulme did not decide to add the northern Hebrides to his empire because there was an imminent danger of the hammer and sickle being raised over Stornoway Town Hall. But the challenge of extending the range of liberal capitalism, of demonstrating to the overheated world of western politics that Leverism could work its beneficial magic even in the most unpromising areas more quickly and more powerfully than any repugnant ideology from eastern Europe, was not only on the mind of admiring merchants from Stornoway. It was part of the mental framework of the elderly Lord Leverhulme himself.

The Leodhasaich saw no harm in extending a hand of welcome. They had no intention of establishing a workers' soviet; they knew of him; they used his soap; he could be no worse than earlier satraps. William Grant offered his newspaper's heartfelt appreciation. Stornoway Town Council and the Lewis District Committee, in joint session, despatched a telegram to Cheshire congratulating Leverhulme on the purchase.

The response of the Lewis Crofters' and Cottars' Association would attract ironic attention at a later, wiser date, but it was merely a model of decorous Hebridean good manners. 'The smallholders and cottars of Lewis,' announced the association's president, Alexander Morrison, 'are delighted that Lord Leverhulme has purchased the island, and they beg to congratulate his Lordship on the historic occasion, assuring him of their hearty goodwill and support. Lord Leverhulme's fame as a just and model employer of labour has reached Lewis before him. The manhood of the island being away fighting for the Empire on the field of glory, where many of them made the supreme sacrifice, the old folk at home desire to send this greeting to his Lordship on this memorable occasion, and they hope that he may be long spared to live amongst them.'

There was no reason for any crofters' representative to say otherwise. The Lewis Crofters' Association was not the Lewis Land League; it had a comparatively moderate remit, to secure for its members the best possible deal from the prevailing situation. Colonel Matheson had proven himself to be indomitably opposed to the extension of crofting tenure and the return of privatised community land. He had been trying to realise his assets by selling the whole kit and caboodle for at least five years. Rumours of official intervention to buy Lewis and translate the island into a crofting paradise were just that: rumours, so much smoke, and crofters had long ago learned to mistrust smoke. One aspect at least of an uncertain situation had been resolved. The new owner had money and a good reputation. Alexander Morrison and his colleagues, while tellingly describing themselves to the proprietor as 'smallholders', must have feared worse.

When William, Lord Leverhulme next stepped onto the pier at Stornoway at Easter 1918 he arrived as heir apparent. His main guide would be – as in the previous autumn – Charles Orrock, the chamberlain, or factor, of what was technically still Colonel Matheson's estate. Orrock duly escorted his new employer into the company of several 'leading men' of Stornoway. No minutes were taken of those meetings and no first-hand recollections have survived. But only a naif could suppose that Leverhulme was not by the April of 1918 at least on nodding terms with the land struggle that had marked Lewis for the last forty years. And nobody could imagine that he was not advised on the nature of this discontent by Orrock and his fellow 'leading men'.

One of those men, the editor of the *Stornoway Gazette*, chose the week of Leverhulme's second visit to editorialise on a recent meeting in Stornoway of the Highland Land League. Whether or not his lengthy diatribe was aimed specifically at the attention of his Lordship, it neatly expressed the views of many of those leading men of Stornoway who would offer advice to Leverhulme in the following days. The 'independent and public-spirited' people of Lewis had apparently 'snubbed' the Land League and all of its doings. There had been a time, conceded William Grant, when the Land League was vital and relevant to local concerns. But that glorious era was now over. A movement which had once been composed of 'patriotic Highlanders' was now dominated by a 'body of London meddlers' whose primary goal was to 'prepare the way for Labour men as candidates for the Highland constituencies'. What right had such people, wondered William Grant, 'to demand a hearing or to command a following in our Highlands and Islands'?

Answer came there: none. The day of the militants was at an end. The reforms which had been won were sufficient for any reasonable man, and Leodhasaich were reasonable men. They would, Mr Grant was confident, reject the impertinences of socialist agitators 'whether Highland born or mere Highland for convenience.'

This was a stubbornly contrary reading both of the circumstances in Lewis and of the Land League's meeting on the island. In fact Mr G.J. Bruce of the Highland Land League had been cordially received in Stornoway on Saturday 16 March. His meeting was chaired by Reverend Donald MacCallum of Keose in North Lochs. Reverend MacCallum, the current chairman of Lochs Parish Council, a veteran of the Highland land movement and by no means a Londoner, wasted no time in attracting loud applause by describing 'landlordism' as an insatiable evil which inhabited the gloomiest corners of the night.

'But long as the night has been,' he insisted, 'and great and terrible as have been the cruelties, there are signs of coming dawn which will break through the darkness in which the land has been enveloped, and bring peace.'

Riding the hall's acclaim, Reverend MacCallum then asked rhetorically why, if sugar-hoarding in wartime were as great a crime as it was made out to be, 'what about [speculative] land-grabbing?' If the freedom of the seas, continued the minister, warming to his theme, 'were regarded as a glorious liberty, what about the freedom of the land and the mountains?' – an observation which provoked more applause. We have the freedom of the seas, he resumed, at which a voice from the audience interjected, 'Not for salmon!' The Reverend happily accepted the amendment. They had the freedom of the seas, he agreed, 'as long as we keep out of the reach of the water-bailiffs'.

When the guest speaker from the Highland Land League managed finally to get a word in, G.J. Bruce advised his audience – 'while expressing regret that an island and its people could be bought and sold in this fashion' – that Lord Leverhulme was not a bad option. The 'London meddler' went on to praise Leverhulme as 'a man of high ideals who looks after the interests of his work people . . . So long as landlords are to be tolerated,' concluded Mr Bruce, 'Lord Leverhulme will doubtless prove one of the best we could have, and the change might be all for the good.'

The meeting had been called to decide which parliamentary candidate would win the support of the local Land League in the next General Election. It was to be an election of unusual interest in Lewis. Due to the war, it would be the first to be held since 1910. No date had yet been set but it was widely understood that the poll would be held at the end of the year or as soon as the war was over, whichever came first (the war ended in November 1918). The Representation of the People Act, which had become law a couple of months earlier, in February 1918, had given the vote to women over the age of thirty. This expansion of the franchise necessitated boundary changes across the United Kingdom. One result, not the least significant, was that the Western Isles of Lewis, Harris, the

Uists and Barra (incorporating a dozen smaller inhabited islands) would for the first time comprise an integral parliamentary seat in their own right. The Southern Isles and Harris were to be removed from the Inverness-shire constituency, and Lewis found itself elevated from being a subsidiary part of Ross-shire to becoming the most populous and influential partner in a conglomerate of Gaelic western islands. Stornoway's votes would no longer be counted at Dingwall. Other people's votes would instead be counted at Stornoway.

The sitting Ross-shire and Inverness-shire MPs remained with their mainland voters, leaving the Western Isles to uncover their own representative. It would be a three-cornered contest. The infant Labour Party was determined for the first time to fight every seat in the country, which was why Mr G.J. Bruce of the Highland Land League arrived in Stornoway in March to attempt to persuade Lewis land reformers to back the official Labour candidate, whoever he (or, in some dreams, she) might turn out to be.

He failed. The local land reformers decided on 16 March to throw their weight behind the Liberal candidate, the Medical Officer for Lewis, Dr Donald Murray. Dr Murray had been born in Stornoway fifty-six years earlier, he had married a Lewiswoman thirty-six years after that, he had served on Stornoway School Board and as a Ross-shire Justice of the Peace. As the island's Medical Officer he had won a great deal of gratitude and respect for his tireless crusade against tuberculosis, which had involved him travelling from village to village advising 'against spitting anywhere, the importance of body washing, good food, windows wide open, pleaded for piped water, drainage in country villages and avoidance of contamination of wells and cows' milk.' Donald Murray was also an Asquithian, 'independent' Liberal, which is to say that he was not one of the Liberals who had followed David Lloyd George into unholy coalition with the Conservatives. Islanders had comparatively fond memories of the old-fashioned Liberal Party, less happy recollections of Conservative governments and little or no experience of the new urban Labour Party.

As the 1918 election year progressed, the land issue was neutralised by the elementary fact that all three candidates declared themselves openly and often to be in favour of sweeping land reform as quickly as possible. Not one of the parties had the suicidal gall to propose a member for the Western Isles who was opposed to land redistribution. The Labour candidate, Hugh McCowan, who was eventually selected by the Stornoway branch of the Independent Labour Party but whose candidature failed to win the endorsement of the national Labour Party, was naturally supportive of land reform. The independent Liberal Dr Donald Murray, who was backed by many of the local radicals, called in his election address for 'a strong and effective scheme of land reform which would result in a speedy distribution of all the available land in the Highlands and Islands among the people'. And the Conservative/Liberal coalitionist William Dingwall Mitchell Cotts, a Dumfriesshire-born colliery proprietor and shipowner who would more accurately be described as a conservative Liberal, appealed for 'a radical transformation of our land system'.

Whatever the inclinations, wishes and advice of such leading Storno-wegians as William Grant, all of the national political parties of 1918 were united in one realistic assumption: the Hebridean land question was not answered, not outmoded, not forgotten, and not driven by the unpopular ambitions of London socialists. It was, in fact, the single electoral issue from which no seeker of votes in the Western Isles could escape.

Leverhulme arrived back in Lewis at the end of March 1918, two weeks after the polite Mr G.J. Bruce had received the decorous applause of that Stornoway meeting. It was not to be his hour of assumption, his coronation tour: that would wait until the last niggling document had been signed and stamped. But it was made in an atmosphere of benign goodwill, among people fatigued by war, whose aspects ranged from cautious anticipation to gazing with shining eyes at the imminent Lewis renaissance. The latter were more likely to be found in the terraces of Stornoway; the former in the farflung countryside.

He drove sparingly – for petroleum was strictly rationed and it was not his way to flaunt his wealth – about his new domain in a motor-car. He met with the eminences of Stornoway. He laughed engagingly at such arch jokes as the one about a Lewisman returning from the south who was asked what he thought of the English and replied: 'I don't know, I only saw [Scottish] heads of departments'. He addressed a meeting in support of war savings, introducing himself as 'a poor Lancashire lad a long way from home' and offering to double whatever was raised locally, up to £20,000. (Given that Stornoway Town Hall, complete with its public library and municipal buildings, had burned almost to the ground earlier in the month, his new island seemed to be making unpredictable calls on his largesse.) After seven days of such glad-handing he went back south again, crossed the Ts of the purchase, took possession of the ancient writings, or deeds of Lewis, and prepared his party to journey to the Hebrides as the courtiers of an island lord.

They travelled on Friday 28 and Saturday 29 June 1918. His immediate cortège – they would shortly be followed by others – included his two maiden sisters and the family of Jonathon Simpson. Stornoway Town Council and the Lewis District Committee had prepared a lavish welcome. A specially appointed sub-committee had draped the South Beach and the steamer quay with bunting, garnished the area with evergreens and hung a banner which read 'Welcome To Your Island Home'. The town's Pipe Band and local politicians waited at their marks and a large crowd gathered.

Sadly, the *Sheila* was delayed. When she docked the witching hour had passed: it was slightly after midnight on Saturday and the Sabbath had begun. The Pipe Band was stood down, the councillors assumed a graver mien and the assembly was muted. Lord Leverhulme disembarked to uncertain cheers and a dignified greeting from Provost Murdo Maclean, emeritus Provost John Norrie Anderson and Charles Orrock. His party then bundled into estate vehicles and drove out to the castle through lines of curious spectators. His Lordship could be seen through the windscreen, smiling, nodding and modestly waving his acknowledgements.

A few days later his 24-year-old niece, Emily Paul, made the journey in the company of her father Alexander, who was an Edinburgh journalist, and her mother, Leverhulme's youngest sister Lucy Anne, for 'great was the interest and excitement of [Leverhulme's] family and friends to hear . . . that he contemplated buying [the island], and in that event intended to entertain at Lews Castle in Stornoway'.

Emily and her parents took the same route in July 1918 as had Uncle William at the end of June, overnighting in Inverness before catching the train west to meet the *Sheila* at Kyle of Lochalsh railhead. 'Owing to the war and consequent naval activities,' she recalled, 'north of Inverness was a prohibited area, and we were not allowed to take our seats in the train for Kyle of Lochalsh before we had produced passports authorising us to travel to Stornoway.' The four-hour train journey under brilliant skies was a revelation to Emily – 'I remember thinking that Heaven itself could not be more beautiful' – which was promptly dispelled by a bilious voyage across the inhospitable Minch.

The landing at Stornoway came as both a relief and a fresh ordeal for a young lady who was neither feeling nor looking her best, and who was consequently grateful for the couple of hours of northern Hebridean midsummer's night at either side of 12.00 p.m. The *Sheila*'s docking . . .

> was effected in the presence of a huge crowd who had come down to welcome their friends and inspect the visitors. In those days the boat arrived so late that daylight was fading for it was quite dark by the time she reached the pier, so no one saw what a sorry sight one looked on disembarking.
>
> Passengers had to force their way through a narrow passage from the gangway to the road, between a sea of gazing faces, which was truly an ordeal for one unaccustomed to such publicity. We were soon packed into a car, and leaving the main street of the town we sped through an arched gateway up the long drive to Lews Castle.

The Paul family was ushered inside Lord Leverhulme's new redoubt, adjusting their eyes to the gloom. They were taken to refreshments in the dimly-lit dining room and as they ate the gas-jet lamps flickered lower and lower until the place was almost in darkness. This was a temporary aberration, they were reassured. It was caused by Uncle William turning on the geyser to draw his midnight bath. When it was full they would once again be able to see each other and their meal.[19]

On the afternoon of Tuesday 2 July, two days after his own arrival, Leverhulme was formally welcomed to Lewis by an assembly of the island's great and good in Stornoway's Masonic Hall: a congenial enough setting for the guest of honour, if one made necessary by the accidental burning of the Town Hall.

The reigning provost, Murdo Maclean, a fishcurer and tradesman of the burgh, greeted his new superior by joking that when the news of his new venture was made public many southerners must quickly have consulted their maps – 'Some people seem to have the idea that Lewis is somewhere adjacent to Greenland, and that the population is in the first stages of evolution.' Quite the contrary, asserted Provost Maclean. The island was a 'nursery for all the learned professions, into which Lewis has sent a constant stream of young men who have taken honoured positions and adorned them'. Nor was all of its potential fully exploited, added the provost to meaningful applause: '[Lewis] has great natural resources that are yet undeveloped, but which we hope to see developed in the future.'

If Leverhulme still needed to be told what was expected of him by the Stornoway merchant class, John Norrie Anderson, a retired solicitor, cleared up any confusion. The new proprietor must grasp the land question by the ears and shake it until it cried pax. Former Provost Anderson assured the gathering that 'there are very serious problems to be solved, and his Lordship will have to tackle them bravely'. Lord Leverhulme must learn to 'take with a grain of salt what some people might say to him . . . The problems of Lewis can be solved if they are tackled courageously and in the right spirit, but if there is to be any progress old traditions must first disappear.' Great remedial measures were imperative, said John Norrie Anderson, if the war heroes were to return to a suitable twentieth-century home, but this was not the time or the place to dwell on such matters, which would certainly be discussed with his Lordship in the forseeable future.

He stood then to address them. His stiff shock of hair now white, his short 67-year-old frame broader than of yore but still unbent, his hearing defective and his vocal delivery monotonous and louder than was required; that gin-trap mouth, stern chin and unblinking gaze as riveting as at any time. He jested that his castle would be as lonely and miserable without their goodwill as any summer sheiling.

He looked back over the island's proprietorial deeds of 600 years past, noting that the owner's title 'is based on service' – 'you have always looked upon your laird as one who can render you superior services . . . I cannot think that there is any logic or reason in the possession of a property such as this if it were not founded upon service – and only to the extent that I can render service should I consider that there was any reason for my becoming possessor of the island.'

The jokes and niceties accomplished, William, Lord Leverhulme then delivered his prospectus for Lewis. With the fresh, unprejudiced eye of the newcomer, the business brain of a self-made multi-millionaire and the unswerving confidence of a man whose instincts had rarely betrayed him, he was convinced that he had identified the road to Hebridean riches. That road lay not on the land, but at sea. The speech that followed on that July afternoon in Stornoway's Masonic Hall indentured all of the fury and disappointment of the succeeding years, issuing as it did from a man who had set in stone as his personal creed: 'I scorn to change or fear'.

'I do feel that we in this island,' he said, 'have been drifting a little away from the modern line of march of science and art . . . There is no blame to any of us in that . . .' But . . .

But: 'We have here in the island of Lewis surrounding us wealth beyond the dreams of avarice —'

A tumultuous ovation from his audience obliged him to pause. Wealth beyond avarice apparently figured large in the dreams of the assembly. His jokes were one thing; what was really needed from the head of Lever Brothers was a step-by-step guide to unlimited affluence.

'And so far from Lewis,' he continued, extemporising, 'so far from Lewis being considered an outlying part of the world as you, Mr Provost, were saying, it is really, so far as the harvest of the sea is concerned, what you may call the hub of the universe . . .' The applause broke out once more, as it would do at every punctuation mark and parenthesis for the remainder of his exposition.

'It is only a question,' he resumed, 'of dealing with this matter on the lines that will enable every inhabitant of Lewis to become better off than at present.' The sentimental philanthropist then broached the concept of adding value at source – presumably, given his earlier remarks, to fish.

> We want to deal with it so that a shilling to every man and woman in Lewis shall be worth more than a shilling . . . There are two ways of dealing with a community. One method is called philanthropy – muddling sentiment, I

call it. I don't believe that the people of the island require any philanthropy . . . There is the other method of dealing with communities, and that
is the one in which there is no philanthropy, but where by the logic of the
situation, by availing yourself of the means placed at our disposal by
science you can enable people to live for themselves and to work out their
own destiny.

Within all of their lifetimes, he insisted – yes, within even the remaining
lifetimes of himself and Mr John Norrie Anderson – Lewis could enjoy 'a
more even distribution of wealth and a higher rate of wealth per inhabitant than any other part of the United Kingdom . . . we can have it!'

This incredible consummation was within the grasp of the Leodhasaich, his wondering audience was assured, thanks to the appliance of
science. It would be achieved through dedication and cooperation.

And it was wholly necessary, he continued, if the 'brave men who have
gone from Lewis' to place their 'bodies in the living rampart against
tyranny' were to return from the Great War 'to a better Lewis than ever
they knew'. The utopian island would be accessible only, however, on
certain terms.

What form the new Lewis may take, said Lord Leverhulme disingen-
uously, 'I cannot say'. But certain unprofitable practices were clearly
incompatible with creating the most affluent district of twentieth-century
Britain.

> More than thirty years ago a Royal Commission considered the Lewis
> problem and their proposal was that 33 per cent should be taken off the
> rents.
>
> I just worked it out and am reminded of the Scotsman who, when he
> saw the pyramids, remarked, 'There's been a terrible lot of building here
> for very little rent.' This Royal Commission takes 33 per cent off the
> crofters – less than one pound per croft if you take in the squatters and
> cottars. In Lewis, families are not smaller but bigger than elsewhere, but if
> they were even of the average size, each person would receive four shillings
> per annum (there would be five persons to a household). But four shillings
> per annum is less than one penny per head per week!

The paltriness of it all exasperated him. Who got out of bed for a penny a
week? 'Now can we do anything in that direction? What can be done with

a penny a week?' He was, as many of the men in the Masonic Hall that Tuesday knew full well, deploying a politician's artifice. The Crofters' Commission rent reduction of the late 1890s had more accurately delivered to the heads of most crofting families an immediate saving of three or four pounds, which was at that time the equivalent of a month or six weeks' income to the ordinary labouring person. Such a bonus would not have been scorned anywhere, and it was not scorned in rural Lewis. By reducing it to the lowest denominator Leverhulme was displaying not so much his ignorance of Hebridean home economics as his determination to belittle them, to hold them up to ridicule before proposing a rational alternative.

And the rational alternative, recognisable enough to the speaker and to much of his audience, was to be found in the form of steady, gainful employment provided by an omnipotent entrepreneur, as he explained:

> Working on the lines of commerce, I hope we can solve this problem in Lewis by providing full occupation at wages not a whit inferior to those paid in other localities. We cannot carry on industries successfully unless we can compete in the open market with similar goods made elsewhere.
>
> If you have got the right material, and we have that, and if you have got wealth at your door waiting to be harvested, and we have that, it is for us to see that we prepare it for the market in such a way that it shall fetch the highest price, and out of that we can pay the highest wages. That is roughly the idea of how I think we can work together.

No such benevolent government, he stressed in words that may later have returned to trouble him, 'can be exercised without the consent of the governed fully and completely given . . . the true liberty is that in which all are governed and all take their part in governing. On such lines I believe we can work out such a condition of things here as will make Lewis the envy of less happy lands.'

Aeroplanes, Leverhulme pointed out in a flight of imagination common and not entirely implausible to an educated, progressive Briton of 1918,

> . . . will so annihilate space that Stornoway might come to be regarded by the people of Glasgow as a suburb where they spend the afternoon and evening. Lewis might in future become a favourite starting place for New

York! That is fanciful, but science has made such strides in the last twenty-five years that he would be a rash man who today would say what advantages a situation such as Lewis might in the future give to its inhabitants.

All I can do will be done. We will work on business lines and we will have nothing to do with philanthropy. We will be able to look each other in the face, and you will be able to say to me: 'We thank you for nothing but the opportunity you have given us, and that is all we want.' [There was applause at this.] And I shall say to you, 'We are good friends. It is a pleasure to live amongst you, and I hope we shall have a long and happy life together.'

Those mild words and the loud and lengthy acclamation they received sounded the death knell in Lord Leverhulme's visionary Lewis of any crofting tenure, let alone an extension of crofting tenure. In doing so they also rang the tocsin for rebellion. His contempt for the prevailing system as uneconomic and unscientific was total. Crofting was clearly not the solution to the 'problem of Lewis', or even a part of the solution. Crofting in the Leverhulme analysis was itself the problem of Lewis. The land question had been approached in a topsy-turvy manner: by appeasement of a medieval life style which not only had no place in a modern utopia, but which also actively dragged its unfortunate tenants back from the future into the muddy embrace of a long-lost century which had never known so much as an automated loom and which would probably, given half a chance, disinvent the wheel. The man from the centre of the industrial world would answer the land question by excising it as ruthlessly as the shacks had been torn down from Bromborough marsh.

This removal of crofting from the landscape would be not so much a product as a precondition of the industrialisation of his estate. Leverhulme had determined, by the time of his fourth visit to Lewis and having spent perhaps sixteen days on the island, that the only important present and future asset of the community lay in its easy access to rich fishing grounds. If fish could be caught and landed in sufficient quantities at Stornoway, then it could also be processed there. This need not be a matter merely of pickling herring by the barrel in brine. If the late-Victorian sugar and soap millionaires had proven anything about marketing, they had demonstrated a simple equation: the smaller the packaged unit the greater the retail return. This was the source of mass employment: on the production lines and in the administrative offices. Many more people would be required to process, advertise and distribute the fish than to catch it. By Highland standards a lot of people lived in Lewis; by any southern urban measure the place was almost unpopulated. Lord Leverhulme's revolution was predicated on a substantial workforce which was ready, able, adaptable, hungry and prepared to live within daily commuting distance of a Stornoway office or manufactory. It did not need employees who were forever slinking back to Tolsta or Leurbost to cut peat or see to the cattle.

It required a deracinated urban working class with no alternative but the poorhouse. It had instead a proud community of insular Gaels from whom over 200 years almost everything had been removed but the independence of their working day, and who owed that surviving, precious independence entirely to the scatter of buildings, grazing rights and patch of family land that they called a croft. Leverhulme's revolution needed the people of Bolton. It got the Leodhasaich.

Clear as his message might have been in hindsight (and clear as it may have appeared to some of those present at the Masonic Hall, whose numbers included the old land warrior Reverend Donald MacCallum of Lochs), it was couched in such positive jargon and recycled through such an agreeable and optimistic section of Lewis society that its import was not yet fully digested. What came across most strongly was that the new proprietor wanted to create well-paid jobs, and no Lewis man or woman was opposed to the creation of well-paid jobs. Even his laceration of the crofting economy would cause little alarm: crofters generally being the first to agree that they were inadequately rewarded.

The meetings continued and the messages of support rolled in. Six days after his manifesto address to the Masonic Hall he assumed his *droit de seigneur* as permanent chairman of Stornoway Pier and Harbour Commission. This position gave the reigning proprietor almost total control of the waterfront and quay, as commission members were almost invariably his own nominees. Flanked once more by provosts past and present, he heard the fishcurer John Mackenzie (who had held the provostship for seven years in between John Norrie Anderson and the present incumbent

Murdo Maclean) advise the meeting that 'the success of the harbour meant at all times the prosperity of the island'. Ex-Provost MacKenzie added that under the lamented rule of Colonel Duncan Matheson he and his fellow commissioners had 'on all occasions had a free hand to act as they considered best'. Lord Leverhulme made no comment.

His territorial scent-trails laid and his intentions outlined he settled nicely into castle life. There was work to be done inside and out. Central heating, a reliable supply of hot water and electric lighting were installed. He enjoyed with his guests the exploration of this gentle land. Lewis at any time was another country; at a time of war, to privileged visitors who understood no Gaelic, it seemed miraculously removed from anxiety, from shell-shock, from the sound of distant guns.

The parish of Stornoway itself had, in truth, little to offer these moneyed sophisticates from the south. His niece Emily Paul – who had been hoping for something at least as exciting as Oban – 'found a very drab-looking town, ill-paved and smelling of herring and harbour. A visitor could buy little except Harris tweed, a few postcards and perhaps a Fair Isle jumper. There were innumerable little shops selling foodstuffs, and clothes of an inferior cut and quality, two chemists' shops, and a picture-house where, as often as not, the light in the projector would fail.'

Only out in the wild beyond Marybank and Arnish Moor would the majesty and thousand little mysteries of the island reveal themselves. Emily would occasionally go along on her uncle's 'business trips' into nether Lewis. On the far west coast she discovered 'a timelessness and healing peace, a dreaming beauty over all which seemed not of this earth'. It was a place to produce giddy fantasy in a lady.

> I well remember getting a real attack of nerves on the Monday morning we returned to Stornoway. We had had no news of the outside world since Friday morning. 'Supposing,' thought I, 'the Germans have landed in Stornoway and we are now running into a town in the hands of the enemy.' By the time we reached the outskirts of the town, I was really worked up about it, with the details clear in my mind as to how all messages to the landward part of Lewis would have been stopped.

Emily's travelling vagary faded with the sight of the smelly old harbour side and the castle turrets. Rural Lewis, not Stornoway, was the realm of midsummer dreams.

Leverhulme made a point of not over-using his motor vehicles at a time of national petrol shortage, but it was necessary to traverse his new domain. Whenever possible he combined his tours of inspection with some official duty. On the last Monday in August he drove to Europie at the Butt of Lewis on the northern tip of the island. There, within sight of acres of commonly-worked runrig arable lands, a couple of miles from the home port of the traditional long-line sailing fleet at Ness, he unveiled a war memorial cross at the restored St Moluag's Church.

On a fine, dry day the unconscripted people of Ness, the old and the very young – many if not most of whom would have been monoglot Gaels – gathered in that silent place to watch and to hear the little Englishman who had come promising so much. They filled St Moluag's until there was standing-room only at the back. But there was to be no talk here of the laughable economics of crofting, no tub-thumping oration about the glittering future of an industrialised fishing industry. The proprietor spoke at length, as usual, but he fittingly limited his observations to the pity of war and the virtue of building rather than destroying. Lewis had, he said, given more men to the armed forces in proportion to population than any other part of Britain, 'but we can look back with pride, and our children's children will look back with pride, on the bravery and self-sacrifice of the gallant dead.'

The Great War, an Cogadh Mor on the memorials of the Gaidheal-tachd, was not yet over. But the last German offensive of the conflict had expired and as Leverhulme spoke at Europie the conclusive Allied assault was underway. Even here, on the far north-western edge of the continent, people were able to hope for the first time in forty-eight months that the torment was approaching an end. The men were coming home.

Leverhulme continued with his duties in an island increasingly expectant, not only of his own proposals, but of the restoration of its surviving young people. He addressed Stornoway Town Council on the subject of replacing the old Town Hall, speaking of a need to combine commerce and beauty in the redevelopment of Stornoway, as had been the case in medieval Venice. He held garden parties at the castle in aid of War Savings.

He celebrated his sixty-seventh birthday on 19th September by distributing the Intermediate Certificates at the Nicolson Institute. The teenaged schoolchildren of Lewis were, he told them, 'about to go out into the world to fight the same battle of life as their fathers and their grandfathers before them had fought'. He had a number of improving and cautionary tales to pass on, such as the parable of the Swiss chemist Nestlé who developed a huge business out of his modest attempts to make his baby's milk more digestible. But many of the bright young minds before him, he knew, would be thinking: 'What chance is there for us here in Stornoway? We must go out into the great world beyond.' He was not sure that they were right. He would tell them a story . . .

There was an Indian boy who became so obsessed with the idea of securing diamonds that he left home and spent his life in a vain search for them. He heard that his old father was in need of assistance on the farm, but he would not return. He heard that his father had died and that the farm was to be sold. But he continued his fruitless search for diamonds, until one day when climbing a mountain where he had been told diamonds could be procured his foot slipped, and he fell to the bottom and was killed. Meantime his father's farm passed into other hands, and here after all were the diamonds which the boy had gone away in search of, for the farm became the famous Golconda Diamond Mine, the richest diamond mine that up till then the world had ever known.

'If you go out into the great world outside in search of diamonds,' Lord Leverhulme told the Nicolson Institute's class of 1918, 'well, you might never find them, while all along there might be acres of them under your feet at home without your knowing it. Whatever there is at home, near your hand, if you can develop it and cultivate it you are far more likely to succeed than by going long distances out into the great world.'

He went to Shawbost on the north-west coast, where young Calum Smith was growing up without English, without his father and three uncles, who were all serving in the Royal Navy, and soon without a croft or a house to the family's name. The proprietor left behind him there a small local controversy about the relative expertise of the fishermen who had been assembled to meet and advise him, and those who were irritated by having missed the visit.

He attended church on the Sabbath, of course. And he delighted in telling the story of being approached by an elder as he left the United Free Church in Stornoway after one morning service. 'Do ye no ken what the Auld Book says?' asked the elder in the Leverhulme family's vernacular version of the tale (which seems to imply that a Dundonian music hall artist had insinuated himself into the Stornoway communion).

'What does it say?' requested his Lordship.

'It says,' continued the aging oracle, ' "Woe unto ye when all men shall speak well o' ye" – and they're speaking well o' ye the noo.'

He was, observed his son, 'brimful of optimism, enthusiasm and determination'.[20] He was also marking time. Everybody was marking time until the men came home. But although he could not yet let his builders and contractors off their leash, his imagination was running wild. After that startling introductory delivery to the Masonic Hall he leaked his intuitions and proposals slowly and carefully, and often away from Lewis. He cultivated the interest and company of the pioneering Lancastrian landscape architect Thomas Hayton Mawson. Mawson – an inspired 57-year-old planner of impeccable liberal Christian credentials whose garden designs were by 1918 in demand all over the world – visited Stornoway that August. The two men drove around Lewis together, the bright-eyed, cadaverous Mawson enthusing his host with rapturous talk of the island's suitability for farming willow trees in sufficient quantities to join the basket trade ('Covent Garden imports three million willow baskets a year grown in Holland. They should be grown in Lewis . . .') and enough soft fruits ('raspberries, strawberries, blackcurrants, gooseberries . . .') to open a Hebridean jam factory.

Upon his return to England Thomas Mawson used the *Manchester Guardian* – a liberal provincial daily newspaper close to both men's heart and home – to describe Leverhulme's ambitions, which had by then ballooned to encompass a railway network and a chemical plant producing iodine. His evidence is valuable as that of a friend and a sympathetic advisor to the early months of the project. It details, at length and in public for the first and only time, the astounding nature of the augurs for Lewis which in 1918 Leverhulme vouchsafed privately to such figures as Mawson and the past and present provosts of Stornoway:

Lord Leverhulme, the new owner of the Isle of Lewis, is setting himself to work in hearty co-operation with the islanders to develop, by the introduction of capital, science and organisation, the natural resources of the island and the waters surrounding it. Lord Leverhulme has discovered a territory much of which is as undeveloped as the western prairies of Canada and with potential wealth proportionately great.

It is the development of the fishing industry to which the new owner will first devote his energies. The production of iodine is also under consideration, and expert chemists are working on the seaweeds which are so abundant round the island. If the residuals or by-products obtained from the chemical treatment of the seaweed prove of commercial value we may look forward to the revival of what was at one time a considerable industry.

But before this or any other industry can be a success it will be necessary to provide better transit facilities by sea and land. Safe harbours are the first essential of all economic developments. Engineers are accordingly at work making preliminary surveys for railways which will connect the principle harbours of the island with Stornoway, their natural base. We may soon have a railway on the east coast, connecting Port of Ness, another railway connecting with Callernish on the west, and possibly a third to Loch Seaforth, connecting the Isle of Harris directly with Stornoway. As supplementary to these the main roads are likely to be further improved and motor routes created as feeders to the railways.

A natural corollary to the introduction of railways and harbour facilities will be an increase in the number and size of the steamers trading with the mainland. A trawling fleet, too, is bound to appear as an arm to the fishing industry. Ice factories, cold storage, and canneries for the curing and treatment of fish for export are already planned, and the work of construction will soon begin.

The solution of travel problems opens up vistas of many other industries which should add to the prosperity of the island. The most important of these, it may be, is the accommodation of tourists, for already Lewis is a fisherman's paradise. Inducements to sportsmen can be considerably increased by improving the loch fishing, and, when it is stated that there are nearly 600 lochs and tarns on the island, it will be seen that the opportunities in this direction are unlimited.

The utilisation of the peat lands, which extend to over 100,000 acres, offers prospects of considerable importance. It is possible to imagine great industrial developments if the peat can be used in the production of power. In the neighbourhood of Moscow it is said that 100,000 horsepower is produced from peat fuel, and therefore the problem has passed the experimental stage. In the meantime the peat is excellent for ordinary fuel, for peat litter and for horticultural purposes.

It is, however, to the conversion of peat lands into cultivated soil that we must look for solid results. The crofters have by a slow process extending over generations reclaimed large tracts of peat lands along the coast, but what is needed is quicker and more scientific methods, and in this direction much research work is already being done. If success follows these experiments Lewis will become a great food-producing island.

Meanwhile huge nurseries are being planned for the raising of forest trees, which thrive on the island. Indeed, had the available forest lands been planted at the same time as the 500 acres around Lewis Castle our war needs for timber would have presented a much less difficult problem. Lord Leverhulme proposes to plant five million young trees each year. These will consist largely of Menzies spruce and Scotch firs. It is also proposed to plant huge areas with the white willow, which grows well on almost any part of the island, and to bring into being a large basket-making industry. It is also proposed to experiment with New Zealand flax, which experts declare will grow well in Lewis. Unfortunately this plant is a long time in coming to the fibre-producing stage, but if success is attained it will bring another important industry to the island.

Those who have seen the productive raspberry farms in Perthshire, which in the fruit season employ thousands of pickers, will not be surprised to learn that fruit-growing on a large scale is to be introduced. Here there is no need for experiments, because raspberries, strawberries, gooseberries, and currants grow splendidly and yield enormous crops. Other fruits, like the loganberry and American blackberries, may also be tried, and along with them the hardy Siberian crab[apple], which is so prolific and so popular for the making of crab and blackberry jelly.

The proprietor further plans an experimental garden, to be devoted to the testing of the growth of plants for distilling, as, for instance, mint and camomile, and also the growth of herbs for medicinal purposes. It is the intention to convert all the raw materials produced on the island, whever possible, into a finished product upon the spot.

It follows that these enterprises will be accompanied by a 'boom' in building both for industrial, commercial and residential purposes, and for the crofter as well as for the merchant and manufacturer. Before the War the population of the island was 31,000. Fully developed, the resources of the island are probably capable of supporting comfortably a population of 200,000.

One wonders how far the Government will encourage this great design to increase the prosperity of Lewis. Will they so reorganise the land laws as to make co-operation between the owners and the cultivators of the soil mutually advantageous, or will they interpose other and more vexatious restrictions than those which at present exist, and which paralyse the spirit of individual initiative and collective effort?

This was Lord Leverhulme's incredible vision of Lewis. Those were the castles built in the air above his motor car as he drove between Stornoway and Shawbost or Lochs. That was the breathtaking summation of his few weeks of observation and conclusion. Its almost unimaginable scale would have made it preposterous from any other source. Issuing as it did from the multi-millionaire creator of Lever Brothers, its giddy immensity seemed almost seductive.

Lewis would become an island of at least 200,000 people – six times more than had ever lived there. Stornoway would be an industrial and trading metropolis to rival Glasgow or Liverpool. Commuter trains would rattle across Barvas Moor carrying thousands of workers home at night. They would pass by fields of fruit pickers and lush acres of flax and herbs. Visiting anglers would wave from the sides of lochans. Forests of willow, spruce and fir would cover the less penetrable central regions. New villages would spring out of the reclaimed land, and older parishes would expand in orderly fashion far beyond the township bounds. And in the distance always, with its – how many? 50,000? 100,000 people? – the great centre of the island's capital would lie simmering in the haze; the horizon broken by the steam from its chemical works, its canneries and its curing factories and the smoke from its peat-fired generating station; the busy surrounding sea populated by its fishing fleet and trading vessels.

The fantastic world created by Leverhulme in cheerful collaboration with such allies as Thomas Hayton Mawson was in fact a mixture of genuine foresight, resurrections from the past and pure nonsense.

The idea of giving Lewis a couple of branch railway lines was neither original nor utterly ridiculous. Just twenty years previously, in 1897 and 1898, two separate private enterprises, the Highland Railway Company and the Highland Light Railway Company, had surveyed and proposed small-gauge lines between Stornoway and Tarbert in Harris and between Stornoway and Breasclete and Carloway on the west coast. The £500,000 schemes had collapsed when the amount of capital required to be raised by private subscription – £290,000 – was not forthcoming.

Seaweed and forestry were industries of the past and of the future. The plentiful quantities of weed which washed up on Hebridean shores had always been used as fertiliser It was known to have various other valuable properties, especially when incinerated and turned into the adaptable alkaline named kelp, which produced soda and potash. A century earlier, during the stringencies of the Napoleonic War, the Scottish Highlands and Islands had experienced a miniature economic boom because of the nation's need for kelp in the making of – as Lord Leverhulme would have known – soap and glass.

The process for extracting iodine from kelp ash, which was being suggested as a local industry by Leverhulme and Mawson, had been discovered in the nineteenth century. It would prove to be a bubble easily burst by the discovery and exploitation of mineral deposits of iodine in Chile and elsewhere. Not that this disappointment signalled the end of the industrial day for this versatile weed. In the 1930s work on seaweed-derived alginic chemicals popularly known as alginates indicated their suitability as emulsifiers and gelling agents in the food industry (as well as the exciting possibility of a 'sodium alginate fibre' which was employed to build one, and only one, experimental De Havilland Mosquito fighter aeroplane entirely from seaweed).

A string of small alginate processing works was established up and down the Hebrides, which repaid crofters who cut and delivered seaweed to their doors. But all of these industries lived and died on the margin. After the defeat of Napoleon and the resumption of international trade, Hebridean kelp was priced out of the market by continental materials. In the second half of the twentieth century the alginate works of Lewis and the Uists struggled in competition with imported goods from as far away as South America and Tasmania to satisfy the demand for high-quality produce speedily delivered. The vision of Leverhulme and Mawson for an island kelp industry was not ludicrous; it was merely overstated.

Overstatement was commonplace. It is tempting to wonder quite how big Leverhulme considered Lewis to be; to speculate that he was deceived by those limitless North Atlantic skies. Where were all those people and their homes and livelihoods to fit, along with the forests, the farms, the fruit gardens, herb meadows and 600 angling lochs? Small forestry plantations would be created by a later generation of Scottish crofters and private owners, but nobody ever again thought it safe or sensible to plant five million young trees a year in Lewis. Peat-fired power generation would remain obstinately on some agendas for decades, but would never seriously challenge the dominance firstly of King Coal and latterly of North Sea oil and gas – and by the time they were running out and peat's day might have dawned the whole family of fossil fuels was considered wasteful and polluting, and was by-passed in favour of such clean renewables as hydro-electricity and – particularly in the Hebrides – wind and water power. Had Lord Leverhulme had access to wind turbine technology in 1918 he would doubtless have overpromoted it gleefully in Lewis. But he did not.

Flax and soft fruit certainly did grow in the islands, but there were reasons why crofters did not already produce them by the sackful, just as there were reasons, not entirely linked to a shortage of equipment and agricultural science, why the same crofters had not already reclaimed the whole of Lewis from peat bog. Leverhulme had visited his island in the winter, but not for very long. Mawson had never been there before the August of 1918. When the distinguished horticulturalist looked about him on fine, dry summer's days, noted the twenty hours of available day-light shining on soil which needed only a treatment of lime to become the ideal habitat for gooseberries, and reported that most of the 770 square miles could be turned into an orchard, his enthusiastic host was neither inclined nor equipped to contradict. Any native could have told them. Lewis had certainly a more destructive rainfall than ever lashed the rasp-berry fields of Perthshire, but its wind was the real difference. The Outer Hebrides are swept by more sustained and violent winds than anywhere else in Britain. Such parts of the islands as Europie at the Butt of Lewis register a greater number of stormforce gales in a year than days of sunshine. Very little had ever stood up to the Lewis wind, which largely explained the popularity of root vegetables among local cultivators. It blew all year round. A raspberry bush – or a white willow sapling – might survive the equinox to be blasted in July. To recognise such reality was not merely the pessimism of the crofters, nor the wilful Presbyterian conservatism so mocked by their lowland critics. To face such facts was the very stuff of survival on Lewis, about which 20,000 sentient adults could have advised Lord Leverhulme at least as suitably as did the well-intentioned Thomas Hayton Mawson.

The last paragraph of Mawson's essay in the *Guardian* betrayed William Leverhulme's fatal concern. His reveries had been disturbed by the news that the Board of Agriculture was intending to resume its pre-war proposals to return private farms to crofting land, possibly on a larger scale than before and with the assistance of new legislation.

The prospect of these 'other and more vexatious restrictions' which would 'paralyse' enterprise on Lewis provoked Leverhulme to write directly to Robert Munro, the Secretary of State for Scotland. Munro had been the wartime Scottish Secretary since 1916 and would retain the position until 1922. For most of that time he was the 'coalition' Liberal/ Conservative representative of the parliamentary seat of Roxburgh and Selkirk in the south of Scotland. But Munro was a Highlander, a Liberal and a Free Churchman. He was born in 1868 at the Easter Ross village of Alness on the Cromarty Firth, a son of the manse and a young devotee of Gladstonian Liberalism. His path from the glebe to the Commons was, not unusually, taken by way of a career in the law. He was one of the generation of Highland Liberals who had seen their home constituencies – in Munro's case, Ross-shire with Lewis – assaulted and usurped by crofters' candidates such as Roderick Macdonald.

Robert Munro may not have been, as a 50-year-old King's Council and member of Lloyd George's coalition cabinet, wholly sympathetic to the Highland land struggle. But he was fully aware of its power. He understood land hunger to be a visceral, organic force which was under normal circumstances virtually impossible to resist, and which a civilised government could therefore only assuage. The challenge presented to him after 1918 was whether or not Lord Leverhulme's presence in and plans for Lewis represented such abnormal circumstances that appeasement would no longer be necessary. Could, in short, Leverhulme convert the majority of Leodhasaich to his own view: that crofting was outmoded and, once supplanted by a thriving wage economy, would soon become undesirable?

The signs were not good. Letters from Leverhulme arrived in Munro's office in the autumn and early winter of 1918 reiterating all of the proprietor's standard arguments about the inefficiency of crofting. But they were read by a man who had forgotten more about crofting than William Leverhulme would ever learn. Munro took heed of them, while also taking care to proceed with the groundwork for a post-war revision of the Smallholder's (Scotland) Act, and while reassuring the Lewis Crofters' and Cottars' Association that he was considering their sugges-tion that Lewis be bought out entirely by the state and converted into their promised land.

News of this state of flux at home may have reached the trenches in Flanders and the ships on the high seas more quickly than it arrived in Whitehall. In October 1918 a serving Leodhasach named Roderick MacLeod, who came from a distressed part of rural Lewis, wrote from the Western Front to his old schoolmaster at home. The young soldier believed that Lord Leverhulme 'evidently means to do well for the island . . . and its people'. He noted sharply that 'the Stornoway Brigade had the barrage on him with all the needs of the situation before he has had time to put his sword and baton up . . . However, let us hope that all the schemes will mature, and that in a few years' time the place will be a busy hive of industry in a network of electric railways.'

And then this moderate, optimistic soul (MacLeod proudly supported the Liberal parliamentary candidate Donald Murray and not the platform of the Land League or the Labour Party) turned to the 'steps necessary for the settlement of Lewismen and others on the island after the war':

> I am afraid that is a question that will take some answering to the satisfaction of everyone. However, I hardly think that it can be satisfactorily solved by forming committees and accumulating funds to ship the people to the backwoods of our Colonies when they could be established on the land and otherwise at home.
>
> Give them a stake one way or another in the country for which they have fought so well and it will awake in them a sense of duty to it that has hitherto been asleep. How can the majority of us be truly patriotic having to fight for countless acres that by right should have been ours long ago, but up to the present have been preserved for the sport and pleasure of the idle rich, to uphold laws that enable the so-called owners to cast our old

folks into prison for trespassing on these lands while we are abroad defending them?

We could do a day's work for a day's wage in any country and under any flag. Let us have something of our very own to fight for in the next war, and there need be no conscription.

There were many ominous sentiments in this message from a Liberal, educated Lewisman. Contempt for the 'so-called' landowning classes was clearly not confined to a few dispossessed malcontents in the Lewis of 1918. More disturbingly for Leverhulme – who would probably have shared the young man's scorn for the 'idle rich' – Roderick MacLeod considered that a mere 'day's wage' was insufficient. He was not looking for the kind of comfortable employment that could be gained 'under any flag'. He was looking for a stakeholding. He was looking for the 'countless acres that by right should have been ours long ago'. He was looking for what he perceived to be justice.

He also made a distinction between settlement of the land struggle and the schemes of Lord Leverhulme. In the view of Roderick MacLeod they were not mutually exclusive. Had they been so, from his faintly sceptical description of 'a busy hive of industry in a network of electric railways' we may suppose that MacLeod would have taken the land ahead of a salaried position in one of Leverhulme's enterprises. But he saw no conflict between the two. Lord Leverhulme, however, did.

From the very beginning, the official version would insist, William Leverhulme found himself frustrated by the dead hand of government. His son, William Hulme Lever, published the first biography just two years after his death. 'His early days in Lewis were very happy ones,' wrote the second Viscount Leverhulme, who spent part of that summer with his father in the Hebrides, 'but they were not to last for long.'

> He encountered the first obstacle in his path in the late summer of 1918, when the Scottish Board of Agriculture declared its intention of taking over, under the terms of the Small Landowners (Scotland) Act 1911, certain of the few remaining farms in the island to meet the demand for further small holdings or 'crofts'. Leverhulme, while he consented to some farms on the western side of the island being taken, was strongly opposed to the splitting up of others . . .

The Government Authorities were obsessed with one sole idea, the provision of further crofts. They admitted Leverhulme's good intentions and welcomed his investment of capital in the island, but they seem always to have viewed his development schemes as being a thing apart and unconnected with the problem of land hunger which had been so long with them . . . It was also said that he sought to 'industrialise' a people who had no desire to be industrialised . . . [but] he had no thought or intention of establishing in the island 'industries' as the term is understood in England.[21]

The son and heir was being filially disingenuous. His father actually was 'strongly opposed' to the reclamation of a single Lewis farm by crofting, on the west or the east coast. Leverhulme pleaded with Robert Munro to prevent the Board of Agriculture from continuing with any of the land settlement schemes that they had initiated before the war, but which had been debated into stalemate by Colonel Matheson's lawyers. The new proprietor claimed to the Scottish Secretary that upon purchase he had been entirely ignorant of such proposals – a fantastic suggestion which implied not only extreme negligence by his land agents, but also an impossible level of ignorance in Charles Orrock and the 'leading men' of Stornoway whose intelligence he had tapped during the lengthy negotiations.

And by any reasonable definition of the term in England or elsewhere, he had every intention of 'industrialising' Lewis. He may not have turned Barvas Moor into the Black Country, but his declared, ineluctable purpose was to increase the population to as many as 200,000. The additional 170,000 would be supported by wage-earners working in chemical plants, fish-processing and jam factories, electricity generators, railway yards, building sites and service industries. When Lord Leverhulme talked – knowledgeably and ahead of his time – of adding value at source to every Hebridean product, he was talking of the industrial processes of refining and preserving and canning.

He was in truth an old man in a hurry. William Leverhulme was as fit and lively as any teetotal 67-year-old who has observed a life-long regimen of sleeping in a bed exposed to the four seasons. But he was only thirty-six months from the end of his three score years and ten. He had never been a patient man and it was clear to everybody that the transformation of Lewis from a sleepy rural backwater to the epicentre of western industry would not be accomplished overnight. Despite his soothing mantra of wanting only to settle down quietly among pleasant neighbours (which was repeated less often and with less conviction as the months passed, until it disappeared altogether from his repertoire), he was – as his son and others reported – a small bundle of seething energy, anxious to make a start, intolerant of delay or scepticism and determined to bulldoze over irrelevant objections.

He had returned to England when the Armistice was signed at 11.00 a.m. on Monday 11 November 1918. Across the whole of the United Kingdom the sweet flavour of victory was cloyed by an unexpected mephitic; a dull, lingering cloud which tempered the celebrations with weariness and sorrow, and which would never entirely disperse from the lives of the survivors.

But celebrations there were on the forenoon and afternoon and evening of that November Monday. Perhaps 5,000 men and women, one-sixth of the entire population of Lewis, had been actively engaged in the conflict. Most of them would at last be coming home. On the west coast of the island 'boys struggled to the housetops to hoist white flags for peace on anything that might serve as a flagpole; even bamboo fishing rods were used.'[22] On the east coast the Home Fleet vessels of the Stornoway Patrol and other steamers blew their sirens in jubilant, noisy discord.

Stornoway Town Council met on the Monday afternoon, in time to receive a telegram which read:

> Heartiest congratulations to town of Stornoway and people of Lewis on victory which brave lads from Lewis have done full share in winning. Hope will be celebrated with happy rejoicings and with dignity worthy of so great a people. All necessary expenses please charge to myself. – Leverhulme.

Tuesday 12 November was a school holiday throughout the island. The harbour was gay with bunting and the pipe band led the men of the Stornoway Patrol and the boys of the Naval Corps on a march around the town. There was an open-air meeting outside the Imperial Hotel which began with a prayer and closed with a rendition of the National Anthem.

In the evening a large congregation attended an ecumenical religious service at the United Free Church.

And then they went off to celebrate, and if they were men over the age of twenty-one or women over the age of thirty, to vote, and to observe as they trickled into the public prints the results of the first General Election since 1910.

The 1918 election was startling both nationally and locally. Across the whole of the country Lloyd George's Coalition Conservative/Liberal alliance, which credited itself with having won the war, swept back into power with a landslide majority of 351. The Prime Minister had at his shoulder 526 members of parliament. The Labour Party had sixty-three MPs, its highest ever, and the Irish Nationalists totalled seventy-three. But the old Liberal Party, the party of Gladstone and Asquith – the party of Scottish Secretary Robert Munro and Lloyd George themselves before they thought better of it, the party which had been in government with a large majority just eight years earlier – was utterly destroyed. It returned just twenty-eight MPs, and it never fully recovered.

One of those lonely twenty-eight Liberal MPs was sent to Westminster from the new constituency of the Western Isles. Herbert Asquith himself may have lost his seat, but Dr Donald Murray of Stornoway was elected with 3,765 Hebridean votes. The Lloyd George Coalition candidate, the Dumfriesshire coal-owner William Mitchell Cotts, came a close second with 3,375 votes, and the first Labour Party candidate to offer himself to the electors of the Western Isles, Hugh McCowan, who had the unenviable task of campaigning with local support but without national Labour Party endorsement, ran in third place with 809 votes.

The ballot was shockingly low. Across the whole of Britain little more than 50 per cent of the voters bothered to tick a ballot paper in Lloyd George's khaki election. In the Western Isles the percentage was even smaller. Donald Murray was elected by a Hebridean turn-out of 43.6 per cent of eligible voters. Only 7,949 islanders bothered to vote out of a total registered electorate of 18,235. The reasons have been glibly ascribed to the number of servicemen still abroad and not bothering with a postal vote (which was available in 1918 for the first time in a United Kingdom general election), or the number of Hebridean women reluctant to exercise their new franchise, or even the inability of Gaelic-speaking people of both sexes to comprehend an anglophone election campaign.

The first two explanations do not hold water and the third is essentially racist. In four of the five further constituency elections over the next thirteen years the Western Isles turn-out would actually be lower than 43 per cent. The troops, as everybody in Lewis and Harris had good reason to know, were certainly home by 1922. By 1931, when the turn-out was just 36 per cent, one may assume that the women of the Scottish Gaidhealtachd were by and large no longer intimidated by the notion of striding down to the parish school and casting a vote. There is certainly no evidence that the people of Lewis, Harris and the Uists were finding English-language electoral debate more difficult to understand as the twentieth century progressed. They had always understood not only as much Beurla as was necessary, but also what a vote meant and where best to cast it. The inter-war electoral malaise in the Western Isles – as, indeed, in the rest of the Highlands of Scotland – seems to have been caused less by illiteracy, by absentee males or by Gaelic female modesty, and more by lack of faith in established party politics.

But in December 1918 Dr Donald Murray of Stornoway, the former Medical Officer and chairman of the School Board and current Justice of the Peace who believed in 'speedy distribution of all the available land in the Highlands and Islands among the people' began his four-year spell as the first Member of Parliament for the Western Isles. Murray would be unlikely to follow the example of Roderick MacDonald and marry into Stornoway Castle, if only because he already had a wife. He took with him to the House of Commons the good wishes and high expectations of such men as Reverend Donald MacCallum of Keose and the serving soldier Roderick MacLeod, and the deep suspicion, bordering on hostility, of Lord Leverhulme and his coterie on the hill.

A state of open conflict between the two camps would be delayed, however. For as 1918 turned into 1919 the islands of Lewis and Harris were violated with such unimaginable severity that politics were made irrelevant, and were left with a suppurating wound beyond the scope of any doctor, landowner, soldier, MP or even minister to heal.

5

FIT FOR HEROES

In the late evening gloom of New Year's Eve 1918 a long line, two men deep, of Royal Naval Reservists stood, lit by the yellow jetty lights and railhead lamps, on the platform at Kyle of Lochalsh in Wester Ross.

Where the railway station ended the mailboat pier began. It stood a minute's march from the train and the carriages, jutting abruptly out into the narrow kyle towards Skye. Between 7.00 p.m. and 8.00 p.m. on Tuesday 31 December 1918, two large boats were tied alongside. They were the regular MacBraynes Lewis ferry *Sheila* and an armed yacht which had been requisitioned three months earlier by the Admiralty, based at Stornoway and rechristened *Iolaire*, which is for Gaelic 'Eagle'. She was a fast, attractive, slim and low-slung ship with a mast fore and aft and a single large funnel amidships.

At an order the line of Reservists divided. Sixty were marched aboard the *Sheila* and the remaining seventy embarked on the His Majesty's Yacht *Iolaire*.

The former would survive. Almost every one of the latter group, as well as scores of their comrades, relatives and neighbours who were already on board the armed yacht, had just a few hours left to live.

They were from Lewis and Harris; some of the 3,000 islanders who had served their country as sailors during the Great War. It is estimated that 6,200 Lewismen joined the Armed Forces between 1914 and 1918. Around 600 were returned emigrants who fought in colonial regiments. The remainder came from elsewhere in Britain and – the great majority – from the island itself, from its total population of 31,000. By the end of the war about 800 had been killed, chiefly on the Western Front. Almost exactly half of the 6,200, virtually all of whom came directly from Lewis, served in the Navy. Those totals represent the largest percentage of volunteer and conscript servicemen to join that conflict from any community in the British Empire.[23]

They returned not in a single joyous group but piecemeal, slowly and steadily, a few hundred at a time in the last few weeks of 1918 and the early months of 1919. The 530 men who arrived by train at Kyle of Lochalsh from Inverness and points south on New Year's Eve 1918 considered themselves to be relatively fortunate. They were 'libertymen', demobilised Naval Reservists who were being sent home within a few weeks of the Armistice and who would arrive back in Stornoway, Tarbert, Ness, Uig and Lochs in time to combine celebrating the peace with that most vital of Gaelic festivals: the advent of the New Year. Kyle of Lochalsh on that day, said Donald MacDonald, who knew several of them and whose township of North Tolsta would lose eleven sons in the early hours of 1 January 1919, 'presented an animated scene as many friends and relatives were reunited, some for the first time in four years. The war was over, and Lewis and their loved ones only forty miles away.'

The 'small, sturdy' *Sheila* could not carry them all. The *Iolaire* was consequently pressed into service. The yacht had only eighty lifejackets and lifeboat capacity for 100 men. Nonetheless 262 island servicemen, mostly from Lewis but including a small number of Harrismen, were ordered aboard. She made good headway northwards with a total ship's complement, including her own officers and crew, of 284, and by thirty minutes after midnight was crossing the Minch in squalls and drizzling rain. Neither the *Iolaire* nor her officers had ever previously entered Stornoway harbour at night.

Shortly before 2.00 a.m. the captain of the waiting pilot boat, Lieutenant W.B. Wenlock, saw distress rockets go up outside the mouth of the harbour. He immediately manoeuvred H.M. Drifter *Budding Rose* towards 'what I considered to be the position from where the rockets were being fired and found a ship in distress on the Biastan Holm rocks, but was unable to render any assistance owing to the heavy seas running'.

James Macdonald was on board the fishing boat *Spider*, which was also sailing northwards back to Stornoway when the *Iolaire* overtook her on the starboard side. He recalled:

> We followed immediately in her wake, and when approaching Arnish Light I noticed that the vessel did not alter her course but kept straight on in the direction of the Beasts [of Holm].

I remarked to one of the crew that the vessel would not clear the headland at Holm as it went too far off its course to make the harbour in safety. Immediately afterwards we heard loud shouting and then knew the vessel was on the rocks. We were passing the Beacon light at Arnish at that time and could hear the shouting of the men as we were coming into the harbour. The night was very dark and a strong breeze from the south raging and a heavy sea running. We were unable to give any assistance as we could not rely on our engine to operate in such rough seas.

The *Iolaire* had struck the rocks known as the Beasts of Holm, less than 20 yards from the shore at the western lip of the harbour mouth. She was immediately holed and foundered, 'listing heavily to starboard after striking'. Some time between 3.00 a.m. and 3.30 a.m. she broke her back and sank in shallow water. In such circumstances and conditions her lifeboats and even her lifejackets were of little use – she was, in the words of Tormod Calum Domhnallach, 'caught between the wind and the sea in total darkness on the one hand and on the other, a steep and rocky shore constantly pounded by huge waves.'[24] The men aboard required shore-to-ship rescue equipment, and that was not available on Holm Point at 2.00 a.m. on 1 January 1919.

Through heroic efforts seventy-nine men were saved. John Finlay MacLeod of Port of Ness threw his boots ashore (he never saw them again), and then followed them with a heaving line, which was used to drag a hawser from the boat to safety, and along that hawser some forty men reached Holm Point. John MacLeod's fellow Nessman Donald Morrison clung for almost eight hours to a mast which leaned out of the water, festooned with redundant rigging and sheets and spars, before he was rescued at 10.00 a.m. by a naval boat.

Two hundred and five men drowned in the biggest peacetime maritime disaster in British history. Among them were 181 naval ratings from Lewis and Harris and almost all of the ship's officers and crew, some of whom were also Hebrideans. The Leodhasaich who perished came from every parish in the island. Twenty-five were from Ness and its west side neighbourhoods. Eleven were from the village of Leurbost in Lochs. The war memorials at Stornoway and Tarbert in Harris – uniquely in the United Kingdom – date the duration of the Great War from 1914 to 1919 in order to encompass the crowning tragedy of the *Iolaire*.

No words in any language could register the pain or evoke the trauma. It was an event so cataclysmic as to affect Lewis and Harris for the rest of the century and beyond. In its immediate aftermath the people of the islands found themselves in the opaque, contorted world of a sleepless nightmare, racked between horror and uncertainty. Some men returned across the moor like ghosts: 'how he got ashore I do not know, but he was like a man out of his mind. And those in the village that had lost men – the mothers and the wives – they were coming in to ask if he had seen any sight of Donald, or Angus, or John, but he could only look at them and the tears coming down his cheeks; and he had two words, I remember that, he had two words that he said often: "Good God . . . Good God . . ."'[25]

Calum Smith's uncle John, whom the boy had last seen returning to the Navy in the company of Calum's father after leave ('quietly smiling as he made some derisive comment about my father giving my mother a farewell peck'), was among the lost. Calum was six-and-a-half years old on New Year's Day 1919:

> A group of us were standing in front of one of the croft houses in North Shawbost when a sailor in uniform came trudging wearily along the street with his head down. We recognised him, and as he went past one of the boys called, 'A Mhurchaidh, an tainig m'athair-sa raoir?' – 'Murdo, did my father come home last night?
>
> We all thought it strange that Murdo didn't lift his downcast head, look round or make any response. Later that day we heard what had happened and that Murdo was one of the survivors, and we understood. When the news did come through my recollection is of everything suddenly going very quiet, of women talking in hushed voices: it was as if there was a feeling that noise would be an offence to the dead.[26]

And so the muted and bewildered first days of 1919 progressed. Survivors with drawn faces had the cuts and abrasions they had sustained on the Holm rocks washed and dressed before peat fires. The bodies of the dead were gradually recovered and laid out for identification on the floor of the ammunition store in Stornoway. The contents of their pockets were put in brown paper bags which were then numbered with the same one, two or three digits, from the number one to the number 200, that were chalked onto the soles of their boots. An endless queue of Leodhasaich filed in and out of that ammunition store on their harrowing quest. 'For months after it was all over,' said a naval lieutenant, 'I saw in my dreams rows of naval issue boots with numbers chalked on their soles.'

As if in someone else's dream, Calum Smith would be able to describe until his old age the monochromatic image of himself as a curious six-year-old on the west coast at Shawbost watching with solemn eyes 'the horses and carts with their burdens of coffins going head to tail along the main road to the Bragar cemetery'.

The pain was intensified by the fact that no complete list had been taken at Kyle of Lochalsh of the *Iolaire*'s passengers, and that scores of the bodies were not recovered for weeks. Mothers and wives were frequently left in limbo, unsure as to whether or not their sons and husbands had been aboard the yacht. In some instances people went to comfort relatives or neighbours on their loss, only for the consolers to be bludgeoned by the news that their own son had also died. There was no escape from cruel bereavement or from haunting fear. Calum Smith's mother was afraid that as her husband had left with his brother John at the end of their last leave, they may also have returned together. Only a frantic exchange of telegrams with the Navy reassured her that she was not a widow.

The *Stornoway Gazette* which appeared in Lewis on Thursday 2nd and Friday, 3 January 1919 carried no mention of the *Iolaire*. It could not have done so: when the Admiralty yacht set sail from Kyle of Lochalsh on New Year's Eve the pages of the *Gazette* were already made up far from Lewis at William Grant's printing works in Dingwall. The few thousand printed copies, carrying their chirpy best wishes for a happy and prosperous 1919, were transported across the Minch aboard a dumbstruck *Sheila* on the second day of the year.

Grant made good his omission a week later. He must have hovered soberly and long over his words before committing them to slugs of hot metal. On his phrasing would hang the reputation and perhaps the future existence of a newspaper which had purported to serve and to represent Lewis for less than two years. He got it right:

No one now alive in Lewis can ever forget the 1st of January 1919, and future generations will speak of it as the blackest day in the history of the island, for on it 200 of our bravest and best perished on the very threshold of their homes under the most tragic circumstances.

The terrible disaster at Holm on New Year's morning has plunged every home and every heart in Lewis into grief unutterable. Language cannot express the anguish, the desolation, the despair which this awful catastrophe has inflicted. One thinks of the wide circle of blood relations affected by the loss of even one of the gallant lads, and imagination sees these circles multiplied by the number of the dead, overlapping and overlapping each other till the whole island – every hearth and home in it – is shrouded in deepest gloom.

All the island's war losses of the past four years – although these number fully four times the death roll of New Year's Day morning – are not comparable to this unspeakable calamity. The bleak tragedy has not a redeeming feature. The surrounding circumstances but add to the horror of it.

Provost Murdo Maclean received telegrams expressing sympathy and shock from the royal family, from the Secretary for War, from the Alness-born Scottish Secretary Robert Munro, from scores of diasporan Leodhasaich, and from Bolton, where the island's proprietor was opening a Wesleyan bazaar and was moved to notice that the chairman voiced his condolence with the disaster in Lewis. 'Bolton people,' telegraphed Lord Leverhulme properly enough, 'would in any case have felt keenly the sorrow that has overtaken the people of the island of Lewis, but at the present moment, in view of the fact that I am directly connected with the island, they feel a closer intimacy and have the keener sympathy with all those who are weighed down with sorrow.'

Carloway School on the west side was closed in the following week, not out of prolonged respect for the *Iolaire* dead, but because the influenza pandemic which would kill millions of people across the world in the winter months of early 1919 had just struck down one of its nine-year-old pupils and an elderly lady in the parish. The boys, the girls and the old people were joining the young men of the *Iolaire* in the burial grounds of Lewis as the unhappiest of years unfolded. Things could only improve as the days lengthened. They could hardly get any worse.

Lord Leverhulme arrived in Lewis two weeks after the calamity. He had not been idle in the interim. His donation of £1,000 topped the bill of the *Iolaire* disaster fund (the second-placed candidate at the recent election, W.D. Mitchell Cotts, followed him with £500). And he was determined to get to work himself and to put the island to work, which this practical man, who was no stranger to bereavement, may have rationalised to himself as the most effective manner of assuaging grief.

In the few short weeks between the Armistice and the tragedy at Holm Point, Leverhulme had registered two companies whose names were self explanatory: the Stornoway Fish Products and Ice Company Ltd and the Lewis Island Preserved Specialities Company Ltd.

On Tuesday 21 January he wrote from Lews Castle to his patent expert in Cheshire asking if the prefix 'Mac' were available for application to brands of fish, such as 'MacTurbot', 'MacCod' and 'MacHerring'. Out of all the projects debated so keenly with friends and advisors, fishing was clearly to have precedence. A visitor to Lews Castle at this time would have observed a curious sight. His Lordship was in the habit of commandeering a downstairs window and placing inside it a can wearing a makeshift label. The label might have been little more than a white background bearing the red message: 'Lewis Canned Fish'. Leverhulme would then stalk around the outside of the building casting furtive glances at the label from every reasonable distance and angle. He was pretending to be Mrs Mary Smith, as he would explain:

> John Smith has been busy in the office all the week (or so he tells the wife), and late home every night. On Saturday he goes home to lunch. Conscience-stricken he tries to make amends.
>
> 'Mary, my dear,' says he, 'you've had a dreary week of it. What about a show tonight?'
>
> Poor Mary is overjoyed. What a considerate man is her John! On the way to the theatre they are held up at the corner for a car – the corner where my shop is. The light from the window shows up LEWIS CANNED FISH most attractively. It catches Mary's eye.
>
> 'I say, John, what a lovely label! Lewis Canned Fish. I like the look of it . . . Just a minute . . .
>
> 'What is this Lewis Canned Fish?' she asks.
>
> 'Madam,' says my salesman, 'it is Lewis Canned Fish and very delightful too.'
>
> 'Can you recommend it?'

'Thoroughly, madam. I believe it is the best canned fish in the world.'

'Thank you. Will you please send along a tin?'

Back from the show Mary is peckish. That can just asks to be opened. They have Lewis Canned Fish for supper. They have never tasted anything so good. They lick their fingers. Nyum nyum!

Monday morning Mrs Smith is in the back green hanging up the washing. Mrs Brown is over the wall on the right.

'Mrs Brown! Do you know! I made the most wonderful discovery on Saturday!' And she lets Mrs Brown into the secret. She also tells Mrs Jones on the left. Each buys a can. And so the great news spreads and spreads. Within a year – certainly within two years – there is only one canned fish that counts in the world, and that is Lewis Canned Fish . . .[27]

On Wednesday 22 January he addressed a joint session of the Stornoway Pier and Harbour Commission and the Lewis District Committee. As chairman of the former body he faced the familiar retinue of Provost Maclean, ex-provosts Mackenzie and Anderson, estate factor Charles Orrock, the 'wool manufacturer' (or tweed baron) Kenneth MacKenzie and several others. What he had to say was not news to them. Earlier in the week he had greased the wheels of this presentation by rehearsing it on at least three of those present. Their responses were therefore preordained.

He suggested that unless Stornoway 'takes immediate and prompt action to provide the necessary harbour modernisation required by modern fishing, then far from going forward the town was 'likely to find itself in a worse position than ever before in its history.'

The cost of the improvements would leave little change out of £250,000. This formidable sum – perhaps £7 or £8 million today – he proposed should be borrowed by the Pier and Harbour Commission from the government, interest-free and repayable over forty years. The government, he insisted, could hardly refuse, given that a modernised harbour would also be an asset to the Admiralty and that 'the percentage of the population of the island of Lewis who, at the commencement of the war, voluntarily joined His Majesty's land and sea forces was believed to be greater than that of any other part of His Majesty's dominions.'

This being so, it is felt that the provision of harbours and roads, and later on railways, throughout the island would make it possible for the island to carry a much larger population than at present, and so prove a still greater source of strength should, unhappily, the country at any future date be plunged again into an equally critical period of history and of war.

Even after the events of early January the concept of Hebrideans being encouraged to multiply as useful cannon-fodder was apparently acceptable to the businessmen of Stornoway. The retired solicitor John Norrie Anderson replied for the Lewis District Committee that he was sure 'his Lordship was not born in Lancashire but in some part of the island of Lewis . . . Lord Leverhulme's wonderful brain has gathered up all the ideas that have been trying to fructify in my mind since I was a young man'. Hitting the government for a grant rather than a loan was an inspired suggestion. The District Committee unanimously supported the Pier and Harbour Commission.

Leverhulme turned then, and for the first time before a public Lewis audience, to his solution to the question of land redistribution which, with the actual and imminent return of those servicemen who had survived, was now pressed urgently upon Lewis and its proprietor. His answer was to move most of them to Stornoway.

> I understand that there are a number of men at present on crofts who, if there were houses in Stornoway, would be desirous of living here. That is, that certain crofters would come to live in Stornoway in houses with allotment gardens attached, and follow the life of fishermen exclusively.
>
> There are, I believe, at the present moment actual applications for crofts in the island numbering 800. Since my arrival last week I was informed that that was an underestimate and that the number desirous of securing crofts in the island is 1,200, or more. The land available in the island, if government exercised all their powers, according to the government scheme could provide only 131 new crofts. Now it is obvious that if there are 1,200 crofts wanted and only 131 can be provided, only one man in nine can be supplied.
>
> The question arises: how is this problem to be dealt with? It is no solution to give one croft to every ninth man. However fairly the apportionment might be made – and I cannot see any other apportionment fair except that of drawing lots – there will be eight disappointed men. They might recognise that they had been fairly dealt with in the drawing of lots, but there would be eight disappointed men for every one man made happy.

Now, if there are men who are not happy on their crofts at present, and if I can put up 300 houses in Stornoway – as I shall try to do this year – then there will be a number of men leaving their crofts and coming to follow a fisherman's life in Stornoway. In this way a certain number of crofts will be vacated, which could be given to men who desire crofts.

Next year I will build another 300 houses, and the year after another 300, and so on until I have built sufficient houses in Stornoway so that every man in Lewis who wants to live in a house in Stornoway can have a house in Stornoway and every man who wants a croft can have a croft. The only way that this can be realised is by my building houses for those who have crofts and do not want them, and by transfer of their crofts to men who have not crofts and do want them.

The whole scheme would be facilitated and administered by a welfare society 'under some such title as The Stornoway Housing and Improvement Association' which would qualify for government assistance and be underwritten by Leverhulme himself. 'I should be very glad of the help of anyone wishing to help,' he concluded to a rising susurrus of assent, 'for we must make Stornoway the finest city – I think we should aspire to this – the finest city in the north-west of Scotland.'

Just one of those present chose then to ask a telling question rather than to marvel at the imminent rebirth of Lewis. Councillor Norman Stewart of the District Committee drew from the feudal superior a significant reply to his request for elucidation on the matter of crofting. 'My ambition is,' a placatory Lord Leverhulme explained to Councillor Stewart, 'that every man in Lewis who wants a croft shall have a croft. But he cannot have it near Stornoway.'

Leverhulme had in this second major philippic once again mis-represented the situation in rural Lewis and, more crucially, mistaken the mood of the island. It was ill-advised of him to believe that in squaring the members of the Lewis District Committee he was satisfying the representatives of all the islanders, or even of the bulk of islanders outside Stornoway. A measure of obstinate naivety was to be found in his slick suggestion that a limitless but undefined number of men who were 'not happy on crofts' would voluntarily uproot and move to Stornoway. Any responsible councillor or other representative who was remotely connected with rural Lewis would surely have disillusioned him. Crofters may have been found who would move temporarily to work and even to live in Stornoway. But very few crofters indeed would have relinquished for a fisherman's pay-packet and an urban allotment all their hard-won tenure on the family acreage and its connected home. For neither the first nor the last time Lord Leverhulme was making no attempt to perceive things as a Hebridean smallholder rather than as a southern industrialist. Projection into the minds of others had never been his strongest point. Asked to decide between a croft at the Butt of Lewis and a ready-made bungalow, garden and salary in Stornoway, he and every single one of his friends, his relatives and apparently his advisers would have fallen headfirst for the address on Matheson Road. Virtually every man and woman in rural Lewis would rather have chosen security of tenure on the windswept plot of turf at Europie. That decision would certainly have been incomprehensible to him. His failure, his great, conclusive failure, was to refuse to recognise its validity.

His statistics were not entirely wrong; just artfully deployed. By March 1919 the Board of Agriculture had indeed received 1,273 applications for crofts and for the enlargement of crofts in Lewis. They did estimate that only 150 new holdings would be created by their current scheme to break up five farms at Galson in Ness, Gress on the east coast eight miles north of Stornoway, Carnish and Ardroil in Uig, and the single unit of Orinsay and Steimreway in South Lochs.

But neither the Board of Agriculture nor the returning servicemen of Lewis had any intention of limiting their land claims to five small properties at the extremes of the island. The Board itself estimated that another 254 crofts could almost immediately be created on a handful of other farm holdings, should the proprietor agree.[28] And so far as the Leodhasaich were concerned the whole broad island, every square yard of it from Kinlochresort to Skigersta was, in justice and in historical truth, theirs to live and work upon. They had fought for four years against what they had been told was an oppressive autocracy, they had watched their brothers die in the name of freedom and a home fit for heroes. They were unlikely to return to Lewis and meekly accept the injunction of a rich arriviste from Lancashire that they could not have crofts on the good land 'near Stornoway'.

A sword was hanging over Lord Leverhulme's head as, apparently indifferent or oblivious to the threat, he continued to formulate his plans. Early in February, having been instructed that the syllable 'Mac' could indeed be applied to families of fish in the commercial arena, he established what would become one of the sturdiest legacies of his Hebridean venture.

MacFisheries was the perfect incarnation of his plans for Lewis. It would be little more than a chain of British fishmongers. As its name suggested, however, MacFisheries was founded to retail the catches of Scotland in general and Lewis in particular (although Leverhulme sensibly retained a large number of the Lancashire boats working out of Fleetwood to make up any shortfall). It was a characteristically ambitious venture. He simply directed agents to buy for him every suitable high street fish shop in the country. The first such outlet, in Richmond, Surrey, was opened immediately. Within three years, by the end of 1921, there were 360 MacFisheries shops throughout the United Kingdom.[29] They were doomed never to be supplied even in small part by a dedicated Hebridean fleet, but they were nonetheless an effective and durable brandname. The chain of stores themselves survived until the late 1960s and the brand itself was revived 'as a symbol of quality' in 2000 by a fish processor from the north-east of Scotland. Two generations of urban Britons grew up in the vicinity of a clinically clean and well-stocked MacFisheries, in happy ignorance of its origin as a notional retail outlet for Lord Leverhulme's island of Lewis.

The fishmongers inevitably brought with them a variety of other interests and holdings. In the early years of the twentieth century wet-fish shops also specialised in selling sausages. This led Lever Brothers to buy the sausage-making company of Ernest Walls in order to keep their 400 MacFisheries outlets dependably supplied. As there was a traditional decline in the demand for pork products during the summer months, and a simultaneous seasonal increase in the popular call for ice-cream, Walls diversified into ice-cream manufacture, wholesale and retail. As the direct result of its founder establishing a chain of shops to sell fish which would someday be caught and processed by the people of Lewis, Lever Brothers found itself within a couple of years to be one of the biggest meat and confectionery producers in western Europe. The small step into the food industry which had been taken when William Lever's company entered the margarine business during the Great War had lurched, almost absent-mindedly, into a series of giant strides.

But in 1919 the men who would catch the fish that would accompany the sausage that would be supplemented seasonally by ice-cream had other ideas.

A month to the day after the incorporation of MacFisheries, on Monday 10 March, the House of Commons found itself debating the Highland land issue. It would have been familiar territory for any surviving member from the 1880s, for they were doing so in the immediate wake of a series of Hebridean raids.

The servicemen were not only returning to Lewis. All over the Highlands and the Hebrides in the early months of 1919 demobilised soldiers and sailors carried their kit-bags for a last time back along the narrow roads and rough cart-tracks to their townships, and once the celebrations had eased all over the Highlands and Hebrides young men began to ask aloud what they had been fighting for. They were armed with a sense of justice, and many of them were also armed with unrelinquished rifles and revolvers. A series of land raids recommenced which would continue throughout the region into the 1920s.

The southern isles of Dr Donald Murray's new constituency consisted of North and South Uist, Benbecula, Barra and some smaller satellites. South Uist and Barra had been for eighty years part of the domain of the Gordon Cathcart family of landowners from Aberdeenshire. Their current mistress was the last in the line, Lady Gordon Cathcart. This proprietress shared her late husband's view of crofting and crofters. Colonel John Gordon had once proposed to the government that his Hebridean islands should be depopulated and turned into a penal colony. The Board of Agriculture had taken a more liberal interest in the Uists and had proposed that – as in Lewis – a few farms should be broken up to meet the demand for crofting land. When (to nobody's real surprise, given Lady Gordon Cathcart's long history of contemptuous refusal to countenance anything beneficial to her crofting tenantry) this failed to occur, and when the men returned, there was a reckoning to be made.

The bill was first presented at Glendale, an isolated district at the southern tip of South Uist. When the farm lease there expired in 1918 local people were given to understand that the Board of Agriculture was considering allocating it to crofting. It shelved the proposal. Glendale Farm was consequently raided, staked out and squatted. Several Uist men were arrested and were still being held in custody when their Member of Parliament Donald Murray got to his feet for Scottish Questions to the Secretary of State in the House of Commons on 10 March 1919.

'The people for whom I plead,' he said, 'are deserving of the help and sympathy of the House.' Dr Murray was, he continued, confident that the heart of Scottish Secretary Robert Munro was in the right place:

> We also want his actions to be in the right place. I would like honourable members to see the Secretary for Scotland bristling with thistles and flourishing a claymore in defence of the rights of his fellow countrymen. The men of the Highlands and Islands are coming back in their hundreds, and land has been promised them. They want to know when these promises are going to be honoured.
>
> When the war was over these matters were going to be settled, but so far as the people see the Board of Agriculture is doing nothing to redeem their promises about dividing some of the estates. In my constituency there have been for years 2,000 applications for smallholdings and in Skye 400 more. The first stone of the foundation for reconstruction in the Highlands and Islands is the settlement of the land question.

Turning finally to the plight of the imprisoned South Uist men, Dr Murray concluded: 'I warn the Secretary of State that if something is not immediately done to release these men it will light a fire in the Highlands and Islands that will not be put out.'

Robert Munro replied with unconcealed sympathy. The case of the Glendale raiders was *sub judice,* he said, and out of his hands – 'I cannot do more in the circumstances than express the hope that even at the eleventh hour some solution might be found which will prevent sentence being imposed upon these men.'

On the broader subject of land settlement, Munro urged patience.

> It should not be forgotten that the system of [allocating] smallholdings was slowed down on both sides of the border during the war . . . Many pre-war

William Hesketh Lever in 1877 at the age of twenty-six

A new kind of packaging: Sunlight Soap aims for the
working man's wife

(Unilever Information Services, Port Sunlight Heritage Centre)

'There's nothing there but slavery' workaday scenes from Port Sunlight

Bringing home the peats in Lewis

The battle of Aignish, 1888

A busy mercantile centre: South Beach Street in Stornoway
in the early 1900s *(The University Library, St Andrews)*

Cottars' cottages on the outskirts of Stornoway, 1900

Members of the Lewis Royal Naval reserve, winners of the
Fleet Rowing Race in 1916 *(National Library of Scotland)*

Baron Leverhulme of Bolton-le-Moors in full Masonic
costume as Junior Grand Warden of England, 1918
(Lady Lever Art Gallery)

Lews Castle from Stornoway harbour

The windswept lighthouse at the Butt of Lewis

The new laird of Lewis: Leverhulme in 1919

Homes fit for heroes: Leverhulme houses in Stornoway

Machair grazing at Coll, north of Stornoway, following resettlement

Obbe in South Harris shortly before being renamed Leverburgh

Tarbert, the main township in Harris

Sir Harry Lauder, Lord Leverhulme and Provost Roderick Smith at the opening of Stornoway's new bowling green in 1922

The Tarbert Hotel in Harris, with one of the estate's Ford motor cars
parked outside

Lord Leverhulme in 1919

A prayer aboard the *Metagama* before her departure for
the New World in April 1923

RACE OF GIANTS ARE HEBRIDEANS; 400 COMING HERE

Men of Party Which Sailed
Yesterday All Five Feet
Nine and Over.

FEAR DEPOPULATION

Sheep Farms and Deer Forests
Replace the Island
Crofter.

By HENRY SOMERVILLE.
Special Cable to The Star by a Staff
Correspondent. Copyright.

London, April 16.—The exodus from
Hebrides commenced yesterday when
400 Islesmen with their wives and
families boarded the C. P. R. steamer
Marloch at Lochboisdale, the solitary
port of the Isle of South Uist, to Canada.

This party is going to form the
Hebridean colony in Red Deer, Al-

The Hebrideans are coming: Canadian newspapers anticipate the
depopulation of the islands *(Toronto Star)*

The opening ceremony at the Lady Lever Art Gallery, 16 December 1922

Viscount Leverhulme of the Western Isles

The castle on the hill

schemes had been in contemplation with regard to Lewis, but all of them had necessarily been held up by the war.

Since then a new development has occurred. The island has been purchased by Lord Leverhulme, who has a number of well-conceived and well-directed schemes in contemplation which would neither sap the independence nor affront the pride of the Lewis people . . .

Privately Robert Munro, as he and his officials had already begun to make clear to Leverhulme, was deeply sceptical about the plutocrat's ability to make good on all of his promises and extremely nervous about his relationship with would-be crofters. On 10 March 1919 they had good reason to be nervous, for three farms on the east coast of Lewis had just been raided as Messrs Murray and Munro addressed the House of Commons.

The raids came in quick succession, at Tong, Gress and Coll. Murray would have been aware of the disturbances when he spoke of an unquenchable fire being lit in the Highlands and Islands, as would Munro when he replied so cautiously. Both of them were in receipt of a warning letter from a group of ex-servicemen which had been posted to Munro and copied to Murray and Lloyd George. It read:

We thought it necessary to inform you of our firmly Determination concerning small holdings in the Island of Lewis. Shortly there is going to be a Lawful or Illegal action to be taken by us regarding Coll Farm. Of course we would rather have it lawful but time and space can't allow us to wait any further, and we are determined to take it by force, without Delay to Fulfil the promise granted by the Government to Demobilised soldiers and sailors, the land ought to be in wait for us we are anxious to know where does the Obstacle Lay's as we are in wait on the land.

As propritors are not willingly to give us land suitable for Cultivation we inform you that there isn't a landlord or even a Duke in the British Isles that will keep the land from us, that has been promised to us by the Primier and the Country at Large without bloodshed. As it is in your power we sincerely hope that you will grant and fulfill the promise made by the Government and at the same time giving us our wish and saving us from any trouble that's liable to come round concerning small holdings.

We desire every farm great or small to be cut down as long as there is any of us without a piece of Land able to call his own with Fair Fixity of Tenure and compensation for improvements . . .

The men who wrote that letter and the Leodhasaich who marked out lots for crofts on those east coast cattle grazings early in March were aware of the fact that they were not acting alone – that in Uist and in Skye and all over the rest of the crofting counties men were demonstrating their lack of patience with the prevarications of landowners and the sluggishness of the Board of Agriculture. Several accounts of what happened in Lewis and Harris over the succeeding five years have attempted to isolate the men who did the raiding from the – supposedly submissive – bulk of the community. But from the very beginning those men were conscious not only of being a present part and the future hope of their own communities, but also of being strong components in a legitimate and justified revival of the entire Highland land movement – a revival which had the support not only of their neighbours and relatives, but also of the bulk of Highland MPs and, it was rumoured, the Scottish Secretary himself. Robert Munro was presiding over a country which just four weeks earlier had seen British army tanks deployed in the centre of Glasgow to discourage urban proletarian unrest led by the returned servicemen of the lowland cities. He was more anxious than most to ensure that his fellow Highlanders remained confident in and faithful to the law of the land. If that meant irritating a few shortsighted landowners, Munro was prepared to be an irritant. Following one set of raids which drove the proprietor to issue furious threats, the Scottish Secretary took Leverhulme's good friend Sir Herbert Morgan to one side. 'Tell Lord Leverhulme that he may interdict these men,' he advised, 'and the judge may send them to prison. But I have the power to release them the same day.'

The choice of targets for the March 1919 land raids in Lewis was significant. If any potential crofting land in the island could be described as belonging to that zone 'near Stornoway', which in January had been declared out of bounds by Lord Leverhulme, it was the littoral at Tong, Coll and Gress. More than that, it was good land. A rare strip of east-coast Hebridean machair unfurled northwards from the head of Loch a Tuath, or Broad Bay, to the Traigh Mhor at Tolsta. It was a gentle, undulating seaboard, running down to dunes and white sand by the shore and rolling back for miles until the reclaimed green turf met the primordial heather and brown peatbog of Barvas Moor. Its unusual fertility was partly created by nature's introduction of shoreline sand to the acid soil, and partly by generations of men who had followed and improved upon nature's example. This patch of coast had traditionally been home to a good percentage of the population of Lewis. It was desirable property.

Tong Farm stood three miles by road and one mile across the loch from Stornoway. Coll was a stone's throw away at the other side of the bay from Tong, and Gress was ten minutes' walk from Coll. The small farm at Tong was pointedly staked out into 30 acres of crofting lots. The farmers' stock was driven away from Gress and replaced by crofters' animals, and some potatoes were planted in newly turned earth. At Coll men and women pegged out the rectangles of notional new crofts, dug the ground and carried fertilising seaweed up from the shore. Nobody was hurt – as the tenant farmers sensibly stood back, nobody was even threatened – and no arrests were made.

Instead Lord Leverhulme arrived. He might have seen the action, with or without a telescope, had he chosen to look from an upper window of Lews Castle. On Tuesday 11 March, the day after the debate in the House of Commons, he engaged in a debate of his own with some of the people of rural Lewis. The schoolmaster at Back, which lay between Coll and Gress, was requested to make free his schoolroom and to preside over a meeting of the two camps.

Leverhulme did most of the talking to a politely sceptical gathering. He commenced as usual by expressing his gratitude to 'every class in the island' for the warmth of their welcome. But not until he assured them that he would 'try to fulfil the reasonable and proper demands of every person living in the island of Lewis' did he elicit a round of applause.

He then proceeded as though delivering to Mr Morrison's ten-year-olds firstly a civics lesson and then (aiming presumably at the weavers of tweed in his audience) a class in basic tailoring. Lord Leverhulme had determined that the source of the difficulty lay in the supposed estrangement of Stornoway from the rest of Lewis. People in all countries, he insisted, 'divide into two sections – those who live in towns and those who live in the country.' He went on:

> I have sometimes met people living in the country who thought that the welfare and well-being of dwellers in the towns did not concern them, and on the other hand, I have met people living in towns who thought the welfare of those living in the country does not concern them.
>
> This is of course a fallacy, for the town depends on the country and the country on the town, and every man living in the island of Lewis will find that his penny will buy more of the goods he requires for himself and his family if Stornoway, as the centre of the whole island, provided with proper harbour facilities and a well-balanced population, is made prosperous and successful. Whatever injures those living in the country will be felt by those living in the towns, and whatever injures those living in the towns will be felt equally and ultimately by those living in the country.

These words appear to have been met by silence from the assembly in Back school. He needed quickly to play to the gallery, and he did so by moving sharply onto garmentry, expressing 'my desire to see that every man in the island who wishes to live on a croft in the country districts shall have his desire . . . We cannot all wear coats of the same size and we do not all wish for coats of the same pattern . . . But while that is true we must cut our coat according to our cloth, and before any of us can have a coat we must see that there is cloth to cut.'

Lord Leverhulme then repeated his 1,200-applications-into-143-crofts-does-not-go equation. But even as he spoke, he said, 'a very large firm of contractors are now landing from steamers at Stornoway the materials for the first instalment of 300 houses. These houses will go up as quickly as material and labour can be obtained. When these houses are erected and all occupied I will build another 300.'

He had, said Leverhulme, enquired into the income made from crofting in Lewis. 'I understand the government officials when assessing for old age pensions take the income that can be earned on a croft at 8 shillings a week . . . we might take 12 shillings as being pretty near the mark. Some of those who have applied to me personally for houses at Stornoway told me they were tired of the drudgery connected with crofting, and they would prefer to make £2 or £3 a week at fishing than work on a croft for 12 shillings.'

Lord Leverhulme then broached the heart of the matter: what would become the chief rationale for his insistence on preventing the spread of crofting 'near Stornoway'. The Lewis Food Control Committee had written to advise him of the shortage of the milk supply to Stornoway. As things stood milk had to be imported from the mainland to the town. How, he wondered, was an expanded borough to cope?

> This is a very serious question for people living in town, for it is absolutely necessary that young children should have milk, and it also affects the invalided and the weak . . . As I am taking land for the building of the new houses from the Manor farm and Goathill, that will obviously decrease the supply of milk while increasing the demand, and therefore I propose to put all the cattle I can on Gress and other farms within motor distance of Stornoway so that the supply produced there can be brought in to meet the needs of the people.
>
> Someone has said to me, [appealing to his earlier theme and to the charity of his listeners], that the country districts have nothing to do with the milk supply of Stornoway. I will never believe that there can be a schism between the people of the country and the people of the town.
>
> Suppose you say you do not care what becomes of Stornoway – let the children of the town die or grow up weak saplings for the want of a proper milk supply – and suppose you take all the farms that are available for holdings. What then? You will have 143 new crofts, and that number is not sufficient for yourselves, and where are you going to get crofts for your children and grandchildren working on the same lines? The problem that has been in Lewis for 100 years will be here 100 years hence in an aggravated form . . .
>
> All my life, I have worked with people and not against them. You might think I am working against you in this matter. I am not, and I feel certain that if my scheme is given a fair trial you will see it is you that have been working against yourselves. If you will not have confidence in me and trust me, I can do nothing . . . It is my sincere intention to do all in my power to see that, as far as the cloth will go and as far as patterns can be made, every man and woman in the island of Lewis will have what they desire for the full development of a happy and comfortable life.

Having accused the people of Back, Coll and Gress of selfish indifference to the malnutrition of Stornoway infants he stood back to polite applause. When responses from the floor were requested a young man from nearby Vatisker spoke up. John MacLeod said that before the war he had been prevented by Colonel Matheson's estate authorities from erecting as a dwelling for himself an extension to his father's home. As a result of this prohibition John MacLeod had been forced to cut four inches off his bed to squeeze it into the small corner of the family home that was available to him. When war was declared, John MacLeod of Vatisker had been the first man from his district called into uniform.

Now he was back, and he had no ambitions towards a cottage in Stornoway and a comfortable salary. 'I want,' said John MacLeod, 'a holding on Gress and a house for myself.'

While Lord Leverhulme drew the meeting at Back to a close by requesting a list of those in need of crofts, a young official from the Board of Agriculture was making his way across the Minch from Kyle of Lochalsh to Stornoway. Colin Macdonald was a 37-year-old Gaelic speaker who had been brought up on a croft in Strathpeffer in mainland Ross-shire. He was, in common with most Board employees, both sympathetic to the crofters' cause and fully aware of the strength of their feelings. He was nervous as he boarded the *Sheila* at the railway pier at Kyle. Macdonald had been in the far north of the Scottish mainland when he read in *The Scotsman* of the raids at Tong, Gress and Coll. 'With a shrewd instinct for self-preservation,' he would joke, 'I tried [then] to get officially "lost" in the wilds of Sutherlandshire. But a rascal of a telegraph operator – a really bright lad – proved too efficient. With untiring tenacity he tracked me to my hidey-hole to deliver the inevitable yellow envelope which contained the curt instruction to proceed to Lewis immediately!'[30]

Macdonald walked down the gangway at Stornoway pier into a 'highly charged' atmosphere.

> Many of those on the pier were old friends and soon I was generally spotted as 'the man from the Board'. Questioners in Gaelic and English demanded to know what the Board were going to do . . . The lads had been led to believe that crofts would be ready for them. Not only were there no crofts ready, but with a hostile proprietor, and a hesitant government, their prospects of being settled on the land were anything but bright. Disappointment, succeeded by intense anger, surged through the island.

Colin Macdonald was thoroughly acquainted with the Hebrides but had never previously met Lord Leverhulme. The proprietor wasted no time before introducing himself to the man from the Board in the second week of March 1919. The Strathpeffer man would find it an unforgettable encounter, and not only because 'he was my first millionaire and Industrial Magnate'.

> At very first glance one would put him down as a rather insignificant little fellow. That impression lasted for a shorter time than it takes to write it. Charm, tact, decision, power radiated from the man's every word, look and gesture.
>
> I had never met a man who was so obviously a megalomaniac and accustomed to having his own way. He had the sort of personality which immediately afflicts ordinary people with a pronounced inferiority complex.

Colin Macdonald was quickly educated in Leverhulme's obdurate refusal to be contradicted or denied. The two men had hardly shaken hands when the proprietor told the man from the Board that – to follow what he perceived to have been a successful debate in the school at Back – he had arranged an open-air meeting with land raiders on the bridge at Gress at 11.00 on the following morning, 12 March. He would like Macdonald to accompany him there. Colin Macdonald had no intention of going to the meeting, and certainly not of attending in the company of Lord Leverhulme. In the whole of the following six weeks he would be given no instructions whatsoever from the Board of Agriculture or from any other branch of government as to what his mission was on the island in that spring of 1919. His own reasonable assessment of his role was to work evenly in the background, collecting information and gauging the public mood. This task was unlikely to be accomplished by sharing a public platform with the proprietor.

So Colin Macdonald told Lord Leverhulme that he had no desire to go to Gress on the following morning. 'But he pressed that I should go. I would not go. "Pity," said he, making for the door, "but I hope you will change your mind. Goodbye."'

Within three hours Macdonald received a telegram from his employers at the Board of Agriculture ordering him to attend the open-air meeting at Gress. No sooner had he finished reading the telegram than a grinning Leverhulme reappeared in the doorway.

'Have you changed your mind?' he asked.

'I have,' said Macdonald.

'Good. I thought you would.'

Colin Macdonald managed to resist travelling out of Stornoway with the landlord's entourage on the morning of Wednesday 12 March. He attended on the ground. Over 1,000 people, mostly men but with a 'fair smattering' of women, waited for Lord Leverhulme on the broad, rolling machair where the Gress River swept quietly down to the dunes and the sea. It was, judged Macdonald, a sullen, resentful crowd which would have been ignited by the smallest spark.

William, Lord Leverhulme may not have understood the Leodhasaich, but he understood massed gatherings of irascible workers. With his Gaelic-to-English interpreter at his side he walked straight into the middle of them, made a circular clearing like a primitive boxing ring among the curious faces, and stood up on top of one of the Gress farmer Peter Liddle's home-made beer barrels. His oration began immediately. As though adapting to his changed environment, his schoolmasterly adjurations of the previous day at Back were lost and forgotten. He addressed the hungry crowd at Gress at once like a politician on the stump and a snake-oil salesman before a hanging magistrate. Colin Macdonald has left to us the most vivid of all of the portraits of Leverhulme at large in Lewis. He began:

> Good morning, everybody! Have you noticed that the sun is shining this morning? And that [a masterly stroke, for no-one else was counting] this is the first time it has shone in Lewis for ten days?
>
> I regard that as a good omen. This is going to be a great meeting. This is going to be a friendly meeting. This meeting will mark the beginning of a new era in the history of this loyal island of Lewis that you love above all places on earth, and that I too have learned to love. So great is my regard for Lewis and its people that I am prepared to adventure a big sum of money for the development of the resources of the island and of the fisheries.
>
> Do you realise that Stornoway is right in the centre of the richest fishing grounds in the whole world? The fishing which has hitherto been carried on in an old-fashioned, happy-go-lucky way is now to be prosecuted on scientific lines. Recently at Stornoway I saw half of the fishing boats return

to port without a single herring and the remainder with only a score of crans between them. That is a poor return for men who spend their time and risk their lives in a precarious calling. I have a plan for putting an end to that sort of thing.

Colin Macdonald recorded that the last two sentences were greeted respectively by ejaculations of assent and expressions of eager interest. Leverhulme pressed on,

> The fact is, your fishing as presently carried on is a hit or a miss. I want you to make it a hit every time. How can I do that? Well, every time you now put out to sea you blindly hope to strike a shoal of herrings. Sometimes you do. Oftener you do not. But the shoals are there if you only know the spot – and that is where I can help you.
>
> I am prepared to supply a fleet of airplanes and trained observers who will daily scan the sea in circles round the island. An observer from one of these planes cannot fail to notice any shoal of herrings over which he passes. Immediately he does so he sends a wireless message to the Harbour Master at Stornoway. Every time a message of that kind comes in there is a 'loud speaker' announcement by the Harbour Master so that all the skippers at the pier get the exact location of the shoal. The boats are headed for that spot – and next morning they steam back to port loaded with herrings to the gunwales! Hitherto, more often than not, the return to port has been with light boats and heavy hearts. In future it will be with light hearts and heavy boats!

A century after the event Lord Leverhulme's ballooning plans for Lewis seem simply hyperbolic; the aerial castles of an old man playing out his final fantasies. They sounded no different at Gress bridge in 1919. Having proposed the ingenious conversion of the Great War's spotter planes to herring reconnaissance duties above the North Atlantic, he returned to well-worn ground. He intended to spend £5 million on Lewis. There would be a great fleet of fishing boats. There would be a great fleet of cargo boats. There would be a huge fish-canning factory. There would be railways. There would be an electric power station. Stornoway would become a garden city. There would be steady work, steady pay and beautiful houses with every modern convenience and comfort . . .

'Seo seo, fhearaibh!' Alan Martin, a prominent raider who had attended the previous day's meeting in Back and who was by the

Wednesday forenoon clearly tired of this yellow brick road, interrupted his feudal superior and addressed his neighbours. Leverhulme stood, quietly uncomprehending, throughout the Gaelic interposition.

'Cha dean seo an gnothach!' said Martin. 'Bheir am bodach mil-bheulach tha 'n sinn chreidsinn ort gu bheil dubh geal 's geal dubh! Ciod e dhuinne na bruadair aige, a thig no nach tig? 'S e am fearann tha sinn ag iarraidh. Agus 's e tha mise a' faighneachd an toir thu dhuinn am fearann?'

In Colin Macdonald's account Alan Martin's stand at Gress bridge around high noon on Wednesday, 12 March 1919, marked the turning point of the meeting, in which case it may also have signalled the watershed of Lord Leverhulme's proprietorship of Lewis. Martin's comments were greeted by 'frenzied cheering' from the crowd, and by understandable bewilderment from Leverhulme atop his beer barrel. 'I am sorry,' he was heard to be saying as the applause died down, 'I am sorry . . . perhaps my interpreter will translate for me . . .'

The interpreter did so. 'Come, come, men,' he pronounced in stirring Anglophone rendition of Alan Martin's interjection. 'This will not do. This honey-mouthed man would have us believe that black is white and white is black. We are not concerned with his fancy dreams that may or may not come true. What we want is the land – and the question I put to him now is: *will you give us the land*?'

It may have been a mistake to call immediately, albeit in a second tongue, for a repetition of Martin's categorical demand. The cheering erupted once more and some wit called out: 'Not so bad for a poor language like the English.' Leverhulme repossessed himself, fixed 'a cold-steel look' on Alan Martin, and said in clipped, staccato tones: 'You have asked a straight question. I like a straight question, and I like a straight answer.

'And my answer to your question is NO! I am *not* prepared to give you the land.'

Colin Macdonald would later remember some protests at this from the crowd, which Leverhulme dismissed with 'a compelling hand-wave' before expounding: '. . . not because I am vindictively opposed to your views and aspirations, but because I conscientiously believe that if my views are listened to – if my schemes are given a chance – the result will be enhanced prosperity and greater happiness for Lewis and its people. Listen . . .' and off he went again, 'the indomitable little artist.'

The Lewis historian Joni Buchanan has identified the next local man to speak at Gress bridge as John MacLeod,[31] in which case he was probably the returned serviceman from Vatisker with the sawn-off bed whom Leverhulme will have remembered from the previous day. He was described by Colin Macdonald as 'a clean-shaven aesthete – a crofter-fisherman' speaking slow, polite English in a strong Lewis accent, 'each word set square like a stone block in a building'.

'Lord Leverhulme,' said MacLeod, 'will you allow me to intervene in this debate for a few moments?'

Leverhulme signalled his assent.

> Thank you. Well, I will begin by saying that we give credit to your lordship for good intentions in this matter. We believe you think you are right, but we know that you are wrong. The fact is, there is an element of sentiment in the situation which it is impossible for your lordship to understand.
>
> But for that we do not blame you; it is not your fault but your misfortune that your upbringing, your experience, and your outlook are such that a proper understanding of the position and of our point of view is quite outwith your comprehension. You have spoken of steady work and steady pay in tones of veneration – and I have no doubt that in your view, and in the view of those unfortunate people who are compelled to live their lives in smoky towns, steady work and steady pay are very desirable things.
>
> But in Lewis we have never been accustomed to either – and, strange though it must seem to your lordship, we do not greatly desire them. We attend to our crofts in seed-time and harvest, and we follow the fishing in its season – and when neither requires our attention we are free to rest and contemplate.
>
> You have referred to our houses as hovels – but they are our homes, and I will venture to say, my lord, that, poor though these homes may be, you will find more real human happiness in them than you will find in your castles throughout the land.
>
> I would impress on you that we are not in opposition to your schemes of work; we only oppose you when you say you cannot give us the land, and on that point we will oppose you with all our strength. It may be that some of the younger and less thoughtful men will side with you, but believe me, the great majority of us are against you.

Lord Leverhulme – you have bought this island. But you have not bought us, and we refuse to be the bondslaves of any man. We want to live our own lives in our own way, poor in material things it may be, but at least it will be clear of the fear of the factory bell; it will be free and independent.

Colin Macdonald noted that 'the loudest and longest cheers of that day' greeted John MacLeod's speech. Leverhulme counted the moments before indicating that he would appreciate silence in which to reply and – 'in moderated, cajoling tones' – coming out for Round Three.

Will you allow me to congratulate you? To thank you for putting the views of my opponents so clearly before me? I did know that sentiment lay at the back of the opposition to my schemes, but I confess I had not adequately estimated the strength of that element till now. My friends! Sentiment is the finest thing in this hard world. It is the golden hand of brotherhood. It is the beautiful mystic thing that makes life worth living . . . and would you accuse me of deliberately planning to injure that beautiful thing? No! No! A thousand times, No!

Then is there, after all, so very much between your point of view and mine? Are we not striving after the same thing? By different roads it may be, but still, for the same goal? We are both out for the greatest good of the greatest number of people on this island. You have admitted that the young men may believe in my schemes. May I again congratulate you? The young people will – and do – believe in my schemes. I have in my pocket now quite a number of letters from young men in different parts of the island, and I have received a great many more of the same kind, all asking the same questions: 'When can you give me a job in Stornoway?' 'When can I get one of your new houses?'

These young men and their wives and sweethearts want to give up the croft life; they want a brighter, happier life . . . My friends, the young people of today will be the people of tomorrow. Are the older ones who have had their day going to stand in the way of the young folk? Are we older fellows to be dogs-in-mangers? No! The people of this island are much too intelligent to take up so un-Christian an attitude.

Give me a chance – give my schemes a chance – give the young folks and give Lewis a chance! Give me a period of ten years to develop my schemes and I venture to prophesy that long before then – in fact in the near future – so many people, young and old – will believe in them, that crofts will be going a-begging – and then if there are still some who prefer life on the land they can have two, three, four crofts apiece.

They cheered him, of course. They cheered him not because, as would be suggested later, Lewis crofters were at heart possessed by 'fervid admiration for an aristocracy'. They cheered because they were good-natured people, because they were amused by the prospect of being offered three or four crofts apiece, because they appreciated the performance if not the message, and because a landowner who was prepared to engage in open debate was a rarity, and they did not want the courageous little soap man to leave Gress thinking that in coming to talk to them he had wasted his time.

Perhaps sadly, that was not the way Lord Leverhulme interpreted their cheers. He raised his hat to the huge assembly and proclaimed that 'the sun did not shine for nothing! This has been a great meeting. This will be a memorable day in the history of Lewis. You are giving me a chance. I will not fail you. I thank you. Good day.'

And he walked back through the gathering to his car to another round of cheers.

Somewhere on the edge of the crowd Colin Macdonald was being mobbed by Leodhasaich eager to know: 'When will the Board be dividing off the land?'

'You do not want the land now,' he said.

'Want the land! Of course we want the land, and we want it at once.'

'But you gave Lord Leverhulme the impression that you agreed with him.'

'Not at all. And if he is under that impression you may tell him from us that he is greatly mistaken.'

'But why did you cheer him?'

'Och well, he made a very good speech and he is a very clever man, and we wanted to show our appreciation – but the land is another matter.'

In his written report to headquarters Macdonald would advise: 'from the Gaelic remarks which I overheard and from statements the men made to me subsequently I am satisfied that their acquiescence was more apparent than real.'

Shortly afterwards Colin Macdonald was able to engage Leverhulme in the privacy of a nearby estate building. The man from the Board of Agriculture found the proprietor in high spirits, and 'began the task of disillusioning him'. He became downcast and muttered darkly of 'double dealing'. Then he perked up again.

'Anyhow, that was a great meeting,' he said. 'They are an intelligent people and I never give up hope so long as I have an intelligent opposition to deal with. Besides, there is not the same enjoyment in things that are easily won. I am enjoying this fight and I shall win them over yet.'

'I am very sorry to have to resort again to the cold-water jug,' said Macdonald. 'But if you could see the position as I see it you would be less optimistic – unless you are prepared to compromise on the question of the land, which I venture to think you could do without material hurt to your schemes.'

Leverhulme's reply was emphatic. 'I shall *not* compromise,' he said.[32]

So commenced the Milk Wars which were credited by Leverhulme at the time and by almost every subsequent chronicler with scuppering his plans for Lewis. His concern about the Stornoway milk supply, although it arrived at the van of his thinking late in the day, had a small element of validity. While the majority of the population in rural Lewis had access to the produce of a milking cow (and were accustomed to consuming very little dairy food), little of this produce was sent for sale in Stornoway, which consequently imported most of its milk from Aberdeenshire. This process usually took a day and a half. The milk imported on Fridays would frequently still be on sale the following Monday.

But Aberdeenshire is and was dairy herd country, which Lewis has never been. The milk which arrived at Stornoway from the mainland was refrigerated and sterilised and only marginally more expensive than elsewhere. The urban people of the Hebrides had been long accustomed to buying and eating imported groceries. Very few of their vegetables and fruits were grown in Uig or South Lochs. Self-sufficiency was a remote aspiration to most individual crofters, who had to supplement their incomes and their family's diet in a variety of ways. For the islanders of Lewis as a whole, self-sufficiency had been left behind in the seventeenth century when they ceased to depend on oatmeal and fish.

Yet Lord Leverhulme, who prided himself on commercial realism, seemed determined to make a massively increased population of Lewis self-sufficient in at least one product. All of the good pastureland on the west coast of Broad Bay would be devoted to dairy cattle, despite the fact that many of the men and women whom he would depend upon to staff his Stornoway operations wanted to build houses and smallholdings on that very land. It was an entirely unnecessary, even a frivolous point of principle, as Colin Macdonald had dared to point out. It became the breaking point only because he elevated it beyond reason. Stornoway could have continued to import – and as things turned out, did continue to import – its milk from mainland Scotland without hazarding the health of its infant population. If Stornoway were to grow so swiftly in size as Leverhulme had projected, it would arguably have been well advised to invest some of its newfound prosperity in an increased trading exchange with the lush green meadows of Aberdeenshire. The dairy farms at Gress and Coll were not essential to a huge industrial fishing fleet, to the pilots of spotter planes, to the labourers at peat-fired power plants and Mac-Fisheries canning factories, to the engine drivers and the railway station-masters, the pickers of soft fruits and the women and boys in the commercial herb meadows of Barvas Moor.

John MacLeod had been correct. The people had no animus against those projects – in so far as they could credit what they were hearing, they welcomed them. But long after Lord Leverhulme had left the Hebrides for one destination or another, John MacLeod and his neighbours would still be there. When that day came they wanted a living space large enough for a full-size bed and enough land to keep them alive. They had achieved security of tenure on crofts just thirty years, or half a lifespan, earlier. They now required crofts to be secure upon.

Leverhulme made a telling admission to Colin Macdonald in their conversation after the meeting at Gress bridge. He found the cut-and-thrust of adversative dispute stimulating. He was exhilarated by the very wit-sharpening process of testing his resolve and his articulacy against 'an intelligent opposition'. To most of the people of rural Lewis this politicking was merely tiresome. Their future and their livelihoods and their native land were not grammar school debating points. They had been engaged in the argument for generations, and had thought it won.

But having reopened the whole, old, blood-soaked box, having engaged himself however unnecessarily in the desperate, blind-alley contention of the land issue, Lord Leverhulme could not be seen to lose. He could never be seen to lose. He 'scorned to change or fear'. He would not – as he had told far too many people for anybody's good – he would *not* compromise. If a dairy farm at Gress was claimed to be an integral, non-negotiable element of his momentous scheme for sextupling the population of Lewis, then integral and non-negotiable it would stay. A thousand people, including many of his employees and the man from the Board of Agriculture, had heard him say, on that sunny March day a few miles north of Stornoway, 'I will *not* give you the land.' How could he possibly recant?

The Board of Agriculture and the Scottish Office found themselves squirming inelegantly on the horns of a dilemma. Had Lewis not been sold, or had Colonel Matheson found almost any other purchaser, they would have progressed as rapidly as the land court allowed with an extensive crofting programme on the island. Many, from Colin Macdonald to the Scottish Secretary himself, believed still that the continuation of such a programme was not only honourable and correct, but inevitable. The magnate from Port Sunlight was however offering to pump riches beyond reason into the depressed economy of the north-west of Scotland, and it was surely the function of government to encourage rather than dissuade such investment. Macdonald's superior, Thomas Wilson, the Board of Agriculture's senior sub-commissioner for the region, had reported to his chairman the essence of their difficulty following a meeting with Leverhulme in the autumn of 1918:

> With his aspirations I expressed the most cordial sympathy and approval. I am satisfied his Lordship . . . has taken up the Lewis problem with the intention of solving it, and he has the energy and resolve to carry his plans to completion. He has great admiration for the Lewis people, who have done such great and noble service for the country in the war, and I think feels he should do what he can for them.
>
> However, his whole life has been industrial, and I question if his experience of three months among the Lewis people has taught him their sentiments or desires. He does not realise that they will never feel satisfied until the farms in Lewis are divided into holdings and given to them . . . What the Lewis man wants is a small piece of land for a house site, two cows grazing and potato and corn growing. That is his ideal and it cannot be eradicated . . .

Wilson's troubled presentiment would have been reinforced when he heard from Colin Macdonald in the March of 1919 that 'it had been rumoured throughout the island that the Board intended to abandon their Lewis schemes to give Lord Leverhulme a free hand, and that the men, including demobilised soldiers and sailors, had made the [Gress] raid as a protest in favour of breaking up the farms into smallholdings.'[33]

Macdonald, an ardent if diplomatic supporter of land redistribution, disliked intensely being on the front line of such a conflict with no apparent resolution. He felt 'an awful ass' at being unable to offer an officially sanctioned solution to the problems thrown at him daily by all parties. 'Would the Board back Lord Leverhulme in his industrial schemes – which ruled out the prospect of any additional crofts – or would they use the power they had to provide crofts for the returned soldiers and sailors? It was an answer to that question which was demanded of me by emissaries of both sides who came in force to see me . . . Easier asked than answered!'

The Scottish Secretary Robert Munro would confess to Nigel Nicolson when they met at a banquet thirty-five years later that he had only once, and briefly, given Leverhulme the benefit of his own doubts – but that any substantial concession of the land issue to the proprietor remained 'politically impossible' throughout. Not only was the House of Commons in favour of crofting resettlement, but the 'deeper family loyalties' of the people of Lewis meant that every time a raid occurred they stood quietly but solidly behind the raiders.[34]

In the meantime, as his contribution to the parliamentary debate of 10 March had suggested, he tried to ameliorate, to keep Lord Leverhulme flattered and interested in pouring millions into Stornoway, and to keep his officials working towards a land resettlement programme in rural Lewis which would satisfy both camps. It was a thankless task. It proved unsustainable only because Leverhulme himself was, as he freely admitted, unwilling rather than unable to compromise.

There followed another uneasy peace. The farms at Coll and Gress remained half-occupied throughout the summer of 1919 and the Board of Agriculture warned of imminent raids at Galson in the Ness district and Carnish and Reef in Uig. Housing began to be built in Stornoway and both a cannery and an ice-factory were raised down by the harbour.

There had long been a peculiar anomaly in the infrastructure of Lewis. There was no direct public road along the east coast between Tolsta and Port of Ness. Lord Leverhulme announced that he would build one – or rather, that he would provide the materials and the wages, and the men of the east coast machair lands would build one. It seemed a neat, if unoriginal, temporary solution. The restless men of Back would be given something to fill their days; they would hopefully realize the delights of a wage economy; and a measure of public good would be achieved. Hiring commenced.

And Colin Macdonald was invited to dinner at Lews Castle.

6

WITH ME OR AGAINST ME

Lord Leverhulme's charm offensive on the island did not stop at Gress bridge and the school at Back. Within hours of his arrival in Stornoway in March 1919 the Board of Agriculture's Colin Macdonald was warned by his old friend Duncan MacKenzie of the Royal Hotel that he would 'be at a dinner at the Castle within a week'.

And he was. Leverhulme intended to enjoy himself in Lewis, and the nature of enjoyment – he had been assured – required more of him than endless meetings and planning and bookwork. He must also go through the motions of relaxation and conviviality. This would not come naturally. His niece, Emily Paul, recalled:

> He never took a holiday in the ordinary sense of the word, and kept to a routine of work even in the island, but the fresh air and numerous drives to inspect new roads, bridges, houses etc must have been of great benefit to him.
>
> He lived very simply wherever he was, and never smoked. He had a tremendous amount of energy and was up at 4.30 every morning, getting a considerable amount of work done before his breakfast, which was served at 7.30 or 8 o'clock.
>
> When in the island he used to take a walk after tea with one or more of his relatives or friends whenever he could spare the time and if the weather was favourable, and on Sunday he went with them to the United Free Presbyterian Church. Should we be dancing on any of the other evenings in the week, he would often join us in the ballroom, entering into both the Highland and the modern dances with zeal and enjoyment. When bed-time came he would run up the stairs two at a time to show us all how young and vigorous he felt.[35]

He threw house parties, where humble functionaries of the local authorities would mingle freely with his glittering guests from the outside world. They could be thirsty affairs. In the first couple of years the teetotal Leverhulme often had to be reminded to pass round the whisky bottle. In 1921 the island of Lewis voted for the prohibition of retail alcohol. This local by-law was agreed upon two years after Andrew Volstead's National Prohibition Act had been enforced across all of the United States. It was not an unusual measure, at the time or later, in the Protestant Celtic fringes of the United Kingdom, and its reverberations would be felt in some of the draconian decisions of the Western Isles licensing authorities throughout the rest of the century. Unlike the Volstead Act, prohibition in Lewis was necessarily an isolated affair. Not only did it take place within a country – within, indeed, a county – where the purchase and consumption of retailed alcohol was in other districts still legal, but its strictures by definition applied almost exclusively to Stornoway, as there were no public bars elsewhere in the island. Only smaller units of strong drink were banned. It remained legal to buy wholesale quantities, such as cases of whisky and casks of beer. This loophole was intended to alleviate the suffering of large hotels (which were permitted to serve drinks with meals to guests) and of the bigger private houses. In practice it gave a new lease of life to the rural village bothan, or shebeen, in Lewis. In many communities a crude but largely weatherproof building was set aside as a drinking den. The men (and it was always men) would contribute to a kitty, wholesale cases and casks would be – perfectly legally – imported, and the bothan would thereafter serve as a private club. This arrangement proved so congenial to the communitarian crofting townships (wholesale alcohol was, after all, cheaper by far than anything bought at a bar or from a shop) that in some cases the shebeen long survived the repeal of prohibition and for decades staved off the introduction of properly licensed commercial premises. In Ness a working bothan survived as a viable alternative to a public bar for more than half a century after 1921, and it was finally put out of business not by a public house but by another community venture: a newly-built social club run by and for the benefit of the local football team.

There was of course no need for Lord Leverhulme to observe prohibition inside the walls of Lews Castle. He decided to do so because he agreed with the principles of prohibition and because he did not wish to offend the parish elders. Before 1921, therefore, drink was sparingly poured at his occasions. After 1921 they became more sober affairs.

He had knocked the castle drawing-room and ballroom into one large entertainment area. Guests would be piped into dinner by Pipe-Major Donald MacLeod 'in full regimentals' – an experience in an enclosed space which young Miss Paul found too ear-shattering for proper appreciation. The entertainment was, in Edwardian fashion, chiefly musical. Pipe-Major MacLeod having discharged his duties and gone away, the stage was prepared for more palatable diversions.

Like many a businessman of his kind, Leverhulme had a fondness for the company of show people. He attempted in Lewis to give this preference a Scottish tone. His visitors from the south became a bizarre melange of the worthy and the baroque of his generation. One after another a succession of septuagenarian celebrities were met off the *Sheila* and hurried up to Lews Castle. The Manx novelist Hall Caine swept down the corridors in voluminous cloak and hat, pronouncing on the links between his popular romances of the Isle of Man and the Gaelic culture of Lewis. That recently-retired ornament of the late-Victorian and Edwardian stage, Miss Olga Nethersole, was chased by cattle in Uig after her bright yellow skirt reportedly annoyed the beasts. The artists David Murray, Luke Fildes and Raffles Davidson took their palettes and paints out to the hinterlands. Charles Coborn, the 'cockney' music-hall performer who had been born into a Scottish family and christened Colin MacCallum, attempted a rendition in Gaelic of the chorus of his international hit 'The Man Who Broke The Bank At Monte Carlo'.

It was a predictable guest-list, imitable down through the decades by any other self-made millionaire with a new country property. Two of its number do, perhaps, shed some light on Lord Leverhulme's perception of and relationship with the Gaels of the Hebrides. Sir Harry Lauder was popular at the castle. (Although possibly not quite so much as his wife Anne, a lively and unpretentious Lothian girl who would insist upon leading the household in song at the dinner table.) Sir Harry Lauder was popular everywhere. The Edinburgh-born former coalminer had become by 1919 – when he was knighted – the biggest entertainer in Britain. Sir Harry had not lost all of his colliery education: before leaving for a day's fishing he would ostentatiously prepare his own sandwiches, giving them to a servant only to wrap and place in his bag. And the songsmith

Marjory Kennedy-Fraser sang her collection of Hebridean ditties to the enthralled gathering, accompanied on the *clarsach* by her daughter Patuffa.

Lauder and Kennedy-Fraser had much in common. They had each made their names, and a great deal of their money, by the travesty of Scottish Gaelic culture. Marjory Kennedy-Fraser had been travelling about the Highlands and Islands since the last decades of the nineteenth century. A trained musician but not a Gaelic-speaker, her stock-in-trade was to note the gist of some refrain or snatch of music overheard in the Gaidhealtachd and then to represent it as a commercially attractive English-language lullaby or love-song. The result was as authentic as Ossian, and equally popular. Kennedy-Fraser's collections of 'Songs of the Hebrides' swept the land. Upon first hearing 'An Eriskay Love Lilt', 'Skye Water-Kelpie's Lullaby' and the 'Uist Cattle Croon' the celebrated music critic Ernest Newman wrote that 'Schubert and Hugo Wolf would have knelt and kissed the hands of their unknown composers'. Schubert may well have paid homage to the unknown composers of true Hebridean music; his opinion of Mrs Kennedy-Fraser's saccharine confections must remain speculative. But for Lord Leverhulme's generation and for many who came later, the 'Islay Reaper's Song' and 'Aignish on the Machair' were not just the most acceptable face of Scottish Gaelic culture – and the veritable acme of that culture – they were the only version of Gaelic creativity accessible to polite society.

Harry Lauder's deception was less devious. He made a fortune all over the English-speaking world by hoisting his tiny frame dressed as a drunken, absurdly-kilted 'Highlander' onto a music hall stage, pattering off a stream of lowland jokes about Anguses, Murdos and Donalds and singing songs like 'Roamin' in the Gloamin'', 'A Wee Deoch an Doris' and 'Stop Your Tickling, Jock'.

There was nothing sinister about Leverhulme's courtship of Kennedy-Fraser and Lauder, but something vaguely sad. Having bought for himself the heartland of the Gaelic language and become the feudal superior of tens of thousands of men and women who wore one of the oldest living cultures in Europe like a second layer of skin, he chose to import as his companions two people whose interest in that culture was exploitative and flawed. It may be frivolous to suggest that such company affected his business plans, but it would be foolish to imagine that Lauder's jokes and Kennedy-Fraser's tunes did not influence and simplify his view of the Leodhasaich.

His relationship with Lauder certainly spilled over into the Stornoway business community. The two men sallied out together to open the town's new bowling green in July 1922, Lauder in full stage regalia from his Glengarry to the *sgian dhubh* stuck in his sock, Leverhulme more conservatively clad in homburg and tweed plus-fours, the two small men like a pair of exotic gnomes beside the (far from lanky) form of Roderick Smith. In the same summer their shared freemasonry took them to Lodge Fortrose in Stornoway. Leverhulme had by then become the Grand Senior Warden of the Grand Lodge of England. On 14 July 1922 more than 100 Stornoway brethren heard Brother Lord Leverhulme, flanked by Brother Sir Harry Lauder, suggest that Lodge Fortrose could become 'the driving force' behind his plans for the rebuilding of Stornoway. The Emblems of the Craft which taught Morality, he said, 'could well be used practically for the benefit of the community. The brethren as Masons could be a powerful influence. Why should we not have a better Stornoway, and produce out of a tangle of relatively mean streets a fine city which would be the Venice of the Western Isles and an inspiration to the whole of the West . . . the inspiration could come from Lodge Fortrose.'[36]

Such dalliances were inevitable. Money found it easier to dine with money. The pity was not in his cheerful enjoyment of 'A Wee Deoch an Doris' and the 'Water Kelpie's Lullaby'. The pity was that on the doorstep of Lews Castle a few thousand others, not least his adopted man from the Board Colin Macdonald, knew all of the words of 'Eilean an Fhraoich' but would never be asked to interpret them.

Macdonald was invited to a soirée at the big house on the evening of the drama at Gress. He enjoyed his party at the castle, once he had learned to jog his Lordship's pouring arm ('I am so sorry . . . the tiniest drop of whisky . . . would make me witless, my thinking would be confused. I cannot afford to let my thoughts get confused . . . But please, please . . .'). Macdonald was not a house guest: he would not join the groups which gathered in the castle yard the following morning to tumble into estate vehicles and be driven with their rods and hampers to some west coast lodge and salmon run. He was there for a purpose. But before the main course came the *petit fours*. Songs were sung and dances were danced, and the young girls pleaded for a turn from their host: 'Lord Leverhulme for the bathing song! Lord Leverhulme for the bathing song!'

At first the great man demurred, refusing to offer 'that dreadful song' and leaving debutant guests such as Colin Macdonald wondering what on earth it was. Then he relented. He could not sing, but Lester Keith's risqué (it 'would make an Irish navvy blush,' considered Macdonald) pre-war hit 'The Bathing Song' was tailored more for lusty recitation. Effectively, he rapped it:

> A sweet little peach from Manhattan Beach
> Was strolling upon the sand,
> And met a young sport from jolly Newport
> Who thought she was perfectly grand
> She murmured to him, 'I'd go take a swim,
> But I am engaged to be wed,
> Though it's very warm, it's very bad form.'
> 'Yours looks good to me,' he said
> She answered right away, 'To Ma I used to say:
> 'Mother may I go out to swim?'
> 'Yes my darling daughter,
> Hang your clothes on a hickory limb,
> But don't go near the water.
> You may look cute in your bathing suit,
> But act just as you oughter,
> Now and then you can flirt with the men,
> But don't go near the water.

'The Bathing Song' was the musical equivalent of the gags he kept written down on pieces of paper in his waistcoat pocket. He followed it with a Lancashire dialect anecdote, gracefully acknowledged the applause, took Colin Macdonald's arm in a steely grip and escorted him to a quiet corner of the room.

'I should like to know,' said Leverhulme, gazing intently at Macdonald, 'exactly how I stand with you. Are you for me or against me?'

'You mean,' said Macdonald, gathering his wits, 'do I think the Board will be with you or against your schemes?'

'Put it that way if you like, but please, *please* do not be evasive. You know, and you know that I know that the Board will be largely guided by you in this matter. Are-you-with-me-or-against-me?'

'I do not yet know. I have not made up my mind. I see both sides. You see only one. Tell me this. You said today at the meeting that you had arranged to spend five million pounds on your developments here. I cannot quite grasp what even one million means, but at least I have an idea that five million pounds is a lot of money. Do you expect to get a return from that expenditure – and how?'

Leverhulme looked horrified. 'I am not a philanthropist in this matter! I would not put a penny into this venture if I did not see that it would be a commercial success. Never have I seen the successful end of a venture so clearly as I do now. Not that I require – or desire – to make more money for myself. I am never sure on a given day just what I am worth in money, but last time my accountant reported to me it was in the neighbourhood of eighteen million pounds. In any case I have more money than I can possibly require. But I derive my greatest pleasure in life from business ventures which call for thought and vision. That is a great game: the creation of wealth – and thereby providing steady work and good wages for thousands of people.'

'I can understand that,' said Macdonald, 'but what on earth is there in this rather barren island that offers economic scope for so huge a capital expenditure?'

'You appear to be intelligent. You probably are. But vision is also required here. You know this island. Did you know that, if you take a map, fix one leg of a pair of compasses in the town of Stornoway and describe a circle of a hundred miles radius, within that circle you have the richest fishing grounds in the whole world?'

'No. I did not.' Macdonald's scepticism was well placed. The fishing grounds of the Minch and the North Atlantic continental shelf were – at that time – good, but they were far from being the richest in the world.

'Quite,' continued Leverhulme. 'Well, you have. That is a very impor-tant fact. Fish is a valuable human food. That is also important. How can

I link up these terminal facts? I shall create the necessary connecting links so that I have a chain leading from the bed of the Minch to the breakfast tables of the world. First I must catch my fish. I shall soon have the best and the best-equipped fishing fleet the world has ever seen.

'My fish must be conveyed quickly to the railheads. I shall have a fleet of fast carrier boats for that. I am in process of acquiring so substantial a block of railway company shares that there will be no danger of my fish rotting at the sidings.

'I am getting on. But am I going to incur all this expense and risk, and then allow another fellow to reap the reward? No. I have already purchased most of the biggest retail fish shops in the big consuming centres. My fish will be sold in my shops. But I shall catch more fish than I can sell fresh. Well, I shall can the surplus . . . Canned fish is like whisky: the longer you keep it (up to a point) the better it gets. When my first cure is properly matured I send a consignment to my principal corner shops with instructions to make a good window display on the Saturday . . .'

'He had all but mesmerised me,' recalled Colin Macdonald 'He was as an evangelist preaching the gospel . . . It needed a real effort to hang on to the one thing I knew to be true – namely, that nothing at that time could effectively stand between the returned Lewis soldiers and sailors and their land.' Macdonald pulled himself together.

'Lord Leverhulme,' he said, 'however much you may convince me . . . it would but mislead you if I said I thought you could convince Lewis men . . . Certainly nothing you can promise them will induce them to drop their demands for crofts. But surely there is a middle way. The retention of the large farms is not essential to the success of your schemes.'

Leverhulme's reply was curt. 'I need them for the production of milk for supplying the greatly increased population which will be one of the direct results of my schemes.'

'You can import milk from the mainland. That is being done now – and better and cheaper milk than you can produce in Lewis.'

'My agricultural expert advises me I must have the farms. In this matter I must be guided by him.'

'I do not question the ability of your agricultural expert to advise you – in England. But with respect, Lewis is not England.'

'But I must have control of my factory hands. How can I have that in the case of men who are in the independent position of crofters?'

Colin Macdonald seems instantly to have realised the significance of the last two sentences. 'That is just the point,' he said. 'That is what was made so clear at the meeting today. These men will not tolerate being subject to your whim or charity. But if you initiate friendly relationships by giving them crofts you will have no lack of men willing to work in your factories. By opposing their desire you will but stimulate their opposition and in the end they will beat you. In one word my advice is: *compromise*.'

There was no possibility of that. Leverhulme 'reiterated again and again: "I will *not* compromise. I *must* control."'

'Then,' said Macdonald, 'I am afraid you are only at the beginning of your troubles.'

The party was almost over.

On the west coast in Shawbost the seven-year-old Calum Smith saw his father return home from the war in May 1919. Murdo Smith began immediately to work the croft, building a flock of sheep to accompany the milk-cow and horse, digging a cart-track to a previously inaccessible lower pasture and planting oats, potatoes and barley. He did so although he knew that his family's days at Shawbost were numbered. Murdo himself came from nearby Bragar. As a younger of six sons he was not set to inherit the tenancy of his father's croft. So when he married he moved onto his wife's croft. She was the younger of two daughters. Upon her father's death her older sister was bequeathed the croft. The older sister's husband, John Macaulay, had also now returned from the war, and they were understandably anxious to settle on their land and in their home.

It was a painfully familiar predicament, and one which was handled with characteristic sensitivity by all concerned. John 'an Ban' Macaulay was 'a gentle, considerate and inoffensive man' who insisted that Calum's family should not leave the croft and the crofthouse until they had somewhere else to go. But there was nowhere else to go. Murdo Smith proceeded to make the barn on the croft as habitable as possible, and he, his wife and five young children moved into it. John Macaulay still pointedly refused to occupy the crofthouse, leaving it available to the Smith family. Calum's mother undertook a series of desperate excursions by bus to the east coast in search of accommodation. There was nothing. There plainly were no crofts, and unfurnished town lets were either impossibly expensive or unavailable to a countrywoman with so many infants. When eventually she found four bare walls and a roof the Smith family had no alternative but to take it. They moved, two adults and five monoglot Gaelic-speaking children, into a single small room in a shack at Coulregrein on the suburban northern outskirts of Stornoway. The room was not big enough to take two beds together with a table and a kitchen-shelf. 'I can never hope to understand,' Calum would write, 'how we all lived together in that little box.' Both Calum and Murdo Smith became life-long socialists.

Even with Coll and Gress still half-occupied, with the government pressing him to compromise and with minor, sporadic, exploratory raids exploding like loose firecrackers across Lewis, Lord Leverhulme's instinct was not to retreat, nor even to entrench, but to expand. So he bought the island of Harris.

In normal circumstances it would have been a logical step. Harris is part of the same landmass. It is separated from Lewis not by water but by a range of mountains which run from between the island of Scarp and Morsgail deer forest in the west to Loch Seaforth in the east, and which peak at the celebrated heights of Clisham. Mountains had been for centuries a more effective barrier to Hebrideans than any stretch of sea, and Harris and the Hearaich were indisputably a place and a people apart.

There were two Harrises. North Harris was the isthmus town of Tarbert and the hills and rock-strewn rough pasture which reached towards the Lewis boundary. North Harris encompassed the busily independent fishing island of Scalpay and the coastal track which straggled hazardously towards Huishinish and Scarp. North Harris had the fantastic apparition of Amhuinnsuidhe Castle, a Victorian *schloss* stuck onto that coast like a child's toy abandoned on the shore.

South Harris was a dreamscape of atoll-yellow beaches, blue and white Atlantic seas and bright green machair on the west and modest hamlets hidden in mazy grey inlets on the east. It was a silent, unassertive place, less noticed by the outside world than many a better publicised island. Its settlements such as Northton, Rodel and Obbe on the coast overlooking the shallow Sound of Harris and the southern islands of Berneray and North Uist were organic outcrops of stone wall and thatch, villages as placid as the night.

∿

Harris had been the property of the earls of Dunmore since falling out of the hands of the profligate MacLeods in 1834. The seventh earl, an explorer and Victorian man of parts named Charles Adolphus Murray, build the baronial edifice of Amhuinnsuidhe Castle by the side of a sensational salmon run in 1865 and two years later divided up his property and sold North Harris – including Amhuinnsuidhe Castle and several thousand acres of deer forest – to Sir Edward Scott. The Dunmores' interest in their surviving holiday estate of South Harris declined as the nineteenth century progressed (Charles Adolphus would transfer his affections to Kashmir and Tibet), but the Scott family managed to combine shooting stags with a degree of philanthropy in North Harris. The school and main road in Tarbert bear their name, for obvious reasons.

Throughout all of these proprietorial comings and goings the nineteenth-century ritual of dispossession was enacted in miniature among the few thousand people of Harris. The clearance of people from the good west coast began under the MacLeods and was continued by the Dunmores. In the words of James Hunter:

> In the 1820s and 1830s the fertile machair lands on the Atlantic coast of Harris – lands which had been occupied from time immemorial – were completely cleared and the evicted population settled on the island's eastern shores.
>
> This was so bleak and stony a district that, as a Harris crofter observed bitterly, 'beasts could not live' in it. Among the rocks on which they were thus forced to set up home, the newly arrived inhabitants of the eastern part of Harris painstakingly constructed the lazybeds or *feannagan* which are still to be seen there and which alone could provide a depth of soil sufficient to raise a crop. More than 100 years later, the pioneer ecologist, Frank Fraser Darling, was to comment of the *feannagan* in question:

'Nothing can be more moving to the sensitive observer of Hebridean life than these lazybeds of the Bays district of Harris. Some are no bigger than a dining table, and possibly the same height from the rock, carefully built up with turves carried there in creels by the women and girls. One of these tiny lazybeds will yield a sheaf of oats or a bucket of potatoes, a harvest no man should despise.'[37]

It was said that at the end of the nineteenth century a person could walk from West Loch Tarbert around the entire Atlantic coast of Harris to Obbe, and pass only three houses – the few lodges and farm dwellings of the landed class. On the stony east coast overpopulation was so acute that the people emigrated in their hundreds.

There was therefore land hunger and struggle in Harris as well as in her larger, more demonstrative sister to the north. There was occasional active resistance to some of the western seaboard clearances. The same appeals for the return of land upon which they could survive were made by Hearaich to the Napier Commission, appeals that were as elsewhere fortified by the teachings of their reformed Presbyterian church. Lachlan Campbell of Scadabay in the overcrowded Bays of Harris reminded Baron Napier and his colleagues that according to Holy Writ, 'He gave the land to the children of men'. Some Hearaich joined the first Park deer forest raid in 1887. Soldiers and sailors from North and South Harris fought and died in the Great War in equal proportion even with the 'loyal' island of Lewis, and men from Harris were among those denied even a short enjoyment of the rewards of peace by the sinking of the *Iolaire*. Those that did return shared identical aspirations. 'When we were in the trenches down to our knees in mud and blood,' said one *Hearach* bitterly in 1919, 'we were promised all good things when we returned home victorious.'

When Leverhulme bought South Harris and North Harris from the Dunmores and the Scotts respectively in the May and June of 1919, he became the feudal superior of 4,500 people who may have lived in a gentle link of the Hebridean chain, but whose calm surface concealed powerful undercurrents.

He arrived in Harris with the highest references. Samuel Scott, the deceased Sir Edward's eldest son, despatched in October 1919 from

Amhuinnsuidhe Castle to his erstwhile tenantry a circular letter in Gaelic and in English. Scott had arranged through a lease-back deal to hold onto the castle as a retirement holiday home. His valediction was therefore delivered to people who may have been curious about his motives; it read:

> In view of the many years during which my family and myself have been associated with you, and the very cordial relations that have always existed between us, I feel I owe it to you to announce that I have ceased to be your Proprietor, having sold North Harris to Lord Leverhulme, and further that I should give you reasons for my decision. Though I have sold the property I have not severed my connection with North Harris. Owing to the increase in taxation and great rise in all expenses caused by the War, I found that it would be impossible for me to continue in Harris as in former days.
>
> 'Till recently it had never entered my head that I should not remain your Proprietor during my life, and it was only with the greatest reluctance that I came to the conclusion that it was in the best interests of all that I should accept Lord Leverhulme's offer, for the following reasons:
>
> First, because after long talks with Lord Leverhulme I was convinced that in him you would have a Proprietor who would further your interests and do all in his power, far more than I could ever do, to help you. At my death the estate would have had to be sold, and I believed it best for you all that the estate should be sold to a man who, I am convinced, will be a good and generous landlord, than that it should be sold after my death to some unknown person who might not have your interests at heart.
>
> Secondly, because I could see no other way of being able to come to Harris, the place I love best in the world, as in former years, and that I should have to let it year by year. I hope now to come to Harris for many years, though only as a tenant; but I need hardly say that my interest in yourselves and your affairs will remain unabated, and I can only hope that in years to come you will look upon me as a friend in the same way as I venture to believe you have looked upon me in the past. I shall do all I can to further your interests both individually and collectively.
>
> I bid you farewell as Proprietor with a very sad heart, and take this opportunity of expressing my great gratitude for the very many proofs of good feeling towards my family and myself which you have always given, and also for the many acts of kindness I have received at your hands; and I earnestly hope that that bond of good feeling and good relationship between us will continue for many years.

Samuel Scott received £20,000 (or approximately £600,000 today) from

Leverhulme for North Harris; Lord Dunmore took £36,000 (approximately £1 million) for South Harris and its distant cousin, St Kilda.

Leverhulme's short gubernation of St Kilda is a less-remarked corner of his Hebridean project. The seventy-three souls, including a minister and a nurse and their families, who inhabited this remote outcrop 60 miles west of Harris had enjoyed an eventful war. Village Bay in St Kilda had been the only community in Britain to suffer a bombardment from an offshore German U-Boat (whose skipper had sportingly announced his intention by megaphone before shelling the place, thereby giving the islanders the opportunity to find safe shelter).

The long-term indigenous human habitation of St Kilda had been the subject of critical debate for the better part of a century. The population had many times been lower than it was between 1860 and 1919, when it hovered around the seventy to eighty mark, but St Kildans had not previously found themselves living their medieval life as citizens of an increasingly prosperous great power. The Victorian pleasure cruisers which brought sweetmeats and spending cash into their bay brought also the unignorable promise of a life of luxury to be discovered on the mainland of the United Kingdom. In 1930 they determined reluctantly to redeem that promise and were voluntarily evacuated to Scotland.

They were Lord Leverhulme's responsibility between 1919 and 1925, although there is no record of him ever once acknowledging the place, let alone visiting St Kilda. He was not the first such negligent proprietor of what was easily the most inaccessible population in Britain. But he was the first to have bought into the Hebrides with the avowed aim of making them thrive rather than stagnate. St Kilda was, however, an island group too far. It had not the population nor the surface area nor the resources to be pulled up by its bootstraps. In coarse entrepreneurial terms it was an economic basketcase. St Kilda has posthumously been made the unwitting symbol of too many lost causes for its own good; it needs no others adding to the roster. It represents only a fraction of Leverhulme's final failure, and that fraction is significant only in one regard. It is that a small number of people called St Kilda home, and would not have left it if presented with a reason to stay. For half of its last ten years of life Lord Leverhulme – the man who announced to the world that he was buying the bigger Hebrides to solve their problems and stem their decline – had it wholly within his power to help the living St Kilda. Like a score and more of others, he failed to act on his promise.

He did not, then, buy Harris in order to obtain St Kilda. He bought it most probably because he had intended all along to bring the entire insular landmass into his estate. There would not be much point to a bustling, industrialised, affluent, densely populated Lewis which stopped at some invisible line between Morsgail and Clisham, south of which was to be found only Third World poverty, migrant labour and eighteenth century agricultural practices. He certainly did not intend Harris to become a bolthole; things just turned out that way.

Throughout 1919, as his purlieu and his proposals expanded, Leverhulme increasingly needed the support of the Scottish Secretary and the Board of Agriculture. The Board's officials, who tended to be of northern smallholding stock, he knew to be largely prejudiced in favour of land redistribution. Robert Munro, however, despite his Ross-shire origins, was like Leverhulme a Liberal lad of parts clambering gamely up the social ladder (Munro would end his life as Lord Alness). He should surely have some sympathy with the proprietor's case.

Munro did have some sympathy. He was constrained not only by his own gut sodality with fellow Highlanders but also by political reality. When the people of Lewis and Harris complained that the land had been promised to them by the government, they spoke little more than the truth. The government had certainly never envisaged breaking up every farm, deer-run and shooting estate in the Highlands and Islands, or even in Lewis. But the government – urged on by the Board of Agriculture – had many years earlier and throughout the war insisted that it was converted to the cause of crofting, and that it would find the tens of thousands of pounds necessary to create enough crofts to satisfy the bulk of legitimate popular demand, especially in such islands as Lewis and Harris where the number of cottars (men and women on unsecured property with no fixity of tenure or controlled rent) was large enough to create serious destabilisation.

Nobody had expected Lord Leverhulme. Once they got Lord Lever-hulme, nobody expected his proposals to be on so gigantic a scale that they promised to eclipse all other forms of social and working life in his domain. And nobody was quite prepared for the dogged tenacity of his refusal to bargain or to compromise.

Munro attempted to keep all the balls in the air. If Leverhulme took home in a huff his sacks of spending cash, it was important that this should not be perceived as the fault of the Scottish Secretary. Leverhulme requested a ten-year moratorium on land resettlement in Lewis and Harris to give his plans time to succeed. Robert Munro's reluctance to grant this demand was denounced at the time and later as unreasonable and ungrateful. But the unreason lay with Lord Leverhulme. When he asked for ten years' breathing space he was almost seventy years old. He had always made it clear that Lewis and Harris were his personal interests and had nothing to do with the Lever Brothers company. There was absolutely no guarantee that after his death, whenever it should occur, the Hebridean schemes would continue to be financed and supported – and every reason to suspect that they would not.

In the meantime the government was confronted by the unattractive spectacle of thousands of Hebridean families who had in the previous decade demonstrated their courage and their loyalty in the most indisputable fashion, being reduced to squatting on a few disputed acres of comparatively worthless peat bog and grazing land.

Leverhulme did not understand their aspirations. He deceived himself. When the islanders said that they wanted a house, they did not mean a rented bungalow in Stornoway. When they said that they wanted land, they did not mean a suburban allotment. They did not need to be given lectures on the paltry income earned by crofters: they knew that better than most.

They also knew that life on the north-western fringe of Europe was uncertain; that kings and queens and landowners and politicians came and went; that great schemes were started and then collapsed. It had been unforgettably proven over the previous century that they, the one human constant in all of this flux, had little security. But if they had a croft they now had – thanks to their living relatives' agitation just thirty and forty years earlier – safe tenure at a legislated rent. They had sufficient land upon which to keep a cow and grow root vegetables. They had a share of common grazing on the hillside, a peatbog from which to cut and dry their year's supply of fuel, and somewhere to draw up a boat. They might never be rich in money, but none of their traditions – their history, their culture, their adaptive religion, their laconic, intelligent view of life – set much store by bulging bank accounts. It is not a difficult philosophy for most people to understand, even to admire. The people of Lewis and Harris were simply the only population of the United Kingdom who had avoided deracination. Some unfortunate north-country ancestor of William Hesketh Lever had in an earlier age been uprooted from her ancestral turf by enclosure or plague or industrialisation or crime. The majority of Hebrideans had in the first quarter of the twentieth century escaped that fate. They understood him – they had the imagination and the experience to project themselves even into his incomprehension. They knew why he could not understand them. He was incapable of returning the compliment. He heard not songs of visceral attachment and yearning, but the vapid lilts of Marjory Kennedy-Fraser; not the considered articulacy of the Free Church lay preacher, but the lampoons of Harry Lauder.

And while they were prepared to compromise, he was not. Like the action in Park of the men of Lochs in 1887, the land raids at Coll and Gress and Tong in 1919 were more of a demonstration than a seizure. When they protested that they had no opposition to his job-creating proposals but wished merely to have a home to live in while he developed them, they were being perfectly honest.

It was, as Robert Munro understood, a reasonable request. There was neither a pressing need for dairy farms to the north of Stornoway, nor any certainty that if they were to be ring-fenced they would efficiently cater for an expanded town's milk demands. If a sizable number of young men with families were to be settled on that disputed machair land, however, then Lord Leverhulme's new projects would have in their immediate vicinity a stable and substantial reservoir of potential employees, without him having gone to the trouble and expense of putting a roof over their heads. The more that Leverhulme's demands were examined the less reasonable they appeared. One or two things were by the end of 1919 starkly clear. His conviction that crofting worked as a drag-anchor on progress in the Highlands was absolute. Crofting was in his opinion not only uneconomic and obsolete: it was positively harmful and retrogressive. Crofting would wither and die on the twentieth-century vine, he was sure of that. But in the meantime it was a deadweight on his own activities, not least because – as he privately admitted – the independence of mind and movement allowed to a crofter was quite incompatible with his own requirement of a docile and malleable workforce. And having announced that his semi-choate plans for Lewis involved the pasture land at Tong, Gress and Coll being devoted to farmed cattle, he would never retreat. It was the received wisdom of Leverhulme's catechism of industrial relations that a personal retraction, a small compromise, would be identified by the labouring classes as a weakness which they would not hesitate to exploit. In fact the independent labouring classes of Lewis and Harris would have applauded such a compromise as the judgement of a sensible man. The weaknesses that they recognised instead were the petty, unworthy flaws of pride, blinkered obstinacy and arrogance.

While Robert Munro was speaking publicly of his confidence in Leverhulme's plans and of the need to accommodate them, he and his officials were working behind the scenes to persuade the proprietor to relax his prohibition on new land settlement 'near Stornoway' and elsewhere in Lewis. Leverhulme not only rejected these overtures; he resented them. Invited to address the Philosophical Institution of Edinburgh on 4 November 1919, he took the opportunity to accuse government involvement in Highland affairs – from the Napier Commission to the Board of Agriculture – of being responsible for the plight of the Gaidhealtachd. Drawing roughly on John Milton, he claimed that:

> Reports from Royal Commissions and visiting commissioners, thick as leaves in Vallombrosa, have been the dominating feature of Government policy in the Highlands and Islands of Scotland.
>
> I will not weary you by detailing them, but the invariable rule seems to have been, where expenditure of public money was recommended by such commissions, for the Government either to ignore such reports or to cut down expenditure so penuriously as only to result in the waste of public money by not spending the full amount required . . . Lewis and Harris have too long been the Cinderella in the Government pantomime.

In other words, Westminster wasted a lot of money in the public charade of commissioning reports on the Hebrides, wasted even more money by part-financing their recommendations, and then wasted the lot by scrapping everything. Whatever grains of truth they might have contained, those were undiplomatic assertions from a man who was petitioning the government for substantial grants towards the improvement of facilities in Lewis and who needed the support of as many visiting commissioners as he could recruit.

In January 1920 demobilised servicemen reoccupied the farmlands at Gress and Coll which they had left the previous autumn. This time they began to build houses. In February 1920 Leverhulme announced that he was ceasing improvement work throughout rural Lewis and would be concentrating his developments solely on Stornoway and in Harris. The small south-coast harbour township of Obbe would, as Stornoway became the Venice of the west, become the Stornoway of Harris.

In gratitude for this unexpected attention the eminences of Obbe had agreed (following an unspecified number of heavy hints and meetings with both his Lordship and the South Harris estate factor) to abandon their thousand-year-old Norse–Gaelic name and give Obbe the new and more fitting postal address of Leverburgh. A Scottish doctor of Highland descent named Halliday Sutherland heard in the south of this proposal. 'Hitherto, no-one in the mainland had troubled about what was happening in Lewis,' Sutherland would recall. 'As soon as the change of name was announced, quiet old gentlemen all over Scotland rose from their chairs and said: "What the devil is the meaning of this?"

'Poor Lord Leverhulme! He was trying . . . to buy one of the things in this world which money cannot buy – an immortality for his name.'[38]

Sutherland was only partly right. A name's immortality may not be for sale, but its Ozymandian longevity is. More than eighty years later the quiet coastal town of Obbe in Harris would still identify itself on most maps as Leverburgh.

The Tolsta to Ness road was abandoned at the northern side of a deep ravine, leaving a symbolic bridge to nowhere across the Geiraha River. The project was not over, Leverhulme would insist, it was merely cutting its cloth appropriately. There were pressures from abroad, as well as an enemy within.

7

NOTHING THERE BUT SLAVERY

In the autumn of 1919 a young man named Arthur Geddes was employed by Lord Leverhulme to assist in an agricultural survey of his Hebridean estate. Geddes, who would go on to become a noted sociologist and historian of rural Scotland, helped Dr M.E. Hardy, who was in his turn treading in the exalted footsteps of Thomas Mawson, to prepare a lengthy report on the natural assets of Lewis and Harris.

It was not part of Geddes and Hardy's brief to look at the sea fisheries. The sea fisheries were taken without question to be a huge unexploited local resource. Once properly worked, the fisheries, assumed everybody from Leverhulme down, would provide the stable foundations of the islands' future prosperity. Without the fisheries, as the proprietor had made clear on numerous occasions, he might never have considered the salvation of Lewis. Without that compass circle drawn around Stornoway, which enclosed 'the richest fishing grounds in the world', he might never even have bought the place. Hardy and Geddes were asked instead to explore such ancillary developments as commercial peat-cutting and market gardening, which might be launched on Barvas Moor as complementary activities to catching industrial quantities of fish, canning and freezing them and sending them off to 400 MacFisheries retail outlets.

Only later did Arthur Geddes observe, from a distance, what was clearly a staggering flaw in Lord Leverhulme's business plan. For a variety of reasons, the demand for and the price of fish was plummeting.

Pondering years later on the fate of the project in which he had played a small part, Geddes found himself wondering exactly why 'the differences of viewpoint' between Leverhulme and the Leodhasaich, instead of being harmonised by two parties with so many interests in common, 'led so soon to friction, deadlock and breakdown'. He dismissed the notion of the 'stubborn crofter', and that of the procrastinating Scottish Office, and even that of the 'impatient or obstinate' Leverhulme as being too simplistic, too lazy a view of what happened in the Hebrides in the early 1920s. Instead Arthur Geddes looked at market forces and suggested that,

> Surely one basic fact remains. In 1917–18, when Leverhulme framed his policy and made his plans, the Scottish fisheries, to judge from pre-war years, could still expect to hold high place in providing for a brisk market in herring and white fish.
>
> True, the value of the Island cure of white fish had fallen from £100,000 in 1900 to one-tenth, £10,000, in 1913; but Leverhulme saw that since fresh fish were now demanded, his capitalisation of equipment with accelerated transit of the catch should bring quick recovery. The herring trade had been active at Stornoway up to the eve of the War; and although the islanders had made leeway following the introduction of steam and of larger motor drifters, Leverhulme thought he saw an opportunity to capitalise the industry, providing 'work for wages'.
>
> This forecast was wrong. Consumption declined, and the market fell. Not only so; the proportion contributed by Scots fishermen to the shrinking market declined even more.[39]

And the proportion contributed by Hebridean fishermen to the Scottish catch also declined. By the start of the Great War the fishing fleets of Wick, Helmsdale, Peterhead and Fraserburgh had been for many years substantially composed of steam-powered drift-net trawlers – which would enable them in times of peace not only to harvest more fish, but also to exploit the waters around the islands which west coast men had previously regarded as their own. The Stornoway fleet only began to make similar mechanised headway after 1918. The post-war domestic market for fish simultaneously declined because peace brought with it the removal of naval blockades and the return of free trade. Fish, which had been in wartime a valuable source of protein, was suddenly competing with a variety of other foodstuffs on the shelves at the same time as it was being caught more efficiently and landed in unprecedented quantities. Its wholesale and retail price collapsed.

The Hebridean boats were also drastically affected by another train of events. Following the Russian revolution in 1917, the Bolshevik withdrawal from the war and the execution of the Romanov royal family,

Britain had imposed a trade embargo on the new Soviet Union. These sanctions had little effect on the greater part of the British economy, which was not reliant overall on doing business in eastern Europe. But they certainly affected the herring trade. Throughout the nineteenth and early twentieth centuries the enormous Russian appetite for pickled herring had largely been satisfied by catches from the great shoals which made their way annually down the Minch. Herring had become a staple of the Hebridean fleet because it was freely available on the doorstep and because there was a traditional and apparently bottomless market. Consequently twenty times as many barrels of herring might be exported from Stornoway in a year than all the white fish catches combined. The domestic market for herring – which was perceived in the south as being a food of rough necessity rather than a gourmet product – was one of the first to collapse after the Armistice. Its disintegration was contemporaneous with British politicians preventing British fishermen from reopening their old herring export routes to Russia.

James Shaw Grant, the son of William, shortly after acceding to his father's editor's chair at the *Stornoway Gazette* in 1932, would tell the visiting poet Louis MacNeice that the post-war collapse of the Lewis herring fishery was also partly caused by Prohibition in the United States. 'The Stornoway herring,' related MacNeice, 'is exceptionally large and tasty and the Americans, being connoisseurs in this matter, used to import large quantities of these herrings, salted, for use in their saloons – the salted Stornoway herring being a great thirst-maker.'[40]

The results were devastating. In the pre-war years more boats had worked the herring fishery from Stornoway and Barra than from Wick and Aberdeen. Some 6,000 fishermen and 2,000 shore workers were seasonally engaged in the Hebrides.

The industry's historian, James Coull, writes that after the war:

> The disorganisation which came in the herring fisheries was particularly severe . . . while the white and other fisheries were less severely affected, they also had formidable problems to face . . .
>
> Other countries had begun to catch up even before World War One, and although the inter-war years were disorganised and at times chaotic for the global economy, competing countries continued to undermine Britain's

THE SOAP MAN

previously leading position . . . Other countries were developing and modernising their fisheries, and the struggle for survival in the difficult market conditions indeed was a stimulus to do so. Norway, Holland, Iceland and Germany all advanced to the first rank among European herring producers, and had in general lower production costs than the fishermen in Scotland.[41]

Just over 200,000 tons of herring were landed in Scotland for salt curing (the staple of the Stornoway fleet) in 1913, which was a bad pre-war year. In 1919 the amount was almost halved to 120,000 tons, and it continued dramatically to decline, as did the overall catch, as did demand and as did prices, throughout 1920 and 1921. It would never properly recover.

The situation was catastrophic not only to the active Lewis fleet of 1919 and 1920, but also to Lord Leverhulme's confident proposals. 'In the early years of Leverhulme's adventure,' recalled Arthur Geddes, 'the fall in total sales and prices of fish brought immediate loss to the keenest and hardest working of the fishermen, and to their financial backers in Stornoway.'

> These losses warned others of the uncertainties of fishing. Now the fall in the fishing industry is not so much as mentioned in [his son's] biography of Leverhulme; nor do we remember a word of it in Leverhulme's speeches. One finds no data to show a substantial endeavour by the Scottish Office to co-operate with Leverhulme in framing policies either to change the trend of European markets or to make local adaptations to combat downward trends. The Fishery Reports certainly record the losses, year by year.
>
> As for the Island fishermen, they shared the feeling expressed by other Scots fishermen, that the old markets across the North Sea, eastward to what had been St Petersburg, could and should be reopened, not closed 'for party reasons' by 'English politicians' . . . In brief, the Scots fisheries suffered after the War as neither Leverhulme nor others had foreseen when first he laid his plans for the island's prosperity . . . [both he and the government] turned their faces away from this disquieting factor of the Baltic markets, though both knew it to be fundamental to the success of Scots fisheries and the island's future.

The very people who were being so forcefully reminded 'of the uncertainties of fishing' were those who were also being exhorted by Lord Leverhulme to dispense with their old attachment to crofting in favour of a new salaried job and a house, both of which would be tied to the fishing industry. Geddes was wrong, as we shall see, to suggest that Leverhulme himself said nothing to indicate that he was aware of the crisis. As the landowner, as an associate of such fishcurers as Provost Murdo Maclean and as the chairman of Stornoway Pier and Harbour Commission, let alone as a capable businessman, it could not plausibly have escaped his attention. Not even his near-monopoly of British high street fishmongeries would help him to evade the pressures of the market, as he appreciated better than most. If MacFisheries were obliged by the rules of capitalism to buy their raw material from Fleetwood or Fraserburgh steam drifters rather than from Lewis, then they would patronise Lancashire and Buchan.

He was slow in pointing to the decay of his foundation stone. He may have hoped that the stormclouds would pass; that the markets would correct themselves. If so he was to be disappointed. Not until late in 1921, when he had already decided that he could supply no answer to 'the Lewis question' and was ready to withdraw, would he publicly confirm Arthur Geddes's suspicions.

By then Leverhulme had become accustomed to crisis and disappointment. The fact that men were reoccupying dairy farms on the east coast of Lewis and that the Hebridean herring fishery had collapsed did not loom large in the concerns of the other shareholders of Lever Brothers Limited in 1920. They had more troublesome regions on their minds.

The post-war international spending boom of 1919 burst like a bubble in the first months of 1920. By March of that year 'the Lever management was noting with some concern the growing stocks of unsold soap, a marked slackening in trade, and above all the considerable fall in raw material prices.'[42] Port Sunlight went onto a four-day week, laid workers off and suffered from strike action. Between February and July 1920 the price of palm kernel oil fell by more than half, from £115 to £55 a ton. In the same six months 'ordinary' palm oil collapsed from £98 to £53 a ton. Lever Brothers were at the time holding stocks of such raw materials which they had purchased for a total of £18 million. They may have lost in half a year as much as £9 million (which eighty years later would be the equivalent of £270 million) in realisable asset value.

Leverhulme – who as the main holder of preferential shares in Lever Brothers found his paper fortune most seriously debilitated – responded as ever to adversity, by acquisition rather than retreat. He bought the Niger Company.

It was an extraordinary purchase at an extraordinary time of an extraordinary business. The Niger Company was a British product of the European scramble for Africa in the late nineteenth century. It originated in the exploits of a kenspeckle colonial adventurer who was, when Lever Brothers inherited his creation in 1920, still alive and venerated as the 74-year-old 'founder of Nigeria', Sir George Dashwood Taubman Goldie. Goldie had made it his vocation to become the Cecil Rhodes of west Africa. He devoted himself to consolidating, and then securing, and then expanding British interests on the extensive banks of the River Niger. Using devices which were becoming familiar – gunboats and disciplined European squadrons and Christian ruthlessness and Sir Hiram Stevens Maxim's rapid-firing automatic repeater rifles – Goldie had by the end of the nineteenth century claimed for Britain the 500,000 square miles of fertile, mineral-rich and well-populated Africa which in 1897 was christened Nigeria.

Goldie's Royal Niger Company had in 1897 been operating for eleven years in Africa under charter, as a quasi-governmental organisation. In 1900 the charter was surrendered, Nigeria became a colony administered directly from Whitehall, and the Niger Company was free to concentrate – as a virtually monopolistic exploiter of considerable resources – solely on making money. It did so with glee, registering throughout the Great War annual profits of £250,000.

Lord Leverhulme's interest in this further great swathe of Africa, a thousand miles north of his considerable Congolese commitments, was largely predicated on the fact that in 1919 100,000 tons of oil seeds passed through the hands of the Niger Company. It was a comprehensible reason for taking a serious interest. It was no justification for acting like a child in a sweet shop.

At their distinguished chairman's urging, in 1920 Lever Brothers paid for the Niger Company much more than it was worth, more than they needed to pay, and more than Lever Brothers could afford to pay. They did so in such a hurry that no real investigation was made of the Niger Company's accounts. When the books were finally examined Leverhulme and his fellow directors discovered that they had bought for an inflated price of £8 million not only the Niger Company's assets but also the Niger Company's substantial liabilities, including an incompetent management and a previously undisclosed overdraft of £2 million which was repayable almost immediately to the bank.

Clarence Knowles, his longstanding director with responsibility for raw materials, was given responsibility for the Niger Company purchase negotiations early in 1920. When Knowles had finalised the deal he received a congratulatory telegram from Leverhulme which acknowledged, 'Price high but suicidal if we had let opportunity lapse.'

Knowles's offer included the bizarre clause – which was also accepted by Leverhulme and the others as part of the necessary cost of their prize – that between January, when the deal was agreed, and July, when the final payments were made, the Niger Company would continue to be run by its old management and directors. This agreement meant that for more than five months in 1920 when the oils and fats market was in turmoil, £8 million of Lever Brothers' money was committed to an enterprise whose pilots were completely beyond their control and who had already amassed at least £2 million of debt.

Unsurprisingly Lever Brothers' broker, Sir Robert Nivison, refused to underwrite the purchase. Leverhulme scraped together the £8 million by floating a new, unsupported share issue and by recapitalising Lever Brothers Limited. Having found the money to complete the Niger Company purchase he was given a few more weeks – until the middle of August 1920 – to repay the £2 million overdraft to the Niger Company's bankers. He turned to other bankers, who politely declined to throw good money after bad. 'It would be in the interests of everybody,' advised one, 'that Lever Brothers should dispose of the shares in the Niger Company.'

Predictably enough Leverhulme responded to this advice not by shedding his Niger Company shares but by bidding for control of another equatorial corporate giant, the African and Eastern Trade Corporation. 'The business,' he explained to nervous associates, 'can well rest after I have gone to view the daisies from the underside . . . I recognise that expansion may not be so rapid after my death.' (He was later persuaded to withdraw from this attempted acquisition.)

Such bravado may have been intended to impress the banks. It certainly failed to mollify them. By February 1921 the £2 million owed by the Niger company had still not been repaid and the creditors threatened Leverhulme with a writ. If the writ had been delivered, considered the company historian Charles Wilson, 'Liquidation would [have been] the inevitable consequence.' It was a situation of unprecedented severity. His markets were slumping, his workers were restless and the banks were foreclosing. 'Holding off the creditors with one hand he negotiated with the other terms for a loan from Barclays Bank – terms which, though onerous, were yet to prove the salvation of the Lever group.'[43]

He got the loan by complying uncharacteristically with all of Barclays' demands. He had no choice. Company results showed that Lever Brothers had in 1920 lost £2 million in the value of raw material stocks alone. 'What the losses of the Niger Company were,' says Charles Wilson, 'it is difficult to say: certainly they were far larger than Lever Brothers' own.'

Business and banking confidence in Lord Leverhulme's judgement, which had for thirty years been beyond sensible reproach, was in 1920 and 1921 shaken to the core. His rash refusal to heed moderating counsel at a time of crisis led to what had previously been unthinkable: people within Lever Brothers began to wonder whether or not the group might be better off without its chairman and founder. 'The Niger purchase had not only changed the structure of the company: by demonstrating beyond any reasonable doubt that the personal autocracy by which the business had [been run] was no longer adequate, it was to change the whole ethos of the business.'[44] A substantial overhaul of the company's management and directorship was commenced in 1921; this would continue for several years and would not be completed until after the grand old man's death.

On 19 September 1921 Leverhulme celebrated his seventieth birthday. It has been tempting for those who observed only one section of this man's encyclopaedic life to assume that he reached that milestone while disturbed chiefly, or even only, by uncontrollable events in the Outer Hebrides. It would be more accurate to say that Lewis and Harris figured small in his concerns. He spent the best part of 1920 and 1921 obsessed not by the question of Lewis but by his company. Lever Brothers was firstly in danger of liquidation, and having survived that threat Leverhulme himself was ever after aware of rumours of regicide, of suggestions that he should relinquish his reins to another driver. It left a seventy-year-old with not much excess energy or sympathy to spend on what had in large part been acquired as a retirement adventure playground.

At this time it became clear that Lewis and Harris, however joined they may have been in geography and their new proprietor's own perception, really were two separate cases. The very size of Lewis, the insular kingdom which had firstly attracted and excited Leverhulme, dictated that only big schemes and ambitious planning could possibly salve its diverse difficulties. For as long as one huge but realisable project such as the sea fishing seemed suited to underpin a score of others, the answer to the Lewis question was in sight. If, however, question marks appeared around the sea fishing project, as they did in 1920 and 1921, then the validity of the whole vast initiative was suddenly in doubt. Herb meadows and commercial peat cuttings were all very well as secondary, supportive activities, but they would not keep 30,000, let alone 200,000 people alive. House building and railway lines would obviously employ workers, but there was no call for houses in Stornoway if the fisheries could not employ their occupants, and no purpose to a railway if nobody travelled on it. Sea fishing had been set in place, with great ceremony and under the sceptical gaze of all of Scotland, as the massive, essential foundation slab of Lord Leverhulme's Hebridean enterprise. If it were removed then very little else could be built in Lewis – and there was a real danger of those few small affiliated structures which had been raised tumbling into dust.

For as long as the equation balanced, Leverhulme could convince himself and others that there was a purpose and a future to what he was doing in Lewis. He could live with, and even thrive upon, the stridency of debate with land reformers, politicians and belligerent returned service-men. But not even his own unquenchable spirit could absorb month after month the realisation that his sums no longer added up, that there were not enough fish in the North Atlantic Ocean to subsidise even a part of his Utopia, and return willingly to the fray. In such circumstances the island of Lewis was in danger of being transformed from a delightful and infinitely challenging social experiment, into just another dispiriting outpost of a troublesome and overstretched empire.

His involvement in Lewis was schizophrenic. It was neither entirely philanthropic nor wholly business-like. It was not solely an old man's whimsy, but neither was it thoroughly planned in advance. He would most characteristically begin from some solid common ground. Once that had been satisfactorily occupied he would proceed to extemporise. His earliest inclinations certainly pointed him towards modernising and expanding the Lewis sea fishery, but after that many of his decisions were made on the hoof; they were fanciful projections no sooner imagined than publicly incorporated into some vast strategy. That strategy in fact never really existed. He knew that whatever could be done in Lewis probably had not previously been attempted by its earlier succession of proprietors. He had a deep faith in his own intuition. If Leverhulme pictured a railway line between Stornoway and Tarbert or dairy ranches at Gress and Coll, then he could see no good reason why there should not be steam trains puffing through Balallan or vast herds of dairy cattle roaming on the machair. If he was capable of projecting a Lancastrian density of population onto the Outer Hebrides, he was not prepared to understand why Lewis may be a better place with a population of fewer than 200,000. He left it to others to sort out the practical details, to lay the rails and erect the fences. He left it to others to fall into line behind his vision. When they proved incapable of doing so his patience expired.

As his exasperation grew he could cushion his retreat with the economic clause. It had always been nonsensical for Lord Leverhulme to suggest, as he so often did, that philanthropy played no part in his schemes. If the fishing had turned out to be as hugely profitable as he had hoped, if his company had enjoyed a post-war golden age of seamless profiteering, if everybody in Lewis had trooped obediently behind him, he would still have found himself injecting millions of pounds of unrecoverable capital. The grandchildren of Lewis may conceivably have benefited. Lord Leverhulme certainly would not. He was prepared to spend money – although, after 1920 and 1921, a severely reduced amount – on a grateful, industrious and receptive island. But he was not going to throw vast sums into a cauldron of discontent. As the fishery failure could be mentioned only obliquely if at all, for to acknowledge it directly would have meant recognising the frailty of his own proposals, he was obliged to fix upon a relatively minor obstacle: the land hunger north of Stornoway. Leverhulme can never have convinced himself that the success or failure of his gargantuan plans for the island hung solely on the question of whether Gress and Coll should be given over to cattle farms or to crofts. But he was in search of an emblematic hard case; he needed a point of principle to illustrate both his own resolve and the increasingly apparent unsuitability of the Leodhasaich to enact his dreams.

He was already embittered in the autumn of 1920 when the raiders withdrew again from Gress and Coll. They did so for three reasons: to demonstrate their preparedness to give their proprietor's grand schemes time to flourish, to give the Board of Agriculture's diplomacy another chance, and because they had less use for croft land in the winter months. His response was to halt the job-creation road-building schemes, to reduce all apparent industrial development in Stornoway, to abandon his plans for canning Lewis fish, to suggest that east-coast malcontents might move to live on the west coast of the island, to voice public criticism of the Scottish Office and to call for a vote of confidence from every parish in Lewis.

He won that vote. At meeting after meeting from Back to Barvas the people of Lewis repeated what they had always said, that they fully supported all of Lord Leverhulme's proposals to bring employment to the island. They saw no contradiction in simultaneously supporting, as they did, the struggle of their sons and daughters to achieve security of tenure on a strip of croftland. As Colin Macdonald had tried unsuccessfully to explain, the contrariety was in his eyes only.

He disengaged himself slowly but inexorably. The process of with-drawal was as complex and stuttering and improvised as had been the happier months of his entanglement. The people, having watched throughout the winter their worst suspicions of yet another fair-weather landowner coming true, moved once again on Coll and Gress (and Orinsay and Galson) in the early summer of 1921. With little left to lose but his authority, Leverhulme now cancelled almost every work scheme in Lewis and pressed Scottish Secretary Robert Munro to take punitive action against the raiders. The castle and the croft were engaged in an elaborate ritual dance, a masquerade of cause and effect from which neither was prepared to retreat. The more he took away, the more they retrieved. The greater his exasperation grew, the firmer was their resolve. The less work he provided in Lewis, the more land they occupied. He launched or relaunched small temporary labouring initiatives, and they took a step back. He stopped them again and they strode forward. Munro, who had ever been prepared to allow for Leverhulme's suggestions, however grandiose or absurd, who had given him more leeway than would have been admitted to any other proprietor, saw finally that this vain schottische must end in exhaustion, and that its finish was in sight.

Leverhulme had lost his argument. The evidence of defeat arrived in small, droll packages as well as in grand pronouncements. One week he shipped a small group of village elders to Port Sunlight, to witness there the bricks and mortar of prosperity, to see how one year's vision could become next year's reality. They were suitably impressed and they admitted as much to their host. But upon their return they agreed with one another that: 'Ach an deigh na h'uile car, cha'neil cal an sud ach an trailleachd.' 'After all, there is nothing there but slavery.'

He lost his castle piper, Donald MacLeod, reportedly in illuminative circumstances. Donald warned Leverhulme one spring evening that in a fortnight he would need to spend a week back at his croft planting potatoes. Leverhulme refused him the holiday – 'You are now in regular employment . . . You now earn as much money in a week as will buy sufficient potatoes for you and your family for a year. I require you here. I cannot agree to let you off for a week to plant potatoes . . . If you go without my consent you should clearly understand that by so doing you will lose your job.'

Leverhulme then repeated this conversation, and Donald MacLeod's apparent consent, to the Board of Agriculture's Colin MacDonald. Mac-Donald was gratified to hear a fortnight later that Donald had left word in the castle kitchen that he had gone home to plant potatoes, and would not be coming back.[45]

Robert Munro received in March 1921 a letter from Murdo Graham, one of the raiders of Gress Farm, which requested:

> Please do not allow our desperate plight to be camouflaged by reference to some minor industrial works at Stornoway. These works may or not mature; the signs are that they will not, as they are liable to be closed down at the slightest excuse. In any event, we are not skilled factory workers and such work would not benefit us or our class. It is necessary we should have land and proper dwellings. The Acts of Parliament passed for providing us with holdings is our Magna Carta, and as long as they remain law we consider it your duty to give effect to them. Once more we call on you to do so.

A month later the Board of Agriculture advised the Scottish Secretary 'that Leverhulme would be glad to get out of his industrial schemes and that he will use the Coll and Gress affair as his justification'.

Robert Munro was as reasonable and placatory a Scottish Secretary as Leverhulme could have hoped to discover. He continued to urge compromise. 'I am satisfied,' he told the proprietor, 'that many if not all the troubles in Lewis would vanish, if you see your way to adopt the suggestions which I make. It does seem a pity that the whole future of the island for years to come should be jeopardised and indeed wrecked on account of a difference in policy regarding two small farms.'[46]

All that the Secretary of State got for his trouble from Lord Lever-hulme were threats of a total capital withdrawal, noisy insistences that Lewis ex-servicemen should be prosecuted for planting potatoes in Lewis soil, repeated and increasingly absurd caricatures of the land raiders as a 'small number of misguided men', and excoriation of Munro himself and all his government's works. The conviction rapidly hardened in the mind of Robert Munro of Alness that he was dealing – that he had always had been dealing – with reason and justice on one side, but with bluster and autocracy on the other.

The decree nisi was served in September 1921, in the unlikely setting of Stornoway Highland Games. 'Three years ago,' Leverhulme told the gathering, 'it was mutually accepted that our relations would be on a strictly business basis; that there would be no odious taint of philanthropy to lower ourselves in each other's esteem.

> No one regrets more than myself that the canning factory, the fish products and the ice companies cannot be opened for work. But the conditions of supply and demand in these industries make it impossible to do so. The business could only make losses, heavy losses if operated at present. We must wait patiently for the world markets to be cleared of surplus stocks before the prices will adjust themselves to the cost of production.[47]

It was little less than a concession of failure. Leverhulme knew that if his Lewis fish industry could not survive one slump, it was unlikely to offer any kind of stable long-term future to the island. And with it went all and any talk of railway lines and fruit farms and forestries and thousands of bungalows in the suburbs of Stornoway. They would never again be mentioned. All that remained was to cut the losses, rescue some pride and manage a dignified retreat.

Robert Munro wrote immediately to acknowledge the capitulation. 'In the circumstances as they are now,' he said, 'I feel that I would not be justified in refraining any longer from putting into operation a generous measure of land settlement.'

In the spring of 1922, thirteen years after the passing of the Scottish Smallholders Act, which had been designed to enable such transactions, the Board of Agriculture completed its purchase of the farms at Coll, Gress, Tolsta and Orinsay and used the land to create 180 new crofts and to enlarge eighty-one existing crofts. Apart from a wilful attempt, which the Scottish Office managed to ignore, to have former raiders excluded from the apportionments, Leverhulme presented no further actual or oratorial barrier to these settlements, which in the remainder of the twentieth century were to become some of the healthiest and best-populated of Lewis communities.

His project was over. The young doctor Halliday Sutherland arrived in

Stornoway in 1923 to find 'a half-built factory on which work had been abandoned, a derelict small-gauge railway, and thousands of pounds' worth of machinery rusting on the shore.' Anxious to uncover the reasons for such a depressing scene, Sutherland approached what was presented in his later transcription as a bellicose old man working a croft in the Back district. The man had no desire, Sutherland said,

> . . . to answer a whistle at six in the morning and work for wages in Lever's factory. No damn fear. Poor as I am, I'm master here, and could order you off this croft.
>
> Why did some of us raid his pasture-land? A dairy farm for the island it was to be. I've another name for that – a monopoly in milk. No damn fear. We are poorer now than we were. Why? Because the line-fishing in the spring has failed. Why? Because of these damned trawlers that spoil the spawn, and half of them are Lever's English trawlers. He makes us poor, and then wants us to work for him.[48]

The divorce decree absolute remained for the time being on his desk; he was not yet finished with the island. He had still to score his swansong to Lewis. He held onto his castle and his position and his honorifics. And he took the high road over the Clisham to Harris.

It was a pleasant road to follow. After the aggravations of Lewis, Emily Paul found the southern way conjured up some of the innocent joys of her uncle's first unspoiled months in the Hebrides. One benefit was immediately apparent. Harris was still wet. There was no prohibition on alcohol in Tarbert and points south. Harris may have been part of the same Western Isles parliamentary constituency as Lewis, and part of the same landmass, but until local government reorganisation in 1974 Harris remained within Inverness County Council while Lewis was a semi-autonomous part of Ross-shire. Prohibition in Lewis was therefore not enforced south of the Clisham. As a result, throughout the early 1920s the Tarbert Hotel enjoyed the unprecedented patronage of parties of Leodhasaich who had braved the one-in-four gradients and hair-raising precipices of the Clisham pass in private cars, hired charabancs, on foot or in the saddle.

Following an invigorating lunch Lord Leverhulme's party – which may still have included, as well as the Paul family, such old friends as Jonathan

Simpson – motored south 'into the brightness of green sandhills, grassy plains and glorious blue sea rolling into beautiful sandy bays.'

There, at Borve Lodge on the western shore of South Harris, Leverhulme had established his southern headquarters. Borve Lodge had been built and renovated on a more modest scale than the castle on Lewis, but it had its attractions. 'Outside,' noted Emily Paul, 'the grandeur and majesty of nature; inside, the comfort and amenities of our comfort-loving age. In the walled garden only a few yards from the never-calm sea, we found flowers and vegetables growing in profusion, such as one might find in any southern garden.' Within yards of the lodge the young men of the party shot deer so tame that they would eat from their hands. Occasionally they left this Eden to explore the nether reaches of the island.

> One day, we went to look over another Lodge called Finsbay, on the east coast of Harris.
>
> A more desolate spot I never wish to see, and one wonders how anyone could ever have built a Lodge in such a stony barren place. Presumably the trout fishing was good. Years before, many of the people and their stock, from the fertile and beautiful west side, had been evicted to make way for deer, and had been allowed to make homes along this forbidding looking coast. What sorrow and desolation must have been their lot in such a change of environment!

Those words are evidence – incidental and minor, but still evidence – of disconnected trains of thought within the Leverhulme party. The sensitive and sympathetic Miss Emily Paul was capable of projecting herself into the 'desolation' of people cleared from their land by earlier proprietors, but not into the efforts of those who attempted to correct the injustice during the suzerainty of her Uncle William.

She could perceive – as who could not? – the pity of the nineteenth century. But when fifty years later the children and grandchildren of those who were despatched from grassy Borve to stony Finsbay (where nobody could possibly have wished to stay unless 'the trout-fishing was good') created waves of discontent, she was happy to agree with some Stornoway merchants and masons, with the editor of the local newspaper and with Lord Leverhulme's party that the landless Leodhasaich were being manipulated by Bolshevik agents. 'There were some,' Emily would insist twenty years later, 'who thought it was a question of politics, and that the crofters were only being used as tools. Certainly some of the letters appearing in the press over signatures of the men concerned, were unlikely to have been written by them. The style and phraseology were entirely foreign to a Lewis crofter, whose mother tongue is Gaelic, and whose English was, and is, always filled with Gaelic idiom.'[49]

The misapprehension that 'a Lewis crofter' was by definition incapable of writing a letter in straightforward English, or that such a person would cheerfully have appended his name to any old incomprehensible communist propaganda at the urging of a Glaswegian agitator, was only possible in a group of people seriously distanced from the actual population of Lewis and Harris. Many people within the islands were also prepared to credit 'red socialists' with causing trouble, but they were strictly identifiable home-grown Gaelic-speaking socialists. The Leverhulme party, spoonfed with the cartoon Donalds and Anguses of Sir Harry Lauder's creation (characters who would never utter a line of English without a liberal sprinkling of mock-Gaelic 'idiom', and whose dumb deference rendered land-raiding quite unthinkable), made their assumptions of political puppetry in ignorance of the recent history and traditions of their neighbours. It was neither a unique nor a passing ignorance. Such prejudice had distorted the southern image of the Scottish Gael for centuries gone and would colour it for a century to come. Embedded in the iron convictions of a landowner who needed to carry with him the hearts and minds of the Leodhasaich, however, it was at best unfortunate and at worst fatally naive.

But Leverhulme was now in Harris, and Harris was different. Harris was smaller and Harris had more modest expectations. He might yet discover in Harris what he had hoped to find in Lewis: the satisfaction of materially improving by the application of Leverist economics the lives and prospects of a small but integral community. Hearaich were as possessed by the same ambitions for homes and a land fit for heroes as their cousins to the north, but on a more manageable scale. It is noteworthy that Leverhulme did not attempt in Harris a scaled-down version of his schemes for Lewis. That would have meant concentrating on the main town of Tarbert as he had concentrated on Stornoway. Tarbert was in many ways a perfect site for expansion. It opened onto both the Minch and the Atlantic; its two natural harbours were deep and sheltered; it was close to the Lewis border. Tarbert had shops and a hotel, tradesmen and a large school. But he eschewed Tarbert in favour of Obbe/Leverburgh. The small bay at Obbe was relatively exposed to the prevailing winds; it was a very long way by a very bad road from Stornoway; the Sound of Harris which it faced was shallow and a notorious graveyard of sea-going vessels. (Emily Paul noted that 'it is exceedingly difficult to navigate on account of its innumerable rocks and strong currents. But my uncle determined to blast some of these rocks away and put lights on others, till he had made his harbour attainable at any stage of the tide by any ships likely to use it.') Obbe had little or nothing, and that was its charm. Whatever he built at Obbe would be an improvement on desuetude. Whatever the inhabitants gained from his injections of capital would be – could surely not help but be – better than before. He had felt obliged in Lewis to excite high expectations in order to gain support. He would presumably encounter smaller but similar ambitions in the urban downtown of Tarbert, Harris. At Obbe, however, he promised them a row of curing sheds and they renamed the place in his honour.

The land raids which took place in South Harris to some extent justified his faith. They were modest and containable, and easily condemned by the ambitious citizens of Leverburgh. They were however no less telling in their quiet insistence. In the middle of February 1921 several men from the Stockinish district of Bays approached the estate factor Norman Robertson at his office in Tarbert to make verbal applications for land at Lingerabay. One of them was a married cottar from Finsbay, a small township lying between Stockinish and Lingerabay, an ex-serviceman whose name was John Macdonald. Macdonald and his colleagues were hardly asking for the earth and all its fruits. Stockinish was one of the most barren but overcrowded areas of eastern Harris. Lingerabay, which to a flying crow lay only six miles down the coast, was equally stony but less densely habited. The men were looking not for rich agricultural soil but for sites upon which to build houses.

By 1921 Lord Leverhulme had heard just about enough of this complaint, and his factors all across Lewis and Harris were under orders to refuse any and all such applications. The men were not surprised. Norman Robertson told the police sergeant at Tarbert 'that they then said they would raid the land and take forcible possession of it'. Mr Robertson thought, reported Sergeant MacGillivray to the Chief Constable in Inverness, 'that a number of men from Stockinish and Cluar will raid this land during the spring'.

Mr Robertson was right. The men who had petitioned him for land had, along with a great many others, been employed by Leverhulme's 'Lewis and Harris Welfare and Development Company' in Obbe/Leverburgh and on one of his road-building schemes. This temporary labour assuaged their hunger without offering them a long-term future. But early in 1921 the majority of workers were laid off from the schemes, in Harris as well as in disenchanted Lewis. Leverhulme could not have sent a worse signal to the Hearaich. Their restraint was obviously irrelevant in the larger calculations of international finance. They were damned if they did raid the land and damned if they did not.

So they raided. Not all of them; not even a majority of them. In Harris as in Lewis there was a strong and stable element of the community which saw a better future in supporting Lord Leverhulme's plans than in annoying him. Throughout the long island these men and women were to be found not only in the shops and masonic lodges and business offices, but in respectable crofting households. Their views and interests were not to be dismissed, at the time or later. They were people of faith, hope and integrity. It was their fate ultimately to be counted out of the historical reckoning precisely because their relative security had deposited them on the irrelevant middle ground. They were in No Man's Land pleading for a unilateral ceasefire; they were caught uselessly between two gigantic historical forces; they were on the horns of a dilemma. In the end they were arguing for nothing other than obeisance. Obeisance to Lord Leverhulme may have served them and many other Hebrideans well. But it would never have resolved the crisis at the heart of their society: the fundamental question of the land.

So their cottar and fisherfolk neighbours raided, and Lord Leverhulme prosecuted them. Whether they expected such a response is doubtful but irrelevant. By the late winter of 1921 the men and women of South Harris would have been aware of their proprietor's changing temper in Lewis, of his hardening attitude. They will also have known of the on–off resumptions of land-raiding to their north, and of the Scottish Office and Board of Agriculture's impatience with Leverhulme. They knew also that the proven way of attracting attention to land hunger in a district was for the people of that district to stake out claims on a forbidden acreage. And they knew that if the worst came to the worst, if the factor and the constabulary acted on their warnings and took legal action, both public sympathy and natural justice were on their side. They had, literally, little or nothing to lose.

So they raided, and they were duly charged. Harris being part of Inverness-shire rather than part of Ross-shire-with-Lewis, they were answerable not to Stornoway Court but to Lochmaddy in North Uist. Rather than ship the accused across the Sound of Harris, the Sheriff Court itself sailed north and convened in the sportsman's hotel at Rodel.

It made an unedifying scene. The bench was occupied by two Justices of the Peace: Dugald MacTavish of Lochmaddy and Norman Robertson of Tarbert – the same Norman Robertson who, in another hat, was Lord Leverhulme's factor and was responsible for reporting several of the accused to the police. Nobody other than Leverhulme himself can have had a greater vested interest in the outcome of the cases, but it was deemed unnecessary for Robertson to acknowledge this by taking a furlough from duty. Having pressed for prosecution, having been a material witness to many of the alleged offences, he then sat in judgement at Rodel.

Along with Dugald MacTavish he surveyed a steady procession of women and men who were prosecuted under the Public Health (Scotland) Act of 1897, for commencing to plant crops or to build dwellings on unauthorised land. They were fined 'modified expenses' of between ten shillings and a pound and given between three and four weeks 'to clear the nuisance'. Their guilt or innocence was never in question. The Rodel hearings of March 1921 resulted in the first criminal records ever to be registered in the name of many of the MacDonald, Morrison and Macleod families of South Harris.

But they failed to stop the raids. Local members of the Lewis and Harris Welfare and Development Company, who were chiefly citizens of Obbe/Leverburgh and Tarbert rather than of the east coast Bays district, felt obliged just two months later to intervene. On the last day of May 1921, two representatives of the LHWDC handed to John MacDonald, the cottar and prominent raider from Finsbay who had been among those refused land by the estate, a letter condemning his activities. MacDonald replied that anybody who attempted to interfere with his plans for crofting at Lingerabay would 'sleep there for an indefinite period', as he was the possessor of a large six-chambered American automatic revolver.

Two days later the Obbe/Leverburgh men reported this incident in writing to Lord Leverhulme at his London home on Hampstead Heath. Following their unnerving encounter with John MacDonald in Finsbay they had returned through Lingerabay, and discovered there a few unearthed rocks 'presumably for building purposes'.

> We trust, [they requested their superior], that your Lordship will not take the least notice of any wild Bolshevik screed which you may receive from this individual. He has been notorious throughout Harris for some years as an individual who glories in causing enmity between landlord and tenant, and also for being always at loggerheads with anyone who chances to employ him, the law courts being his happy hunting ground, although he invariably comes out on the wrong side.
>
> We can assure your Lordship that we have no intention of breaking our promise to desist from land raiding for the ten years period required by you, and we shall make it our business that no hare-brained 'red flag socialist' like Macdonald will be allowed to carry on land raiding to any extent, however small, to the detriment of the whole of Harris. We are keeping an eye on all his movement, and if he begins building or any other illegal proceeding we shall immediately take steps to render his handiwork valueless. We believe that we can safely guarantee that you will not be troubled by land raiding in South Harris and we again take the opportunity of expressing our loyalty to your Lordship and our determination that Harris men will always remain men of honour whose word is as good as their bond.
>
> We are
> Your Lordship's Obedient Servants . . .

Within days the police constable at Obbe/Leverburgh, James MacRae, had taken himself over to the east coast to investigate John Macdonald's 'big American revolver . . . with a view for a report to the Procurator Fiscal for being in possession of firearms without holding a certificate'.

Macdonald told the policeman that he had no such revolver. The Finsbay man had, he protested, merely been employing a figure of speech which had been misunderstood by the deputation from the south coast. 'What he meant was that he had an American fountain pen, and would use same to seek protection in event of any persons interfering with his proposed works at Lingerabay.

'In my opinion,' reported PC MacRae, 'he is not in possession of firearms. There has not been any raiding yet with the exception of unearthing a few stones with the intention to build . . . In my opinion the Police authorities should not regard this as actual raiding.'

Just over a month later, on 13 July 1921, James MacRae was obliged to concede that 'actual raiding' had commenced. 'With reference to my previous report regarding land raiding at Lingerabay, Harris,' he informed his Chief Constable, 'I beg to report that I visited that part of my district today, and find that the aftermentioned persons are proceeding with the construction of houses and ultimately intend to use the soil.'

There followed a list of six names, comprised of two men from Stockinish and four from Finsbay. The first name on the list was that of John Macdonald.

'These persons,' explained PC MacRae, 'are all ex-servicemen. They have every intention of holding onto this part of the estate.'

They had, continued the constable, apparently been offered house sites elsewhere by Leverhulme, and an acre of land apiece, and building materials worth £250 with fifty years to repay – but they

> absolutely refused. They wish crofts under the Crofters Act and have nothing to do with the scheme put forward by his Lordship . . . Mr Robertson, Estate Factor, tried to reason the question with them but I understand found it impossible.
>
> Macdonald is the ringleader and I understand does not want the land, but his idea for such illegal proceedings is to stop all developments by the

Lewis and Harris Welfare and Development Co Ltd, which I understand
from the public he frankly admits . . . These persons have already cut out
crofts, but I cannot say what acreage has been raided.

Once again due process was observed. On the instructions of the estate
the six men were prosecuted and sentenced to forty days in Inverness
Prison. That did not stop the raiding. One of the most striking
expressions of land hunger in Harris occurred at the beginning of 1923.
Six men from the Geocrab district of east Harris, just south of Stockinish,
applied in the spring of that year for holdings on the island of Killegray.
This tiny scrap of greensward amounted to roughly one square mile in
area, and lay three miles out from Obbe in the middle of the Sound of
Harris. It fell within the boundary of Leverhulme's estate.

The Geocrab men stressed that their main ambition was to build
family homes. In Bays at the time one of them shared a house with fifteen
other people. Two of them shared their crofts with another three families.
One of them lived with his wife and six children in a single-storey
building 17 feet long and 10 feet wide. They were refused holdings
because Leverhulme believed that 'the crofting system is opposed to the
best interests of the island'.

The six men thereupon sailed out to deserted Killegray, built a shelter
there and began to prepare the soil for cultivation. The estate factor in
person and their new MP, Sir William Mitchell Cotts, by letter tried
unsuccessfully to persuade them to leave. They voluntarily evacuated only
after receiving an assurance from the Board of Agriculture that it would
try to establish them within a year on crofts being created at Cheesebay in
North Uist and at Talisker in Skye.

The Board of Agriculture chose throughout the 1920s largely to
ignore pleas for crofting settlement in Harris itself. The result was that by
1925 North and South Harris had by far the lowest number of satisfied
requests for new crofts in the Hebrides. Only fifty-nine new holdings were
created or existing crofts extended in Harris between 1912 and 1925. In
the same period 337 applications had been lodged. The percentage of
'settled demand' was therefore just 17.5. In the same period in Lewis,
Skye and the Uists an average of 40 per cent of 'demands' for crofts were
settled, although many more requests were made in those islands than in

Harris. By 1925 in Lewis 540 demands had been met out of a total of 1,344. In Skye the figure was 502 out of 1,304, almost all as the result of Board of Agriculture intervention. If Harris had enjoyed a similar degree of attention 150 crofts rather than 59 would have been created or expanded. But they were not, and as a direct result young Hearaich left – or more accurately, continued to leave – their island.

They left it even before Lord Leverhulme. If Harris voted with its feet on the issue of Leverhulme's proposals for the island, then his Lordship lost the poll. Overcrowded islands such as Taransay were left for new settlements such as the one at Cheesebay in North Uist which was offered also to the Killegray raiders. In 1923 the Board – frustrated by its inability to solve the problems of Leverhulme's islands within Lewis and Harris – bought the farms of Drynoch and North Talisker in north-west Skye, turned them into sixty-eight crofts and filled all but five of those crofts with immigrants from the other side of the Minch.[50] Four hundred people, mostly from Harris, subsequently established themselves as fisherfolk, crofters and progenitors of the only commercial home tweed industry outside the Western Isles in the district of Portnalong. And as well as leaving for Skye and Uist, Harris men and women joined their neighbours from Lewis in a strangely revived twentieth-century version of that famous old Hebridean reel, the dance called America.

They took much of their fate upon their own shoulders. The windows of the Church of Scotland at Croick in Strathcarron, Easter Ross, are scratched with graffiti made in May 1845. The messages were left by families from nearby Glencalvie who had been cleared from their land and who huddled on the consecrated ground for temporary shelter and relief. Perhaps the most celebrated line there reads: 'Glencalvie people the wicked generation'. It is remembered because to later eyes it presented a conundrum. It was surely not the Glencalvie people themselves who were wicked, but the factors and landowner who had driven them to sanctuary in that place. But given a nineteenth-century churchgoer's understanding of the word 'wicked', which would incline it more towards 'sinful' than 'malevolent', and given the metaphysical sense of human responsibility held by the Glencalvie people and their church, there seems no reason not to take those words at face value. For such evil misfortune to afflict us, an over-simplified interpretation might read, we must have done something wrong.

Some similar anguish may have been at work on the spiritual consciences of the people of Lewis and Harris in the early 1920s. That generation was certainly fated. They had been born and brought up among dispossessed families. They had suffered and died to a dispropor-tionate degree in the most murderous war of modern times. Despite the apparent support of government and public opinion, despite winning for half a century every debate from Westminster to Gress they had, not once but time and time again, been refused house sites and smallholdings in the land of their fathers. Two hundred of their brothers and neighbours had survived the war only to drown together a few yards from the coast of Lewis. The benevolent businessman who had arrived from the south promising security and affluence had put a padlock on his chequebook. They were self-sufficient people, trusting only in the Lord and His weather. They were temperamentally disinclined to blame others for their misfortunes. They looked with sadness at themselves in 1922 and 1923, perhaps seeing there a sinful and obscurely reprehensible generation. What, after all, had they done to deserve all this?

And with heavy, reluctant hearts but without censure, obeying both the laws of economics and the dynamics of disillusion, from the northern tip of Lord Leverhulme's Lewis to the south-eastern edge of Harris, they began in mass to emigrate across the North Atlantic Ocean.

8

DIGNIFIED RETREAT

All things considered, Donald Murray's defeat in the General Election of November 1922 came too late to be of much help to the proprietor of Lewis and Harris. The Stornoway man had been an active Member of Parliament in support of his constituents' interests, which Dr Murray had always taken to include their access to the land of the Western Isles. He had not liked Leverhulme and Leverhulme had not liked Murray.

Murray fought the 1922 election as a sixty-year-old whose health was so troubled that he had, in fact, only eight months left to live. It was a two-cornered race between himself and his main opponent from 1918, the Coalition Liberal (and recently ennobled) coalowner, Sir William Dingwall Mitchell Cotts, Bart. Thanks to the returned servicemen the electorate had risen since 1918 by almost 2,000, and Murray's share of the Western Isles vote increased by almost the same amount. But the vote of Sir W.D.M. Cotts almost doubled, another low turn-out of 54 per cent giving him a majority of 939. Having entered parliament as a traditional Liberal against the national tide, Murray was evicted just as his party made enough of a recovery in the rest of the United Kingdom to present – along with the rapidly growing Labour Party – a troublesome opposition to the new Conservative Prime Minister Stanley Baldwin.

Murray was accompanied through the exit by Robert Munro, the Liberal Scottish Secretary. Baldwin replaced Munro with Viscount Novar. In his earlier life as Robert Crauford Munro-Ferguson, Novar had been briefly the Member of Parliament for Ross-shire-with-Lewis. He had been dismissed from that post when the Third Reform Act had enfranchised sufficient crofters to elect their own MP in the General Election of 1885. Robert Crauford Munro-Ferguson had then been sent south with the warning ringing in his ears never again to oppose the crofters' interest. He would not do so.

The office of William Mitchell Cotts as parliamentary representative of the Western Isles was short, unexpected and unique. It lasted for only a year, it usurped a widely respected sitting member and it returned to Westminster the closest thing that the constituency ever had to a Conservative MP. Baronet Cotts would never have described himself as anything other than a Liberal, albeit a 'National' or Coalition Liberal. But he served under the Conservative administrations of Andrew Bonar Law and Stanley Baldwin.

The significance to the land issue of his election was partly muted by the persistently low turn-out, by the lull in turf hostilities in November 1922, and by the fact that Cotts himself always agreed that a respectable, negotiable amount of estate property in the islands should be returned to crofting tenure. He was neither so fiery nor so effective on the subject as Murray, but he adhered to a substantial measure of land reform. He could hardly fail to do so: it was the official policy of his party. But Cotts was undoubtedly the Leverhulme candidate and the champion of the professional merchant classes. As a titled southern industrialist he had far more in common with the proprietor (who shared with him, it should be recalled, a distant Liberal pedigree) than did any Stornoway doctor. Cotts was also the favoured son of William Grant's *Stornoway Gazette*, which spent a great many of the post-war years shrieking like a maiden aunt about reds under her bed.

In 1922 a total of 21,089 men over the age of twenty-one and women over the age of thirty were franchised to vote in the Western Isles. Sir William Mitchell Cotts was endorsed by 6,177 of them. As Murray received just 5,238 votes this was enough to elect Cotts as the MP for a disturbed constituency in a chaotic time. There would be five General Elections between 1922 and 1931. The 53-year-old Cotts stood down at the next one a year later in December 1923. His term of office had been unremarkable, distinguished more by his substantial leaves of absence in southern Africa on business affairs (during which hiatuses the long-suffering mainland Ross-shire MP Ian MacPherson would attend to Hebridean constituency matters) than by legislative achievement.

In the election which followed Cotts resignation his Conservative/ National Liberal Coalition Party promptly suffered a series of electoral losses which resulted within two months in defeat in the House of Commons and Ramsay MacDonald's Labour Party establishing its own coalition government with the Liberals.

The Western Isles was one of the seats which contributed to this shift of national power at the end of 1923. In place of Baronet Cotts it returned a straightforward traditional Liberal MP named Alexander MacKenzie Livingstone. The 43-year-old Livingstone was the son of a family from Applecross in Wester Ross and was married to a Mary MacAskill from Skye (after Mary died in 1946 Livingstone took as his second wife a widow from Stornoway named Maggie Clark). His work as the head of a family exporting business had taken him to London, and he had first stood unsuccessfully for parliament at Dover in 1918. He revived his Highland political interests by standing in 1922 for Inverness-shire as a cohort of Donald Murray in the Liberal interest. Like Murray, Livingstone was defeated in 1922. His candidature for the Western Isles one year later was his next testing of the electoral water.

He won a three-cornered race against Conservative and Labour opponents, after another tired turn-out of 40 per cent of island voters. The fatigue, the widespread satiety of Leodhasaich with the land issue and with the tiresome unnecessary controversies provoked by Lord Leverhulme was made evident by Alexander Mackenzie Livingstone's earliest parliamentary activity: he devoted himself to challenging illegal east-coast trawling in the inshore fishing grounds of the Western Isles and the 'inadequate' postal service to Stornoway. The question of the land, which was now apparently back in the hands of the Board of Agriculture, bothered him hardly at all.

Illegal trawling and the Lewis mail were enough to satisfy the bulk of his electorate. On 9 October 1924 the shortlived minority Labour government lost a House of Commons vote and the country trooped wearily into the polling booths for the third time in three years. Labour suffered only slightly in the resulting Conservative landslide, but once more Livingstone's Liberal Party collapsed, from 155 seats across the country to a mere 40. And once more, the Western Isles kicked against the traces. Its Liberal candidate, Alexander MacKenzie Livingstone, was not only one of the forty to be returned – he was the only one to be re-elected with a substantially increased majority. In a similarly low poll to that of 1923 he increased his personal vote and his majority from 233 to 2,161.

And so Livingstone sat, as a member of what was suddenly, mysteriously and irretrievably the third party in British politics, in opposition to Stanley Baldwin's second Conservative administration, until 1929, when he retired from the Western Isles seat to make way for another Liberal.

Thereafter, not insignificantly, the Ross-shire businessman Alexander MacKenzie Livingstone and his former constituency of the Western Isles followed a similar political projectory. In 1930 Livingstone joined the Labour Party. He would serve his new allegiance faithfully, as a national administrator and a City of London councillor, until his death in 1950. The island voters would have patience with his Liberal successor for only another five years. In 1935 they returned the Labour candidate Malcolm K. Macmillan. For the remainder of the twentieth century, apart from a seventeen-year interregnum between 1970 and 1987 when the seat was held by a popular local representative of the Scottish National Party, the Western Isles would elect a Labour Member of Parliament. For most of this period the Labour Party was regarded as an instrument of the urban proletariat. Its persistent popularity in the most rural constituency in the United Kingdom posed therefore a psephological puzzle. At least a part of the solution was perhaps to be found in those dispiriting years which followed the First World War, during which a generation of Gaelic smallholders discovered that their interests coincided to an unsuspected degree with the concerns of their fellow ex-servicemen from the south – who had also returned to a land fit for heroes, and who had also discovered there instead a dystopia of homelessness and unemployment dictated by the epilepsies of high finance.

In the opening months of 1923 Lord Leverhulme, having congratulated his fellow baronet Mitchell Cotts on his election and returned to the challenges of Lever Brothers, stepped carelessly into another Highland morass. The resignation Honours List of David Lloyd George in November 1922 had offered him a further step in the peerage. He was made a viscount. As with his baronetcy, the viscountship traditionally required the suffix of a place or a district. He decided upon the Hebrides. Despite everything, despite all the disappointments and misjudgements and retreats, he would recognise his happy months in Lews Castle by becoming Viscount Leverhulme of the Western Isles in the counties of Inverness and Ross and Cromarty. 'When I was first raised to the Peerage,' he would explain, 'I took the title of "Lord Leverhulme of Bolton-le-Moors", which is my birthplace and place of my ancestors . . . I viewed Bolton in the position of mother, and I viewed the Western Isles in the position of wife.'[51]

In the furore which followed it was often asserted by Leverhulme's party that 'most of the people' of Lewis and Harris 'were pleased that he chose to include them in his title'.[52] There is no evidence of this, although the *Stornoway Gazette* was staunch in its editorial support, and it was probably true that a majority of islanders either wished the little soap man well in whatever vanities might make him happy, or were so inured to the pretensions of feudal superiors that they neither noticed nor cared.

Sadly, there were people other than Viscount Leverhulme, David Lloyd George and their sovereign who set great store by such titles. Their first shot was fired on 23 January 1923, when Mr Alexander N. Nicolson, the secretary and treasurer of the Gaelic Society of Inverness, rose to address his colleagues. The Gaelic Society of Inverness was in January 1923 entering its fifty-second year. It perceived itself with justification as the most venerable Highland pressure group in the country. It had in its history been unashamedly political. Lairds flocked as ardently to the Gaelic Society of Inverness as did radicals, but it had nonetheless managed in the land wars of the 1880s to align itself uncompromisingly with the crofters – one of the Society's founders, William MacKay of Glenurquhart in Inverness-shire, manipulated its 'cultural' remit to present to the Napier Commission evidence of traditions 'which showed that the land in the Highlands was considered to belong to the crofters who worked it'.

In its fiftieth anniversary year of 1921 the Gaelic Society of Inverness had appointed Alex N. Nicolson as its secretary/treasurer. For almost another forty years Nicolson would be a mainstay, almost the personification, of the institution. He did not believe in a modest profile.

With Alex Nicolson, wrote Mairi A. Macdonald in her centennial history, 'a fresh wind blew into the Society . . . at times, this wind could be a perishing nor' nor' easter, causing chaos and bitterness, but it blew, and eventually fanned a steady flame of continuous activity.' Viscount Leverhulme was among the first to feel its chill.

Leverhulme had, asserted Alex Nicolson, 'been badly advised when he adopted the style "of the Western Isles" . . . It was a great pity that his Lordship should depart from the propriety with which Englishmen, who had bought estates in Scotland, had for many generations respected the sentiments of the Scots. [Mr Nicolson] did not know of any case in which the sentiments of the Scottish people had been offended as they had been in this instance.'[53]

Alex Nicolson was undoubtedly over-egging his pudding. It is unlikely that there was much more popular discontent with Leverhulme's chosen title in Gorbals or Kirkcaldy than was evident in Breasclete. The Lancashire man had simply displayed yet again his ignorance of Highland history. His new title encroached on the honorific Lord of the Isles, which was (as the Gaelic Society delicately pointed out) at present the property of the Prince of Wales, the future King Edward VIII. It also trod on the toes of Sir Alexander Bosville Macdonald of Sleat in Skye, the titular head of Clan Donald, who was entitled to style himself Macdonald of the Isles.

More seriously, both of those established handles referred back to the same honoured memory of the Lordship of the Isles, the quasi-independent medieval Hebridean principality which for over 300 years before the end of the fifteenth century had represented the only autonomous Scottish Gaidhealtachd in history. It was a fabled estate, an insular emirate which had in its bloom reached from Lewis to the Isle of Man. The head of Sunlight Soap may as well have bought Cornwall and called himself Leverhulme of Camelot. He was not to know – although he could have been told by friends other than Sir Harry Lauder – that it was difficult to resurrect some hope of independent renewal in the Scottish Hebrides without stirring buried embers of the Lordship of the Isles.

And there was snobbish outrage that an upstart merchant's boy from Bolton should assume such dignity; and more palatable annoyance that he chose to throw his seigneurial cloak across the Hebrides at the same time as he was apparently losing his interest in the future well-being of Lewis. There was existing disquiet about his 'colonial' renaming of Obbe as Leverburgh. And there were too many people in too many offices with nothing to do but pen irate letters.

'Sir,' wrote Alex Nicolson, Secretary, from the Gaelic Society at 6 Queen's Gate, Inverness, to his fellow Scot, the Right Honourable Andrew Bonar Law, Prime Minister, at 10 Downing Street, London, on 26 January 1923:

> We deeply regret to trouble you over the subject matter of the enclosed copy of a resolution passed by this society *re* the style adopted by Lord Leverhulme on his being created a Viscount, viz., 'of the Western Isles'.
>
> While, however, we regret the necessity of troubling you, we strongly feel that action should be taken to prevent this outrage on the feelings of all Scotsman, particularly on the feelings of Highlanders, not only at home but also in the Dominions.

The last point was a diplomatic one. Although he represented a Glasgow constituency and had been raised by his maternal family in that city from the age of eleven, Andrew Bonar Law was born and had learned to walk in the dominion of Canada.

> We desire, [continued Nicolson], to bring to your notice that this matter is causing a great deal of feeling, and, in the interests of all concerned, it is hoped that the matter will be rectified and this cause of offence removed . . . even if he did possess the whole of the Western Hebrides it would not justify the assumption by him of any title which suggests the ancient title of Lord of the Isles: especially when that title is held by His Majesty the King.

Andrew Bonar Law was an old, extremely busy and rather sick man. His private secretary despatched to Inverness a brusque reply regretting that the Prime Minister could not 'take any action in regard to the matter'.

Lord Leverhulme himself was more combative. He responded to a similar plea by requesting further explanation of the Gaelic Society's objections. Alex Nicolson obliged. He wrote to Hampstead Heath on 9 February 1923, after careful examination of the industrial patent procedure with which his correspondent would doubtless be familiar:

By the use of the words 'of the Western Isles', your Lordship is employing what would be, under the Merchandise Marks Act, be called a 'colourable imitation' of the words 'of the Isles' . . .

The title 'of the Isles' belongs to the heroic age of Scottish history, and is enshrined in the song and story of the West; consequently, its use – or the use of anything approaching it – by any other than the Royal House or the descendants of its ancient holders is bound to give offence to all who cherish the traditions of our race . . . In any case, I think I am right in stating that the islands of Uist, Benbecula, Barra etc., do not belong to your Lordship; therefore you are not entitled to include them in your territorial designation even though the term 'Western Isles' comprehended the Outer Hebrides only.

Alex Nicolson received for his pains an extraordinary manifesto from the proprietor of Lewis and Harris. Swiftly rebutting any suggestion that his honorific was unsuitable – 'In my opinion the title indicates service and nothing but service' – Leverhulme moved on to a lengthy vindication of his efforts in Lewis and Harris. It was as clear an indication as survives of his state of mind in February 1923, eighteen months since he had frozen all major developments in the islands and washed his hands of rural Lewis. It illustrated not only his continuing willingness to do battle with anybody who questioned his will or his judgement, but also a certain condition of denial. He wrote in part as though it was still a sunny day in 1919 and he could see the future of Lewis laid out on a clear horizon, as though Gress and Coll and the Niger Company and the fishery collapse had never happened, as though the milk farm argument were still there to be won, as though the only obstacles to health and prosperity were the purblind meanderings of a few pesky bureaucrats. He wrote as always in an effort to win hearts and minds, confident that all and any exception to him would be swept away by the power of logic and enlightenment. The members of the Gaelic Society of Inverness read with baffled fascination this further rationalisation of the rebirth of the Outer Hebrides. He wrote as though, at the age of seventy-one, he could start all over again.

May I call your attention to the reports of Royal Commission after Royal Commission on the state of the very fine people of Lewis and Harris and other portions of the Western Isles. No finer manhood or womanhood exists. In reading history I find that the condition of my native county of Lancashire was very similar two and three centuries ago.

What has raised Lancashire to its outstanding position and what has raised the mainland of Scotland is the service the people render to the world at large in manufactures. In my boyhood days hand loom weavers in Lancashire still existed in the cottages and up the valleys through the country: hand loom weaving has now ceased. Today we find in the Western Isles the native industries are hand loom weaving and fishing.

My problem is to try to make these staple industries for the people. The women take naturally to hand loom weaving; the men take naturally to fishing. Crofting today is entirely an impossible life for these fine people. In considering an old age pension the Government, I understand, assess the value of a croft at 8s per week. Crofting and the life on a croft undoubtedly were substantial and reliable two or three centuries ago, but since then the cost of clothing, tea, coffee, sugar, and other items which are necessities today, but which were luxuries then, are out of the reach of the crofter because the income from the croft is practically *nil*. The produce of the croft is merely a portion of the food consumed.

The service I wish to render is that of an attempt to introduce a higher scale of living and of greater opportunities for happiness and well-being to the fine people of the Western Isles. I have travelled around the world and I find Lewis and Harris men and women honoured and respected and filling the highest positions in Canada, Boston, New York, and elsewhere throughout our Colonies. It is only in their own native Island that they are living under conditions of squalor and misery . . .

Unfortunately, the Scottish Office, notwithstanding the adverse reports of Royal Commissions . . . that farms are essential to the life of a community, are determined to convert the farms into crofts, thus hampering me and crippling me in the work I have undertaken . . .

There will soon be no farms left in Lewis; the Scottish Office have given me notice again this week to take another farm. They have the power to do so, and disregard the warnings of their previous experience of following this line of policy. It can only lead to the forced exile of the rising generation – the sons and daughters of the people of Lewis and Harris.

The service I am proposing to render is to make it possible for the rising generation to find congenial and profitable employment in industries native to the Island, and then it will still be possible for the adventurous spirits to emigrate to Canada, New Zealand, or elsewhere if they so desire.

What I resent very much, and what I know the people of the Island resent, is the forced exile under present conditions owing to lack of employment. I got a most pathetic letter from the wife of a crofter about Christmas time, which to me was more like the wail of a drowning person crying for help than any words of any letter I have previously received, and this wail was from the wife of a crofter in the very district in which the Government are proposing to take the only remaining farm to convert into crofts.

. . . you might know that the people of Lewis and Harris have expressed their pleasure that I added these words, and I have not had a single dissentient word from the people of Lewis and Harris.

Leverhulme was in many ways an unusual landowner. But he held in common with the great majority of his predecessors and successors the inability to distinguish between what he was allowed to see and hear of his tenants and their actual opinions and ambitions. His personal armoury consisted not only of a refusal to comprehend opposing voices, but also the unwillingness to recognise that just because no crofter was self-destructive enough to tell him that he was arrogant and misguided, it did not mean that no crofter thought such things.

Forced against their intention to debate with Leverhulme on the future of the Hebrides and on the views of Lewis and Harris men and women, the Gaelic Society soldiered on. At its annual dinner six days later the Society's chief, Sir John Lorne MacLeod, noted with asperity that 'Lord Leverhulme is not in the lonely furrow he thinks he is about his plans for the welfare and prosperity of the Islands'.

On 26 February the indefatigable Alex Nicolson replied once more to Leverhulme: 'even though the people of Lewis and Harris were unanimous in their approval, and we know that they are not, they only represent *one* of the Western Isles. Consideration must be given to the opinions of the inhabitants of over 200 other islands.'

Nicolson added a sentence of advice which may have been directed at more than the views of Leodhasaich on Viscount Leverhulme's title. 'It is well known,' he said, 'that Stornoway seldom, or never, represents Lewis opinion.'

This quaint debate was pursued for a further month, increasingly with more enthusiasm from the Gaelic Society's secretary than from Lord Leverhulme, and reached the delighted columns of the southern newspapers. Leverhulme signed off by huffily refusing to change his title and describing Alex Nicolson's entreaty as 'a request that should never have been made'.

Nicolson took pleasure in two last words. On 5 March 1923 he informed Viscount Leverhulme that he was 'flaunting public opinion . . . from all parts, including your own district of Lancashire'. Three days later the Gaelic Society of Inverness decided that as the peer seemed bent upon error, there was no further point in writing to him at Hampstead Heath or Port Sunlight. Instead they agreed unanimously that all Highland Members of Parliament, the Scottish Secretary and the – increasingly ailing – Prime Minister should be circulated with a request to revoke the title 'forthwith'.

So Andrew Bonar Law, two months before ill-health forced him from the premiership and seven months before his untimely death, received from Alexander Nicolson in Inverness another request to 'cause the removal of this gross insult to Scotsmen in general and Highlanders in particular . . . This is not an agitation on the part of a few perfervid individuals . . . If you, Sir, can obtain the removal of this blot, and restore to us, unsullied, a title which belongs to the heroic age of Scottish History . . . you will earn the deep gratitude of the members of this Society and of thousands of others.' Poor Bonar Law found the request impossible to meet.

It was in the end just another Highland exasperation for Viscount Leverhulme. The public merriment which surrounded the press coverage of his spat with the Gaelic Society of Inverness (and with the Clan Donald Society of Glasgow, which petitioned chippily on behalf of its chieftain Sir Alexander Macdonald of Sleat) was an unexpected irritant. He had been certain that his benevolent intentions at least entitled him to a degree of goodwill. Compared with other proprietors past and present, he should have been a popular hero. He was restrained in pointing this out, as to do so would have involved describing all manner of Highland lairds (whose honorifics were never questioned) as rogues and vagabonds. He would eventually be driven to do just that, but in the short term he restricted himself to describing in detail his own efforts and left the public to draw the appropriate conclusions. His ally William Grant at the

Stornoway Gazette was first to articulate the real sense of grievance in the Leverhulme camp; in February he wrote:

> In all the circumstances of fact and of right, those who object to the claim are left with little but sentiment to justify their attitude and action. But in this case the sentiment must be very thin and far-fetched. When we face the historical settings of the matter, what have we to commend the title 'of the Isles' to our modern sense of honour and of chivalry? Clan Macdonald may boast of its Lordship connections as it pleases, but what have their so-called Lords done for the Highland people?

The attentions of the people of Lewis and Harris were still focused on what their present proprietor was doing for them, and too often they found it to be too little. While people in Harris were being told that in order to have crofts they must leave for Uist or Skye, the Board of Agriculture was having difficulty in keeping pace with the scale of the housing problem in Lewis. Landless families such as that of young Calum Smith had been squatting since 1921 in huts on the Marybank and Coulregrein grazings outside Stornoway. Early in 1923 Leverhulme's estate finally initiated action at the Sheriff Court to have them evicted even from this undesirable terrain. The Board of Agriculture considered applying to the Land Court to have the squatters' camps reassigned as legitimate housing sites. A survey of the Coulregrein grazings, however, revealed that they were too wet and badly drained to qualify for building consent. Like the squatters themselves, the Board searched desperately for alternatives. Calum Smith's family, which by 1923 included seven children, moved from their small shack at Coulregrein to a thatched two-roomed cottage a mile away at Newvalley. 'For occupation by a family of nine,' he would recall, 'it couldn't be described as anything other than a rural slum . . . My family survived, like all islanders, because of perpetual hard work on the land and sea, and because of the system of mutual communal aid that obtained at the time.'[54]

Others went farther afield. Advertisements for shipping lines and passages to America jostled beside advertisements for Sunlight Soap in the columns of the local newspaper. Australian government agents disembarked at Stornoway and urged Leodhasaich across the length and breadth of the island not to forget the charms of the Antipodes. 'It is to be hoped,' enthused the *Gazette*, 'that the opportunities offered by the Australian Government will be seriously considered by many in the island of Lewis who have not had a chance in the past of taking up agricultural pursuits under such good conditions.'

Some did, but most of them paid greater attention to the entreaties of the representative of Ontario at meetings in Balallan, Leurbost, Ness, Barvas and elsewhere. Two poignantly symbolic events took place within fourteen days in the spring of 1923. On Saturday 7 April Leverhulme, who was making his first visit to the island since the controversy over his new title, announced plans to build a new town hall and art gallery in Stornoway. Two weeks later, on Saturday 21 April, the SS *Metagama* dropped anchor in the harbour, took on board 260 Lewis men and women and set sail with them for Canada.

The first of those occasions took place over a long and distinguished luncheon party at the Waverley Hotel. Leverhulme was presented with an illuminated address signed by the chairmen of every parish council in Lewis and Harris, congratulating him on becoming Viscount 'of the Western Isles', and with a telegram from Sir William Mitchell Cotts which regretted that following his recent business trip to South Africa the Member of Parliament had returned to so much work in London that he was unable to take the night train north.

Provost Kenneth MacKenzie, a tweed manufacturer, assured the proprietor that whatever had been said or written during the past few months, there had not been 'a murmur of dissent' in Lewis and Harris about his new title. On the contrary, 'there is entire satisfaction'.

If there was any surviving doubt as to whether the old man had been hurt and embittered by Alexander Nicolson and his colleagues in Inverness, Leverhulme cleared it up with bravura. He was extremely annoyed. He was no sooner on his feet than the jibes commenced. He had uncovered, he said, 'the previous record of some of the gentlemen who assumed the title "Lord of the Isles", and I must say they do not seem to have been a very attractive lot.'

The packed tableside at the Waverley Hotel burst into laughter. And better was to come. 'I quite understand that Inverness will have no more of them,' he continued. 'On one occasion a Lord of the Isles burnt

Inverness to the ground. And on another occasion one of them seized the Castle of Inverness and levied toll on the inhabitants. Why? To keep an illegitimate son of his! I can assure the people of Inverness I have no intention of burning Inverness to the ground or of seizing the Castle, or levying toll on the inhabitants.'

Viscount Leverhulme returned then, in almost elegiac tones, to a summation of his plans, his philosophy and his feelings for Lewis. In an adjusted version of his epistle to the Gaelic Society of Inverness he spelled out in one more sad account his detestation of the crofting system. 'It reduces the people in health and strength; it is a hotbed for the breeding of consumption.' Cutting farms up into crofts 'looks to me like certain men who do not go to sea at all casting their eyes on a beautiful haul of fish landed by other men, and, instead of going to fish themselves, say: "Let us help ourselves to these fish here, it is so much easier!" – and the Scottish Office supports this.'

Equating Lewis people with common thieves and describing the Scottish Secretary as their accomplice in crime was the language of a man who intended to go no further on this island. No more evidence was by April 1923 required of the gulf which yawned between Lord Leverhulme and his Hebridean tenants. Above all, perhaps, he stubbornly refused to comprehend their visceral attachment to the 1886 Crofting Reform Act. This measure had been won by these people and by their parents not forty years earlier. It was perceived accurately by them as being the fruit of their longsuffering testimony. When land raiders said – as they invariably did say – that they wanted not tied estate bungalows, but a croft 'under the 1886 Act' with security of tenure and compensation for improvements, they were not being sentimental or unrealistic. They were expressing their refusal to relinquish so quickly what they considered to be the basic human right of freedom from eviction.

Many of the men squeezed tightly around a dining table in the Waverley Hotel that day laughed and applauded their landowner when he repeated his comparison with fish-stealers. (The line had, first time round, evoked no reported response.) There were Morrisons present, and MacLeods and MacKenzies, as well as a William Grant. Perhaps they were so far removed from their origins and their constituents as to accept the analogy without flinching. Perhaps – we have no way of knowing – their hilarity was slightly forced and their handclaps muted and uneasy.

He moved on. He chewed unhappily and at length over the perfidy of Robert Munro, the brutal ignorance of the raiders and his own unimpeachable intentions. He said that the present wave of emigration was due entirely to the insurmountable obstacles which the Scottish Office and the land raiders had erected before his development schemes. He recapped the sorry tale of seizure and retreat and re-seizure at Gress in the far-off days of 1921. He mellowed towards his conclusion. He would, he said, like to see a park in Stornoway. He presented his plan for a new town hall, and asked the gathering to notice that it included space for an art gallery. He was presented in return with the illuminated address congratulating him on his latest honour. He stumbled a little in his thanks. He would never have adopted 'of the Western Isles', he said, 'if I thought it would give pain to a single human being'. The illuminated address was then passed around an admiring table. As it made its way from hand to hand Leverhulme spoke again. 'It is a beautiful work of art,' he said. 'But I value it most for the heart-throbs in it.'

He was consoled by Provost Mackenzie, by his old friend and former provost Murdo Maclean, by Reverend Alex White of Stornoway United Free Church and by John Mackenzie of Tarbert. He was told that the men who had raided his estate farms in pursuit of crofts were both untypical of Lewis and Harris and a disgrace to their compatriots. He was informed by Murdo Maclean that the raiders were the 'lowest element' of their community, and that they alone bore responsibility 'for thwarting all of the objects that Lord Leverhulme had so much at heart'. He was reassured at length by John MacKenzie that far from resenting his adoption of the Viscountship 'of the Western Isles', everybody in Lewis and Harris welcomed the honour unequivocally. He was, Lord Leverhulme was told, 'a prince . . . a man who had shown that his sole interest and desire was to promote the well-being of all who served him'.

A fortnight later the *Metagama* left with its human cargo for North America. It was not the last vessel to sail out of Stornoway carrying such a doleful burden. In 1923 and 1924 1,000 Leodhasaich would leave in similar ships. The *Metagama* became emblematic of them all because in

April 1923 it appeared to present such a stark and final solution to the post-war problems of Lewis. Her departure took on the aspect of an exodus. Thirty-five journalists and photographers from the national press attended the ceremony. They witnessed astonishing scenes. On the Sunday before the sailing Reverend Alex White drew his sermon at the United Free Church from Genesis 12: 'And Jehovah said unto Abraham, get thou out of thy Country and from thy kindred and from thy father's house unto the land I will show thee.' Reporters from Glasgow and Edinburgh saw the country buses – 'motor vehicles of an antique pattern, with box-like open wagonette bodies' – begin to roll into Stornoway on Friday night, along roads which 'resembled scenes of refugees fleeing before an advancing army'.

The emigrants, chiefly 'young men with sunburnt faces and new suits' (there were 242 Lewis men and 18 women on the *Metagama*), wore maple leaf badges and were each presented with a Gaelic bible. The pipe band marched and played and psalms were sung on the pier. They were assembled on the quarterdeck of the *Metagama* late in the afternoon, and before she hauled anchor two Free Church ministers, from Ness and from Garrabost in Point, addressed them in their native language. Then they swung cautiously out past the Beasts of Holm and eastwards into the Minch before the liner set her course north, to round the Butt of Lewis and make headway into the North Atlantic Ocean.[55]

The 260 people who sailed on her, along with a few dozen from other islands and from the mainland, were certainly in search of a livelihood. But it would be misleading to suggest, as had been the received wisdom in the Waverley Hotel two weeks earlier, that they were driven from Lewis because of the frustration of Lord Leverhulme's schemes for industrialisation. Just 14 per cent of them were from Stornoway. The remaining 86 per cent departed home addresses in every rural parish on the island. They had been the passengers on those wagonettes, the refugees on the Stornoway road out of Point, Ness, Tolsta, Lochs, Barvas and Uig.

They did not travel to Ontario to look for a job on a factory line or a salaried office position. Overwhelmingly, they emigrated in search of land. They left Lewis because they were promised smallholdings, on the

Canadian prairie or in the Australian outback, from which they could not be evicted and upon which they could build houses. Pastoralists they had been, and – whatever sorrows and disappointments, whatever other great and good and immensely rewarding careers they and their children would eventually discover in the newfoundlands – at the point of departure, pastoralists they intended to remain.

Viscount Leverhulme was no longer in the Western Isles on the day the *Metagama* sailed. He did not need to be present to recognise the immense symbolism of the occasion. Nothing between him and Lewis could ever be the same again. It was not even a private severance. Those three dozen pressmen ensured that this bleak, emotional and highly visible conclusion to all his loudly touted plans and proposals and enthusiasms for the future of the Hebrides was splashed across newspapers from London to New Brunswick. 'These isles are now being emptied,' announced one Canadian journal. 'Only the old are left behind.' British editorial columns, which a few short years before had acclaimed him as the saviour of a benighted region, were now discoursing mournfully on the pity of emigration and the tragic circumstances of the land whose very name and titles he had assumed. There had been many beginnings to this end, but Saturday 21 April 1923 represented the final chapter. Had he only realised it, after the sun set on that spring night there was no longer any point even in trying to apportion blame.

Since his frank admission at Stornoway Highland Games in September 1921 that the real reason for shelving his improvement projects was the unfavourable 'condition of supply and demand' in the fishing industry, he had hardened into a condition of what later dictionaries would define as denial. His later statements and speeches were studded increasingly with self-justifying protestations, which bordered occasionally upon the maudlin, of his inculpability, of his helplessness in the face of events beyond his foresight or control. Crotchety and frustrated, the old proprietor rarely again referred after September 1921 to the economic situation which had forced his hand. As the months and years passed he felt obliged to uncover scapegoats, individuals, malevolent human explanations for the legendary industrialist's defeat by the market. It might one day be the raiders, Murdo Maclean's 'lowest element' of

Lewis. It might another day be the Board of Agriculture. It could be Scottish Secretary Robert Munro. Munro's successor, Viscount Novar, was surely an unlikely candidate for blame, but in the twilight view over ruined dreams from the turrets of Lews Castle any mirage was possible.

He brooded throughout the summer in London and in Harris and in Cheshire. His decision finally to relinquish Lewis was probably reached in July. At a meeting at the Scottish Office in London on 14 June called by the landowner to protest against the transferral of Galson Farm to crofting tenure, the chairman of the Board of Agriculture Sir Robert Greig hinted to Leverhulme's representative Sir Edgar Sanders that the government hoped to continue providing new croft land in the Hebrides. To this end, farms might in the future be sequestrated.

Both Viscount Novar's office and the Board of Agriculture subsequently insisted in writing that they had no intention of turning all of Lewis into a crofting estate, or even in the months to come of reallocating any more of Leverhulme's farms. What had been said, insisted the Scottish Under-Secretary John Lamb, was 'not a statement of policy, but merely an expression of Sir Robert's fear that so long as there was any land available in Lewis there would be a demand for it and a danger of raiding. My recollection on this point is confirmed by Sir Robert.'

Viscount Novar and Sir Robert Greig appear to have felt compelled more to explain the realities of life in north-western Scotland than to issue Bolshevik threats. But Sanders and Leverhulme seized upon Greig's vague and unremarkable repetition of the Board of Agriculture's desire to ease the lot of land-starved Hebrideans. They decided to ignore Lamb's placatory letters from the Scottish Office. An imaginary menace issuing from a wearily disputatious meeting therefore became, conveniently, the straw which broke the camel's back.

'It would be madness for me,' Leverhulme would claim, 'to disregard this clear intimation from the Scottish Office that under certain circumstances they might be compelled to take for crofting every farm in Lewis except the Manor Farm' (which, as the estate's Home Farm, was immune to reassignation). He had been given no such intimation. He had on the contrary been reassured that the Scottish Office supported his own proposals, if not his detestation of crofting. But they were out of patience with him, and he was out of patience with Lewis.

His options were limited. The traditional recourse of an estate owner at the end of his tether was to sell his property. Leverhulme searched for an alternative to this. Property prices were still in recession. Whatever relatively small sum he might be offered for Lewis would mean little to the personal fortune of a multi-millionaire approaching the end of his life. To sell, to hand those proud deeds over to somebody else, would moreover be the final personal admission of defeat. It would also carry with it the unconscionable danger that a new proprietor might prove to be more popular and more successful than Viscount Leverhulme of the Western Isles.

So he determined to divide the island into separate estates, falling broadly into the categories of town and country, Stornoway and the outlying districts – the very parishes which he had once insisted to the people of rural Back were indivisible. Having done so he would offer Lewis as a gift to its people.

There can have been no single, easily identifiable reason for this decision. It was in 1923 an unprecedented gesture. It came from a man who had insistently railed against the threat of Bolshevism and the nonsense of socialism. All of Leverhulme's working life had been interpreted as an exercise in benign capitalism, as a practical demonstration of the benefits of that apparent oxymoron, liberal autocracy. His efforts in the Wirral had been intended to prove that healthy and well-housed urban workers were happier and more profitable to their employer. His efforts in Africa had been attempts to give colonialism a human face. His efforts in the Hebrides had been unashamedly inspired by the desire to set twentieth-century market forces loose in a 'backward' agrarian part of the United Kingdom, and thereby prove to the world that everybody – Merseyside proletarian, northern industrialist, Lewis crofter and Highland landowner – stood to gain by the intelligent application of capitalist principles.

This was the man who now suggested turning Lewis, one of the biggest private estates in Britain, into a couple of autonomous workers' soviets. It has been suggested that he considered himself to be handing a poisoned chalice to his erstwhile tormentors, that he expected to provoke either their refusal to accept such responsibilities, or their catastrophic failure to carry them out. If so he was half-rewarded. He may have considered the crofting Hebrides to be ungovernable by any other person or persons. He may (as he privately suggested to at least one English friend) have wished to pre-empt any attempt by the Board of Agriculture to bring them into state ownership. He may also (as he said publicly and privately on several occasions) have nursed a reluctant regard for his formidable 'enemy'; he may have believed that these proud and God-fearing and articulate people, with the exception of their 'lowest elements', had earned the opportunity to mould their own future.

And he may, at the end of the struggle, have allowed most characteristically that sentimental, philanthropic part of his nature to well up and spill out in a dramatic demonstration of unrequited love. The Western Isles, he had said, were like a wife to him, and he was ever a devoted husband.

Leverhulme called virtually every public representative in the island to a meeting at the Town Council Chambers in Stornoway on Monday 3 September 1923, sixteen days before his seventy-second birthday and two years after he had announced that both his own affairs and the national fishing industry were in such crisis that he could no longer continue with most of his Lewis investments. He had arrived on the *Sheila* a few days previously. Harley Williams, the recently-appointed Medical Officer for Lewis who would later become a successful author, was among the curious gathered at the waterside and sensed 'a certain coldness in the welcome . . . A respectful crowd thronged the wharf, but I remember there was no cheering, no enthusiasm, and the thickset grey-combed figure moved up the gangway and drove away between silent throngs.'[56]

Some of those present at the meeting on the following Monday were familiar to some degree with the purpose of the assembly; everybody was aware of being witness to something of great moment. Leverhulme was introduced with grave ceremony by Provost Kenneth Mackenzie. He rose from his chair to the shuffling silence of a church service.

> I never had a more uncongenial burden laid upon myself than the one which devolves upon me today, which is to explain fully and without reserve the position I find myself placed in with regard to my relationship

with the island of Lewis to all my friends – you in this room, and the greater number outside this room – with whom I have had such agreeable and friendly relations for over five years.

As I explained to you at our first meeting together, I am not attracted to Lewis by any love of sport such as fishing, game shooting or deer stalking, but entirely by the possibilities I thought I recognised here, in Lewis, of doing something in a small way, within the limits of my capacity, for the permanent benefit of the fine people living in the island of Lewis and who have for centuries won the admiration of all who have known them.

Many people warned me before I came here, and before I finally decided on the purchase of the island from its then owner, that I should find the people difficult, and the usual slander was uttered that I should find them not only difficult but lazy. Neither in my own experience, nor has it been so in the experience of others who have written on the subject, have I found the slander of laziness to have any foundation in fact. We have all of us our natural aptitudes, and, if we do not understand each other, we cannot draw right conclusions. I know for a fact that letters have been addressed to English papers, by working men, asking the question: 'Did anyone ever hear of Lord Leverhulme doing a hard day's work in his life?', notwithstanding the fact that my day's work begins by rising at 4.30 in the morning . . .

There were no punctuations of applause at this fateful meeting, no outbursts of supportive laughter. He passed on from praise for the diligence of Leodhasaich to sing yet again of the unrealised potential of Hebridean fisheries. He pronounced dead the days of the cottage industry and the small crofter. Then he turned to land raiding. It had been made absolutely clear, he asserted, that Scottish Secretaries of all political persuasions were opposed to the imprisonment of raiders – 'the raiders made their own law, and the Scottish Office permitted it'. In such intolerable local circumstances had he been obliged to wrestle with the enormities of international economic depression.

In September of 1921 in speaking in Stornoway I called attention to this and also to the economic conditions which then prevailed and which of themselves made it impossible for me at that moment to resume development work . . . It would have been as mad for me to have said I would resume at that moment as it would be for any captain of any ship on the ocean that encountered fog to persist in going all speed ahead, but, just as surely as that the fog will lift and the mists disappear so surely would such economic conditions pass away, but I was given no opportunity for this to occur.

The Scottish Office had interpreted Leverhulme's suspension of his improvement programme as the landowner defaulting on his gentleman's agreement to press on with job-creation in return for a ten-year holiday from croft-creation. This supposedly crucial arrangement was never much more than wishful thinking. Even if Robert Munro had felt himself able realistically to promise such a lengthy hiatus in land settlement, any successor in the Scottish Office would have been free to overturn it in an hour. All the major political parties were in favour of granting crofts to Highlanders, especially to Highlanders who had served in the Great War. Of all the leading figures in this drama, only Lord Leverhulme was opposed to crofting and an advocate of sending land-hungry holders of the Distinguished Service Medal to jail. For so long as he guaranteed to replace smallholdings with respectable and secure salaries, the government might try to humour him. The moment he announced that he was not only cancelling his future schemes but also curtailing those few labouring projects which were already in operation, the government had no choice but to revert to its previous position and answer the cry for land. This was duly interpreted by Leverhulme as the Scottish Office stampeding to betray him. It was, he told his audience in Stornoway on 3 September 1923, nothing short of Shakespearean tragedy:

> I am now left without any object or motive for remaining here. For me merely to come each year as an ordinary visitor to the castle, and knowing that I could take no interest in fishing or sport, would be meaningless. I am like Othello with my occupation gone, and I could only be like the ghost of Hamlet's father haunting the place as a shadow. Under these conditions, I should feel rather depressed than exhilarated, and so I am proposing now to take one of two courses.
>
> The one of these two courses would be that I should sell the castle and all the sporting properties. I am informed that these would sell readily at a price which, under the circumstances, would be satisfactory.
>
> The other course, and the one that would be more congenial to myself, would be that I should make a gift of the whole of the island of Lewis as I purchased it from the late proprietor, Colonel Matheson.

Without binding myself at this moment . . . I suggest that Lewis is divided into two spheres of influence for the Trustees. One sphere being all issue, crofts, etc, lying beyond a distance of seven miles radius from the Post Office, Stornoway, the other sphere being within this radius.

In the sphere beyond the radius of seven miles from the Post Office, Stornoway, as to all existing crofts, including the crofts proposed to be cut out of Galson Farm, but excepting crofts occupied by ex-raiders, shall be given as a free gift from myself to their respective cultivators, being resident occupiers of same.

All farms not yet taken for crofts, together with all sporting and fishing rights with their lodges and houses . . . together with all crofts in the possession of non-resident crofters, and all crofts the resident occupiers of which do not wish to avail themselves of this offer, and together with all crofts occupied by ex-raiders . . . I wish to give to Trustees nominated from time to time by the Lewis District Committee.

All crofts, farms, castle grounds and policies within the seven-mile radius from the centre of Stornoway would similarly be given to Trustees nominated by Stornoway Town Council and elected from the Parliamentary Voters Lists. Both bodies were requested to give him their acceptance or refusal within five working weeks, by Saturday 6 October.

The original seven-mile radius proposed by Leverhulme was just enough to put Gress within the Stornoway Trust and Tolsta without it. To the east it encompassed almost all of Point but the busy headland township of Portnaguran. To the south, most of North Lochs would have been governed by one body but all of South Lochs by another. To the west there was little controversy. Enough of the lowlands of Barvas Moor were contained within the township trust to keep their summer sheilings and peat cuttings in the reach of east coast crofters. And enough of the high wasteland of Barvas Moor was included to ensure that eighty years later, when a local resource which had escaped the attention even of Lord Leverhulme was ready for exploitation, the Stornoway Trust was in a position to help develop wind turbine electricity generation on the far hills beyond the suburbs of Newvalley and Coulregrein, where once young Calum Smith and his family squeezed into a single living room and wondered how a living was to be found in 1920s Lewis.

The seven-mile radius and the selection of trustees were rationalised in the following weeks. Tolsta and the whole of Point were taken into the

Stornoway fold. Lochs, North and South, were excluded. The boundary now ran to the south of Arnish Moor. Everything else would be within the purlieu of a 'country' trust, half appointed by the Lewis District Committee and half elected. The 'town' trust would take the same form, with its appointees put forward by Stornoway Town Council.

Leverhulme finished his speech that day with both a scripted and an improvised text. His prepared lines concluded:

> I am leaving Lewis with deep regrets. I am carrying with me the happiest recollections of my five years' residence among the people of Lewis, and my most profound gratitude for the full and generous welcome and support I have always received practically unanimously from all, because support and welcome came from all but less than 2 per cent of those living in Lewis. I hope you will receive my proposals as indicating my desire when leaving Lewis to do all in my power to secure the future welfare, prosperity and happiness of its people.

He then set down the script and addressed his audience – which had finally managed a round of applause – extempore. He would now be leaving the room, he said, so that in whatever discussions took place they would not be impeded by his presence. He felt they would want to discuss the matter amongst themselves, and in going he would save 'some little pain' to himself and it would be convenient for them. He did not want any votes of thanks (he got one anyway, albeit brief, from Provost MacKenzie). It was a very serious matter for all of them. As far as he was concerned his desire was that they should accept. He would have no difficulty in selling on the open market – 'but I would rather that the experiment is first tried of ownership of the island by the people of the island.'

And so Viscount Leverhulme of the Western Isles divorced himself from the island of Lewis, beaten down by international market forces and the – in his rendering, equivalent – vandalisms of a group of land raiders from Back. The size of this crucial band of subversives remained always open to question. At times they could be claimed by allies such as Murdo Maclean to be as few as ten or twelve. Leverhulme had once informed the Board of Agriculture that this 'small group of misguided men' were about thirty in number. On other occasions, most notably following the meeting at Gress bridge, he had perceived them as being in four figures.

He presumably deliberated before settling, in this keynote final delivery, for the total of 'less than 2 per cent'. Not 1 per cent, which would have indicated 300 people, or a rounded 2 per cent, or 5 per cent, but 'less than' 2 per cent. Should we say, 500 men and women who from a population of 30,000 had failed to offer him 'support and welcome'? He did not know; he never had known and never would know. Ten, 30, 500, 1,000 or 30,000: they were as invisible as conscience, a guerrilla army of ghosts, only rarely recognisable and quite impossible to count. They had not defeated him. The bulk and top-heavy weight of his own overblown schemes and expectations had rather collapsed about his feet. They had merely been there at the beginning, asking for promises to be honoured, as they would be there at the end to pick up the fragments.

They would however, most of them, defeat his final scheme. He was offering to the crofters of rural Lewis owner-occupancy. He wanted them to relinquish their titles as tenant smallholders and become little private freeholders. For a number of reasons which would become evident as the weeks (and indeed the years) passed, almost all crofters were unwilling to take this step.

There was never much doubt that Stornoway Town Council would accept its part of the bargain. They were being offered the freehold of some considerable amenities, they would be buoyed by substantial urban rates and duties, and they would be responsible only to the croftlands to their immediate north. Within a week the Council had met and agreed 'to accept the gift subject to the adjustment of details'.

Beyond Barvas Moor and south of Arnish matters were more complicated. Murdo Morrison, a Justice of the Peace from Bragar on the west coast, described how:

> During the first flush of the excitement [following Leverhulme's offer] no possible drawback seemed probable. Complete freedom and independence – so dear to Lewis hearts – was ours for the taking. Not a cloud on the horizon, and we were to be happy ever after – like the ending of all good children's stories.
>
> But on the morrow, after sleeping over it for a night, the awakenings brought misgivings. Questions of managements and economies forced themselves forward. Miniature parliaments and legislative assemblies soon

became the order of the day, and 'ways and means' were discussed in a manner that does credit to the Lewis crofter, and as it is generally known that the parish of Barvas is not self-supporting, the various sources of revenue suggested, which were never before tapped, are highly interesting, and some of them appear quite feasible, the object being that the crofter may not have to pay in taxes as much as he now pays in rent and taxes combined . . . At the moment the general impression is that it would be a crime against all Lewismen, both 'Burghers' and 'Outlanders', if the offer is declined.

One thing was quite out of the question. The 'outlander' crofters of rural Lewis (and for that matter, the 'burgher' crofters of the Back machair) were not prepared to sacrifice their rights under the 1886 Act. And the 1886 Act was framed to protect them as tenant smallholders. Once they had become owner-occupying freeholders, the 1886 Crofters Act would cease to apply in Lewis.

There was some sentimental attachment here, and some financial acuity – for a croft was a small and difficult patch of land to hoe, and its crofter might ever prefer to be under the protective umbrella of a larger conglomerate. But there was also an atavistic intuition about the precious nature of crofting. It was a peculiarly communal livelihood. It allowed the crofter an enviable combination of independence on his own small turf and free association with his neighbourhood. Many crofting activities, such as gathering and shearing sheep from the common grazings, or cutting the year's peat fuel supply, or renewing thatches, had always been and would continue to be embarked upon in large and cheerful groups. Sometimes this was necessary – a gang of men and boys and dogs was unquestionably more efficient at a gathering. Sometimes, however, it was not – no time and motion study could ever prove that a family group of three which spent six weeks cutting and drying its own peat would be slower and more inefficient than a township group of eighteen which devoted six successive weeks to cutting each others' peat. They chose the latter (or some approximation of it) because it was more enjoyable that way.

To reduce a crofting community to a series of independent freehold-ings would be to fracture and ultimately atomise that collective. This was understood perfectly well by crofters throughout the twentieth century. It was not that they idolised a laird. They did not, and were almost always happier and more secure once their landlord became the state, in the form of the Board of Agriculture or any of its heirs. Rather, they valued the egalitarian communion of their crofting townships, not only for its workaday practicality, but also because without it the system of crofting would lose its very soul and independent value, and its practitioners would be no better and no worse than a million other self-absorbed peasants competing for a livelihood on the worst soil in Europe.

The most widespread demonstration of this attachment was made fully ninety years after the passing of the 1886 Act, and half a century after the commotions in Leverhulme's Lewis. In 1976 the Labour Government, acting chiefly on the advice of William Grant's son James Shaw Grant, who had followed his father into the *Stornoway Gazette*'s editorial chair and thereafter into a series of quasi-governmental Highland authorities, passed another Crofting Reform Act. James Shaw Grant was an intelligent thirteen-year-old student at the Nicolson Institute in Stornoway when Viscount Leverhulme made his offer in the Council Chambers in 1923. Between 1963 and 1978 he was chairman of the administrative and advisory body, the Crofters' Commission. The main plank of Grant's 1976 legislation was designed to give all crofters across Scotland the right to do what Lord Leverhulme had recommended to the crofters of Lewis: buy their own crofts. For an easily attainable sum, a small multiple of their annual rental, they were given the legal capability to become owner-occupiers.

Despite the loudhailing by an uninquisitive media of this 'bargain of the century', they refused to do so on a massive scale. Almost every crofter in Scotland simply failed after 1976 to accept this apparently generous offer of promotion up the social scale from dependent peasantry to landowning freeholder. In the whole of the Western Isles especially, hardly a croft was bought by its tenant. Ninety years after its passing, they still preferred William Gladstone's Act to that of the son of William Grant.

If rejection of the 1886 Act was unacceptable in 1976, in 1923 it was unthinkable. 'The view of the crofters of Lewis,' said the Aignish parish councillor George MacLeod in the days after Leverhulme's offer, 'is that they would rather be under the Crofters Act than be their own owners.' MacLeod was himself an ex-serviceman who had been involved in re-establishing a democratic local grazings committee in 1919. 'Under the Crofters Act,' he explained, 'the crofters have the power to rule their own villages, with regard to the grazings, by men appointed by the people . . . My idea is that when everybody will be his own master, everybody will put his cattle where he likes and when he likes, and there will be no law or order in the place. What I want is law. It doesn't matter whether it is under Lord Leverhulme or anybody else, as long as it is going to benefit the poor as well as the rich.' 'There is doubt in some minds,' agreed the headmaster from Knock in Point, 'as to whether those accepting their crofts . . . will thereby continue to enjoy the benefits of the Crofters Act, and to have the status of crofters.'

In the weeks that followed packed meetings throughout rural Lewis confirmed those sentiments. Even in the Stornoway satellite township of Laxdale it was unanimously agreed 'that we should abide under the protection of the Crofters Act and not become owners of our own crofts.' A massed gathering of the citizenry of North Lochs at Fidigarry School heard Neil Mackenzie of Crossbost disown any scheme, 'no matter where it originated, that departed from the legitimate rights and privileges conferred on him by the Crofters Act'. Alexander MacRae of Ranish concurred: 'I have not met any crofter yet who agrees to accept the proposed scheme. The Crofters Act with all its disadvantages is much better than individual proprietorship.' Roderick MacLeod of Ranish 'failed to conceive of any benefit to be derived from accepting the crofts as individual proprietors'. The meeting unanimously agreed that 'we wish to remain within the four corners of the Crofters Act.'

The country districts, the 'outlander' regions of Lewis which were being asked to form a trust through the District Committee, also carried the full weight of landlessness. This was no mean burden. There were perhaps 3,000 registered rate-paying, rent-paying and tax-paying crofters outside the burgh of Stornoway and Back, and an estimated 1,800 squatters or cottars who were unable to contribute at all to the common weal. In sharp contrast to the gas works and steam laundry, the rents from rateable businesses and individuals of Stornoway, almost all that the district parishes could depend upon for an immediate annual income was the letting of shootings and riparian rivers.

Their answer clearly was to turn the dependent cottars into contributing crofters, but so little had been accomplished in this direction under the Leverhulme regime that, five years on, it represented a daunting problem. The crofters of rural Lewis were fully aware that a succession of previous governments and Scottish Secretaries had accepted that the responsibility for solving it lay upon their own varnished desks, and not with the hard-pressed neighbours, relatives and friends of the landless. It appeared now as though they, the crofters of Lewis, were being asked not only to resolve but also to subsidise a monumental failure of official policy and landowning philosophy.

Set against this was their comprehension of both the scale of the opportunity and the caricature of themselves which would be painted if, having protested for so long that the land belonged to the people, the people declined to take 'free' ownership of the land. Bailie George Stewart, one of Leverhulme's sternest Stornoway supporters, pointed out with relish that: 'A refusal to accept would prove the old slogan "The Land for the People" to be a meaningless and insincere shibboleth.'

Bailie Stewart was being mischievous. They wanted the land, but not on anybody's terms. While the Stornoway Town Council, unperturbed by such difficulties, ran smoothly towards acceptance of their own offer and the establishment of a Stornoway Trust, the Lewis District Committee battled bravely to tie up loose ends and balance the books.

They quickly decided that they needed a little help from the government. On the night of Wednesday 12 September 1923, ten days after Leverhulme's offer, two officials from the Board of Agriculture and two from the Board of Health disembarked at Stornoway and went on the following afternoon into urgent consultation with the District Committee. The meeting closed by reaffirming the Committee's desire

> to co-operate in carrying out Lord Leverhulme's public-spirited and generous proposal that the landward part of Lewis Estate should be handed over to a Public Trust to be administered for the benefit of inhabitants . . . but we foresee certain difficulties in administering them arising partly from the possibility of any considerable number of crofters

electing to accept their crofts while common grazings are to be vested in
the Trust, and from the prospect of a somewhat narrow margin of revenue
for carrying on the administration, seeing that public burdens will exhaust
the greater part of revenue.

They wished to be able to co-opt onto such a trust representatives from
the Boards of Agriculture and Health, as 'the public departments most
closely associated with Lewis'. They also desired to meet in Edinburgh
with the Scottish Secretary, Viscount Novar, just as soon as he was able to
accommodate them.

On the night of Monday 17 September the Town Council called a
meeting of Stornoway's ratepayers in the Drill Hall. It was so well
attended that the doors were shut behind a packed assembly before the
appointed hour. Provost Kenneth MacKenzie and his fellow councillors
confirmed what everybody had guessed: whatever difficulties their
colleagues on the District Committee may be having in reconciling the
acceptance of rural Lewis were not shared by Stornoway Town Council.
Their half of the figures added up. The fish processing factories could
not, as Leverhulme himself had so painfully discovered, be depended
upon to provide any substantial income. The Fish Oil Works were, said
Provost MacKenzie, 'a more or less uncertain source of revenue . . . being
entirely dependent upon the fishing – we, therefore, leave these out of
account.' The cannery and ice-making plant had never been opened for
business. But other estate ventures which would fall into the hands of the
Stornoway Trust, such as the town's steam laundry and especially the gas
works 'would be sufficient to maintain the castle and policies'. The
crofters of Back, Coll and Gress, if they did not wish to divorce
themselves from the crofting system by becoming owner-occupiers (they
did not), would instead become tenants of the publicly-elected Trust.

It was settled without serious dispute. Provost MacKenzie left the
Drill Hall to convey two messages to Viscount Leverhulme. One
congratulated him on his seventy-second birthday. The other informed
him that Stornoway said yes.

On Saturday 29 September four representatives from the District
Committee, led by their chairman, ex-Provost Murdo Maclean, met the
Scottish Secretary in Edinburgh.

Viscount Novar was presented with a statement which declared that the Committee thought it to be 'in the best interest of the people of Lewis' if they accepted the offer of the land. It added that the crofters 'throughout the district are likely to elect to remain tenants', and that the notional Lewis District Trust would require for its first few years of life government assistance in both administrative personnel and financial solvency.

The latter was most important. Murdo Maclean insisted that given the right people and policies, the trust could make itself pay after a short period of time. 'Our object,' he said, 'in coming here this day is to see whether the Government will encourage us and remove the bogey of finance that lies between us and accepting Lord Leverhulme's gift.' His vice-chairman Alexander Maclennan 'did not see why the island should not be self-supporting . . . the great thing we cannot lose sight of is – we feel that without immediate financial assistance we will not be able to carry on the trust, even for a year, on the face of the figures that we have got.'

The anticipated amount of short-term subsidy was small. According to the estate's own figures it ran to a total, for the whole of rural Lewis, of £1,365 9s 2d a year.

Viscount Novar had made up his mind before meeting the delegation from rural Lewis. Murdo Maclean would later bitterly reflect that the Scottish Secretary, having heard the lengthy case proposed by the Leodhasaich, in reply produced and read aloud from a written statement which had clearly been composed before the meeting took place. 'Therefore,' submitted ex-Provost Maclean, 'we concluded that his decision had been arrived at before we went there.'

He rejected outright any possibility of his office, either directly or through the Boards of Agriculture and Health, delivering members or financial subsidy to a non-governmental trust. He alluded delicately to the occasion thirty-eight years previously, when as the 24-year-old Ronald Crauford Munro-Ferguson of Novar he had spent a year as Member of Parliament for Ross-shire before being kicked unceremoniously out of office by, among others, the newly enfranchised crofters of rural Lewis. 'My associations with the island of Lewis in parliamentary and county affairs were very close at one time,' he said, 'and though seas have divided us I have never failed to follow with deep interest the affairs of the island.'

Despite that deep interest, 'only one answer is possible to the suggestion that the two Boards should each nominate a representative to serve on the proposed Trust. It is not possible for me to accede to that suggestion.' There would otherwise be, he insisted, an unacceptable conflict of interest.

As for the District Committee's proposal 'that if such a Trust were constituted the Government should give financial assistance to it for a few years at least . . . I might say at once that it is impossible for me to entertain the proposal that payments for the purpose of meeting such a deficit on the working of the estate should be met by the Board of Agriculture, the Board of Health, or any other department. This decision rests on general grounds of principle, and I do not think it can cause surprise.'

Viscount Novar was saying that it was, in 1923, impossible for him to differentiate between an estate which was owned and run by a private proprietor, and one which was operated by and for its tenantry. As a private landowner could not expect a rates subsidy, neither could a Lewis District Trust. On that 'ground of principle' he withheld any possibility of the Board of Agriculture – which was regularly spending tens of thousands of pounds to acquire Highland estates and farms and turn them into crofting communities – doling out a few thousand pounds over a few years to assist the community ownership of almost the entire island of Lewis. By withholding the possibility of such a subsidy he was, as he must have known, effectively eliminating any possibility of a District Trust, for without underwriters the individual trustees themselves would have been personally responsible for any estate deficit, which could have forced a number of serving members of the Lewis District Committee into bankruptcy.

It was an unhelpful position to adopt. It may have been worse than that. The District Committee member Donald MacLeod of Breasclete, who was not part of the Edinburgh delegation, would later muse with some conviction that: 'I think if Viscount Novar had cast about him he would have found a precedent that is not very remote . . .' He could have added that it was within the prerogative of Scottish Secretaries to set precedents. Novar's successors in Scottish government eighty years later, who found themselves answering requests for millions of pounds from populations anxious to buy out their comparatively small acreages of Hebridean land, may have regretted their predecessor's profligacy.

The deflated delegation returned to Lewis and called a full District Committee meeting for Friday 5 October. Twelve members, representing Breasclete and Shawbost on the west coast, Dell and Europie in the Ness district, Back and Stornoway assembled under the chairmanship of Murdo Maclean. They had twenty-four hours in which to convey their decision to Leverhulme, who had been informed of Viscount Novar's lack of cooperation but who found himself unable to extend his deadline beyond 6 October.

In the depressing circumstances their debate was creditable. Not a single member disagreed with the basic principle of a Lewis District Trust. But no-one could adequately answer vice-chairman Alexander Maclennan's admission that 'I fail to see how we can get over this deficit that we have from the figures supplied.' Mrs J.M. Fraser protested that: 'We have been hearing from infancy the cry of "the Land for the People and the People for the Land", and now when we have this unique opportunity I do not see how we can refuse it.'

It was not easy, conceded Alexander MacFarquhar of Dell. But

> when it comes to the government, the government has withdrawn back, and doesn't seem to help in any way. It seems very strange to me, that attitude, and I must say it is heartsore . . . For my own part I cannot see – although it is difficult and although it is disagreeable, and I would certainly like to be the first to accept the gift if I saw my way clear, but owing to this deficit, and not sure of what might take place, there's a certain amount of risk in it – I cannot personally see my way to accept.

John Mitchell of Shawbost, where the schoolboy Calum Smith and his family had been made homeless and landless, found that: 'I cannot refuse this offer.' Murdo Maclean answered with feeling: 'The sole difficulty with us is the financial difficulty. If that difficulty were removed then I would say with all my heart, accept . . .' 'Faith will remove mountains,' interjected Mrs Fraser.

Mrs J.M. Fraser moved that the District Committee should accept Lord Leverhulme's offer of the whole of the landward area of Lewis. She was seconded by John Mitchell. Alexander Maclennan moved an amendment which stated that 'in view of Viscount Novar's decision not to meet the deficit on the working of the Estate, [the Lewis District Committee] much regret that they cannot see their way to become the nucleus of the proposed Trust for the sphere lying beyond the radius of seven miles from the Post Office of Stornoway.' He was seconded by Alexander Macfarquhar.

The motion to accept attracted three votes, from Fraser, Mitchell and Ranald Macdonald of Europie. The successful amendment recommending rejection drew six votes. It was supported by Maclennan, Macfarquhar, Malcolm Mackenzie of Crossbost, Allan Morrison of Back, Donald Macleod of Europie and John Macleod of Stornoway. Aside from chairman Murdo Maclean, three members abstained. They were the clerk Hugh Miller, Donald Macleod of Breasclete and Hector Smith of Europie. 'If I were a younger man,' said Hector Smith, 'I would have no hesitation whatever in facing it.'

Lord Leverhulme was instantly notified by Hugh Miller of the committee's decision. The proprietor's reply arrived in Stornoway on the next day, Saturday 6 October. 'Note with regret decision arrived at by Lewis District Committee,' the telegram read, 'which I am confident had circumstances permitted they would have preferred to have been otherwise. Please accept my sincere thanks for the consideration given to the matter. I must now proceed to deal with the situation in such other alternative manner as I may be advised.'

His advisers were short of profitable ideas. The 56,000-acre Galson shooting, farming and crofting estate was sold for the throwaway sum of £500, or twopence ha'penny an acre, to Mr Edward Valpy, an acquaintance of Leverhulme who had been an occasional visitor to Coll and to the Castle. Galson Estate contained an unfurnished but substantial lodge, several trout lochs and rivers, wildfowl shooting and twenty crofting townships. Its total annual rental income was £1,638 and its 'rate-burden' was £1,242. Edward Valpy said afterwards that he had 'expected' his offer to be accepted, and that he had no plans for Galson other than recreational shooting and fishing.

Valpy may have had a realistic eye on the property market, for the auctioneers Knight Frank and Rutley were unable to win any acceptable offers for the estates of Park, Morsgail, Grimersta, Soval, Carloway, Barvas or Aline. When Lord Leverhulme had, in stressing the philanthropic motivation behind his proposed gift, assured the people of Lewis that he would otherwise have no difficulty in selling the island piecemeal for a tidy return, he had clearly miscalculated. He could in the end sell virtually none of it. Those seven benchmark sporting and crofting estates comprised between them 540,000 acres. In 1923 and 1924 £50,000 would have bought the lot. But £50,000 was not forthcoming. With the exception of the grateful Edward Valpy, private speculators apparently agreed with the Lewis District Committee that they were not worth the risk.

So the aging widow Mrs Jessie Platt, who had in 1887 attempted to admonish the Park deer forest raiders and had run into a stone wall of Gaelic, was allowed to remain in grace and favour residence at Eishken Lodge. A lodge and part of its estate at Uig were given to Leverhulme's niece Emily and her new husband, the Lewis doctor, Donald Macdonald, who would in future years become a popular historian and folklorist of the island. 'Two bays of the canning factory,' writes Nigel Nicolson, 'which had never produced a single can, were dismantled and transported in sections to Leverburgh, where they joined the ice factory, which had never produced a cube of ice.'[57] Leverhulme made another half-hearted attempt to persuade Lewis crofters to become owner-occupiers. Forty-one of them agreed to do so. Three thousand declined.

On November 8 1923 Stornoway Town Council met to consider, and to approve, the draft deeds of property which would become the estate of the Stornoway Trust. They noted with satisfaction that the 'seven-mile radius' had been amended to exclude all of the inhabited parishes of Lochs south of Amhuinn Leuravay, and extended northwards to encompass all of Stornoway parish. At a further meeting on January 28 1924 Provost Kenneth MacKenzie told his fellow councillors that he had received the complete Deeds of Trust from Viscount Leverhulme's Edinburgh solicitors. This democratically accountable body was now the proprietor of much of Stornoway and its environs, and was the crofting landlord of the entire Back machair from Tong to Tolsta by way of Gress and Coll.

The Stornoway Trust, unlike the thwarted Lewis District Trust, actually anticipated a surplus of revenue. They intended to invest any such profits

> in developments on or in connection with the Trust estate calculated to promote the material and social welfare of the community; in improving means of communication with the island by land, sea or air; in afforesting certain portions of the estate; in encouraging higher education by the provision of bursaries to enable deserving scholars to proceed to secondary schools and universities; in improving the medical service of the community by assisting in the employment of medical practitioners, nurses, and for the building and equipping of hospitals or dispensaries; in the improvement or construction of roads and bridges.

An interesting restriction had been written by Leverhulme into the trust deeds applying to Lews Castle. Sir James Matheson's towering symbol of ownership should 'never be let as a hotel or club, nor as a private residence for a tenant of sporting rights.' It would become in due course a Technical College, which would carry the name of the building – if not the building itself – into the twenty-first century.

The Trust would be composed of ten members. Five of them would be ex officio: the Provost, two magistrates and two senior town councillors. The other five would be elected to represent 'those holding lands within the trust area in their own right on tenure, or who appear in the Valuation Roll as paying rent for subjects within the said area in their own rights'. This enfranchised the crofters. On Thursday 28 February 1924, the Stornoway Trust, the first substantial community-owned estate in the Highlands and Islands of Scotland, held its inaugural elections. Polling took place briskly in Stornoway itself at the Nicolson Institute and the Drill Hall, and at schools and other public buildings at Tolsta, Back, Aird and Bayble in Point. The Stornoway doctor J.P. Tolmie won most votes. He would be accompanied onto the Trust by Mr J. McRitchie Morrison of Stornoway, the Stornoway shipping agent and councillor Murdo Maclean, Norman Mackenzie of Bayble and councillor Angus Smith of Holm.

In October 1923 the local Nursing Committee at Ness re-formed itself into an Emergency Relief Committee. The headmaster of Lionel School grew so concerned by the malnourished condition of his pupils that he issued a public appeal for funds to provide them with a midday meal. Sir William Mitchell Cotts MP appealed unsuccessfully to Lord Novar to resume the Ness to Tolsta road works which had been abandoned by Leverhulme. Almost a full year of preternaturally wet weather resulted in the failure of the potato crop throughout the Hebrides and the west mainland. In Lewis itself only a handful of days in May, June, July and August had been completely dry, just one day in September had seen no rain, and in the whole of October and November there was 'not recorded one single instance of twenty-four consecutive hours dry'. Peats and corn had been too wet to harvest properly. Cut hay lay blackening on the ground. Severe equinoctial storms blew down the few stooks of fodder and wiped out most surviving crops in certain west coast districts such as Callanish. The fishing industry remained in deep depression. Clothing and food parcels were distributed throughout the islands by charitable organisations and Highland societies. People said that matters had never been worse since the Hungry Forties of eighty years before.

The fishing township of Cromore in Lochs was reported late in 1923 to be in a condition of 'destitution . . . there is no place, even in Lewis, where things could be worse'. A meeting at Back Free Church warned of 'starvation in many homes. The people have nothing to fall back upon owing to the failure of the fishing industry, the complete failure of the potato crop, and the lack of work of any kind.'

At Westminster in the new year of 1924 the freshly elected radical Liberal MP for the Western Isles Alexander MacKenzie Livingstone pleaded urgently but in vain for a Commission to be appointed to investigate 'the exceptional economic conditions prevailing in the Western Isles'. The first Labour Scottish Secretary, William Adamson, who took office following the December 1923 General Election, acknowledged the 'exceptional distress in Lewis this winter' and announced that the government would be supplying the Highlands and Islands 'at a reduced cost [with] seed oats and seed potatoes for use this spring'.

Across the other Hebrides land raiding resumed. In Lewis a

generation continued to emigrate. On Saturday 26 April 1924, the Canadian Pacific Railways liner *Marloch* put into Stornoway and carried away with her to the New World 290 young Lewis men and women. Most of them travelled on the government of Ontario's Assisted Passages Scheme. The men were bonded to become farm labourers until they had repaid the debts of their passage; the women to be domestic servants. They left amid the precedented noise and bustle of southern reporters, pipers, prayers and weeping relatives. 'A greater number,' opined the *Stornoway Gazette*, 'will certainly follow.'

9

THE REQUIEM

The proprietor had attempted to leave that sorrow behind. He would return like Banquo's ghost just one more time to Lewis.

Leverhulme planned at the end of 1923 to winter in Australia, but before doing so he made a well-semaphored further visit to the Hebrides. On the afternoon of Thursday 25 October 1923, he arrived by train at Kyle of Lochalsh. He stayed overnight at the railhead, and at 6.00 a.m. on Friday morning he boarded the SS *Plover*, which made straight for Tarbert, Harris.

As the *Plover* entered the long sea roads of Kyles Scalpay rockets were sent up into the sky from the surrounding shores. When she approached the pier at Tarbert flags were seen to be waving and a crowd was cheering. As the small ship berthed more rockets were despatched from the Tarbert waterfront and from her own decks. A piper played gaily at the harbourside, and the little old man was escorted to his car beneath a banner which read: 'Ceud Mile Failte do Viscount Leverhulme'.

The local steamboat agent John Mackenzie, who would be dubbed 'the Tarbert Demosthenes', then put in a deliciously composed public plea for North Harris. They had waited too long, he said, to offer such a greeting to their landlord. They had watched with interest his proposals for South Harris. Now, surely, it was their turn:

> Robust Calvinists that we are, we cannot help believing that in these dark and cloudy days when unemployment with its attendant evils, hardships and distress, roams rampant throughout the length and breadth of the land, and when we ourselves are faced this winter with a situation – created by the failure of the sea and land harvests and other causes outwith our control – such as the oldest among us never encountered the like of before, we say, we cannot but believe that Providence has so ordered it that we should have as our laird one who has brains, heart, and wealth, and further we have cause to raise our Ebenezer to that kind and benevolent Provi-

dence that these three powerful attributes for good are, as they happen to be in your Lordship's case, beautifully blended and actively engaged for the material welfare and comfort of your tenantry.

That remarkable sentence won, as well it might, a round of applause on the Tarbert harbourside. Leverhulme thanked the gathering for their memorable greeting, assured them that given ten years' grace he could transform their island, and warned them sternly not only against taking part in land raiding, but also against letting anybody else do any land raiding ('I would take that as a sign that you were not sufficiently interested in my schemes to justify my staying in Harris'). Just before getting into his car he remembered exactly where he was. 'My developments at Leverburgh do not mean that I am going to neglect Tarbert,' he said hurriedly, to another round of applause. He asked them to have faith, and was driven away to Borve with a chorus of 'For He's A Jolly Good Fellow' ringing in the wake of his exhaust.

He returned from the Southern Ocean in May of 1924, this time anticipating a later vehicular ferry service by driving to Uig in the north-west of Skye and having one of his own steam drifters carry him from there to Harris. He examined the slow but steady progress at Obbe/Leverburgh, where a concrete pier and wooden wharf had been completed, two lights had been put up in the Sound of Harris, a coaling hulk moored offshore, twelve drift-netters were almost ready to go, and a posse of fashionably dressed young female office workers imported from the south were of absorbing interest to the community.

Tarbert began to get restless. After a week of glancing fruitlessly down the southern road the village was relieved to see Viscount Leverhulme arrive to open their new Recreation Hall, which he had subsidised. Once more there were rockets, and John MacKenzie once more assured him of the fealty of the people of Harris. Leverhulme once more replied in vaguely disconcerting terms, by praising the immense potential of the fishing parish of Leverburgh and barely mentioning North Harris.

He did, however, agree to meet half of the costs of the Scalpay and Scarp roads. Until 1924 the westerly route ended at Amhuinnsuidhe Castle. The isolated township of Huisinish and small inhabited island of Scarp, six miles to the west, were consequently isolated. There was no passable road east from Tarbert to Kyles Scalpay, leaving that island similarly cut off. Leverhulme helped to finance the extra lifeline stretches of tarmacadam which would connect them to the rest of Harris. This delivered to him another extraordinary example of Hebridean courtesy. On a morning in June 1924 the 82-year-old Angus MacInnes left his home in Scarp, took a boat to the Harris mainland and then walked over 20 miles to Tarbert. He was waiting at the door of what had become known as the Leverhulme Recreation Hall when the viscount and his party arrived for a meeting. The old man jumped the queue of dignitaries and launched into an exposition – in English, the quality of which impressed Lord Leverhulme – of the difficulties of life in Scarp without a road. His proprietor was much affected, and wished Angus MacInnes a safe walk back to Scarp.

He returned for a third time at the end of August 1924, to open the annual sale of work of the Tarbert Branch of the Women's Rural Institute, and afterwards to attend to graver matters further north.

A year had passed since his eve-of-birthday address in 1923, when he had proposed to give his bigger island to its people. He had tidied up some affairs and left the castle in October, never since returning. But in September 1924, on the cusp of his seventy-third birthday, he was still the proprietor of Lewis, and the proprietor of Lewis must attend the unveiling of the island's war memorial.

This striking 85-foot high cenotaph had been, of course, funded by Lord Leverhulme. It was erected atop a small green hill to the west of Stornoway, so situated that from its summit could be seen portions of every parish in Lewis.

He was due to preside over its inauguration on Friday 5 September 1924. His final appearance and his final speech in Lewis would be in memoriam of the blasted hopes of a generation, at a service which united the entire community in stoical sadness. On the morning of that Friday Stornoway once more asserted itself as the natural capital of a great island. As they had done so many times before for so many different reasons, people from the country districts poured into its grey streets from north and west and south and east, not this time carrying placards, red flags, or luggage to stow in an emigrant ship, but plainly dressed, soberly mannered, and finding their eyes constantly drawn up and out of town towards the monument above the road to Marybank.

In the early afternoon a long procession wound its way up that road from the town to the memorial hill. The Girl Guides led the Seaforth's Pipe Band, who were followed by a detachment of soldiers from Fort George on the east coast of the mainland. Then came the Sea Cadets with their pipe band, a guard of honour from the Royal Navy, and the innumerable ex-servicemen of Lewis, their honours from the war attached to their civilian clothes and glittering in the bright sunlight.

Among them all, scattered here and there on the fringes of this slow and purposeful procession, small groups of dignitaries made their way towards the hill. Three chairs were laid out beneath the memorial. Lord Leverhulme took the central seat, with the Provost of Stornoway Kenneth Mackenzie on one side and the chairman of the Lewis District Committee, Murdo Maclean, on the other. Councillors, ministers, businessmen and other worthies were assigned their lesser places on the pantheon, and the great mass of the general public covered every square foot of ground on the crest and spilling down the sides of the mound.

Reverend Kenneth Cameron of Stornoway Free Church led them in a Gaelic prayer, and Reverend Murdo Macleod of Uig Free Church read from the Book of Joshua ('and these stones shall be for a memorial unto the children of Israel for ever').

Viscount Leverhulme spoke with so strong a voice in the sunlit silence that 'even those on the outskirts of the crowd were able to follow clearly'.

> These outer islands, of which the Lews is the largest and most populous, provided a greater number of volunteers for service, from the very instant of the firing of the first gun in the Great War, in proportion to population, than any other part of His Majesty's Empire . . . the men and women of these islands have proved for all time to be like strength of oak and granite rock, to withstand all attacks of storm and stress, and to resist without flinching all assaults of man.
>
> And the people of these islands have accomplished this in spite of the fact that no people so dearly love or are so deeply attached to peace and the arts of peace and to their beloved native island. Lewis men love their home, their wife, their children with a passionate ardour that few can realise who have not lived in these wind- and storm-swept isles . . .

The author of the celebrated Canadian Boat Song, he said, must surely have been a Lewisman –

> From the lone sheiling of the misty island
> Mountains divide us, and the waste of seas,
> Yet still the blood is strong, the heart is Highland,
> And we in dreams behold the Hebrides.

He turned to the ex-servicemen who stood bare-headed and proud around him, whose comrades' desperation for housing and an acre of land had supposedly undermined his work in Lewis.

> You have returned from the War demobilised but not demoralised. You and we all must live our lives bravely and worthily of the sacrifice the dead heroes have made and set ourselves to perform our task . . . Farewell, brave dead! . . . With parting words we pray that your brave lives and noble deeds may for ever endure fresh and fragrant in the memories and lives of all living and of countless generations yet unborn.

The memorial was then unveiled by two west coast veterans: Seaman Donald Macleay of Upper Shader in the parish of Barvas, who had lost his right leg and his right arm in the second month of the war, and Corporal Donald MacGregor of Tolsta-Chaolais, who had been been severely wounded at Beaumont Hamel on the Western Front in July 1916.

They withdrew the white and red ensigns which covered the entrance door and the inscriptions whose dates acknowledged the wreck of the *Iolaire* – 'Chum gloir Dhe agus mar chuimhneachan air muinntir Leodhas a thig am bhatha seaghad anns a Chogaidh Mhor. 1914–1919.' 'To the glory of God and in memory of the Lewismen who gave their lives in the Great War. 1914 – 1919.'

Leverhulme was thanked by Provost Mackenzie. He replied solemnly, perhaps tiredly, that the invitation had been all the thanks needed. 'Although I am not today as closely connected with Stornoway and Lewis as I was twelve months ago, my heart is in that Canadian Boat Song.'

The pipers played 'Lochaber No More', the National Anthem was sung, and the gathering dispersed. A fitting sense of humility may be discerned in that valediction. Viscount Leverhulme left Lewis for the final time a sad and somewhat lonely figure. A story which may or may not be apochryphal, but which is certainly credible, was later told of him passing time before the *Sheila* left that night for Kyle of Lochalsh. He walked in the dark to the half-dismantled factory on the waterfront and looked emptily at the building which had been intended to provide a million Mrs Mary Smiths somewhere in southern Britain with 'the best canned fish in the world'. His companion stood slightly behind him, and 'suddenly saw the outline of the great shoulders trembling with sobs'.[58] They then walked silently back to the mailboat and shook hands at the gangway. Leverhulme never again set foot in Lewis or Harris.

He would spend the winter of 1924 and 1925 in the Congo, making regretful comparisons between the signs of progress at Leverville in Africa and his comparative difficulties at Leverburgh in the Hebrides. He returned to England in the middle of March and made plans to visit Harris for a fortnight on 11 May. In the last week of April he went down with a chill which developed into pneumonia. He died at his Hampstead home in the early hours of the morning of Thursday 7 May 1925. On 11 May, instead of crossing the Minch to Borve Lodge, William Hesketh Viscount Leverhulme of the Western Isles was laid to rest beside his wife at Port Sunlight.

The union flags which flew over Lews Castle and Leverhulme Hall were lowered to half mast on 7 May, giving many in Stornoway and Tarbert their 'first intimation of the sad intelligence'. On the Monday of the funeral all shops were closed in Lewis and Harris. Shortly after midday the Nicolson Institute sent its students home, and the Lewis Pipe Band paraded on the terrace before the castle playing the laments 'Lochaber No More', 'The Flowers of the Forest' and 'Cumha nam Marbh'.

Stornoway's United Free English Church hosted a joint religious service. Reverend Donald John Macinnes told the congregation:

> Our chief interest in Lord Leverhulme is the connection he had of late years with ourselves as proprietor of the Long Island. His schemes and ideals for Lewis miscarried, and there may be differences of opinion as to the causes of failure. A man of his career and experience would be more than human if he did not sometimes want his own way and a free hand; but no one can imagine that he had selfish ends in view. He was genuinely anxious to do the best he could for the people. There is no reason to doubt the sincerity of his words when he said that he loved the Lewis people.

Leverhulme had made no provision whatsoever for the future of his substantial holdings in Harris and Lewis in the event of his death. There was to be no bequested body devoted to the care of the islands and the continuance of what developments had survived. On the contrary, he had signed an agreement with Lever Brothers which absolved them of any responsibilities in the Hebrides. As part of his estate they would be inherited by his son, the second Viscount Leverhulme, who, as his father knew, had no affection for them.

Lever Brothers and the new Viscount Leverhulme instantly pulled the plug on Lewis and Harris. All developments at Obbe/Leverburgh were halted and all employees were given a week's notice. The new chairman and board pounced with almost indecent haste upon their opportunity to consolidate their real assets. As the old man himself had foreseen, the time for the company to relax and cease from adventurous enterprise arrived with his death.

Lewis and Harris were sold off piecemeal over the next few years, successfully this time, for Knight Frank and Rutley were under instructions to consider even the most negligible offer. The port installations at Obbe/Leverburgh were bought and scrapped by a demolition company. The crofting estate of South Harris was sold for £900. Amhuinnsuidhe Castle, the Harris Hotel, 6,000 acres and all the policies of North Harris went for £2,000. The country areas of Lewis became a jigsaw of privately owned sporting and crofting fiefdoms, each answerable to a different laird and each subject to the whims of the open market.

Both Colin Macdonald of the Board of Agriculture and the travelling doctor Halliday Sutherland returned to Harris in the years after Leverhulme's death. 'Leverburgh never attained the status of a town,' Macdonald would observe. 'Just a score or so of houses and some scars on the moor (now healed by kindly time and vegetation) where streets and buildings were meant to be. And the pier – that imposing structure of piles and planks that seemed to cover acres. Three years ago, when I landed there off a motor boat from Berneray the piles were rotting and the planks sagging to such an extent that we were glad to get off them onto firm land.'[59]

'At Obbe,' reported Sutherland in the 1930s, 'there is now no industry, some of the houses built by Leverhulme have been bought by retired officials, others are occupied by squatters, and one of the half-built villas is used as a cow byre by a crofter living in a black house.'[60]

'Those who believe,' a later chronicler would conclude, 'that Lewis would have been transformed if Leverhulme had been left alone to get on with his plans, have not looked at Harris.'[61]

By the time that Sutherland and Macdonald wrote those words the demands of those who wished for crofts in Lewis and Harris were beginning to be met. The Board of Agriculture requisitioned several sporting estates on the west coast of Lewis and in South Harris, and brought them into the Crofters Act. In the early 1930s the Anglo–Irish poet Louis MacNeice travelled the Hebrides from Barra to Lewis. ('You seem to have a mania for going north,' rebuked his infamous friend, Anthony Blunt.) He was subsequently provoked to write a lengthy piece of doggerel about Lord Leverhulme's Hebridean escapade.

> I'd hand them happiness on a plate,
> If only the fools would co-operate . . .
> But blind with Celtic mist and phlegm
> They cannot see what is good for them.

All that remained at Lever's death, the poet decided, 'Was a waste of money and a waste of breath:

> Far below in the Western Seas
> The moors were quiet in the Hebrides,
> The crofters gossiped in Gaelic speech
> And the waves crept over the lonely beach.[62]

Louis MacNeice drew and publicised his conclusion – which was actually little more than an idle common prejudice left undisturbed by his brief visit – that nothing had altered in the islands because its inhabitants were dogmatically averse to change. His journey through Harris had taken him up the west coast, past Borve Lodge and the great sands of Scarista. He noted there with amusement young bare-foot children running out of ramshackle houses to wave at his passage.

MacNeice was incapable of noting that just fifteen years earlier such a sight would have been impossible, for between Luskentyre and Northton there had been no houses other than the estate lodge, and no children other than those on holiday with the proprietor. The Board of Agriculture first settled families from the east coast onto the machair at Scaristavore in 1928. Following insistent raiding it repeated the process at neighbouring Scaristabeg and further north at Luskentyre, and eventually at Borve itself. It was to the thankful incoming families from Bays not so much an emigration as a retrieval. They were returning home.

There is an attraction in Ozymandian monuments. The half-hearted industrial shells at Obbe/Leverburgh and the abandoned whaling station at Bunavoneader in North Harris stand as some kind of requiem in stone to Leverhulme's vain ambitions for the northern Hebrides. But so in all justice, whether he intended it or not, does the continued benevolent presence of the Stornoway Trust as a Sargasso of calm and accountability in the forbidding and unstable ocean of private Highland estates.

The people who welcomed him with caustic eyes, who greeted his good ideas and opposed his foolishness, knew exactly what they wanted to leave behind. The well-populated crofting townships which swarm over the landscape from Tong to Coll to Back to Gress and Tolsta became home, throughout the twentieth century and into the third millennium, to a huge proportion of the population of Lewis. The clusters of white crofthouses on the greensward now harbour inscribed plaques and sculptures which pay tribute to the land raiders who came back from the First World War. They are modest remembrances of the fathers of these enduring townships, but they are more than was ever anticipated. Such people neither wished nor expected their ambitions to be eulogised in stone. The ex-servicemen, as Lord Leverhulme acknowledged in his final address to the people of Lewis, were looking for no testimonial and had in prospect no reward other than this: the security of their children's children at peace on the soil of their island.

NOTES

1   *The History of Unilever*, Vol I, Charles Wilson

2   ibid

3   ibid

4   *The Second Disruption*, James Lachlan Macleod

5   ibid

6   *My Life*, Angus Watson

7   *Tales and Traditions of the Lews*, Donald MacDonald

8   *Men of Stress*, Dr Harley Williams

9   *The History of Unilever*, Vol I, Charles Wilson

10 *Lord Leverhulme*, W.P. Jolly

11 *Land For The People?*, Ewen A. Cameron

12 ibid

13 *The Crofters' War*, I.M.M. MacPhail

14 *Land For The People?*, Ewen A. Cameron

15 *Around the Peat-fire*, Calum Smith

16 *Lewis – A History of the Island*, Donald Macdonald

17 *Twenty Years of Hebridean Memories*, Emily MacDonald

18 *The Western Isles*, A.A. MacGregor

19 *Twenty Years of Hebridean Memories*, Emily Macdonald

20 *Viscount Leverhulme*, William Hulme Lever (the first Viscount Leverhulme's son)

21 ibid

22 *Around the Peat-fire*, Calum Smith

23 *Call na h-Iolaire*, Tormod Calum Domhnallach

24 ibid

25 Donald MacPhail recorded by BBC Radio in 1959

26 *Around the Peat-fire*, Calum Smith

27 *Highland Journey*, Colin Macdonald

28 *Land for the People?*, Ewen A. Cameron

29   *The History of Unilever,* Vol I, Charles Wilson

30   *Highland Journey,* Colin Macdonald

31   *The Lewis Land Struggle,* Joni Buchanan

32   *Highland Journey,* Colin Macdonald

33   *Fit For Heroes,* Leah Leneman

34   *Lord of the Isles,* Nigel Nicolson

35   *Twenty Years of Hebridean Memories,* Emily Macdonald

36   *A History of Lodge Fortrose No. 108 Stornoway,* George Clavey

37   *The Making of the Crofting Community,* James Hunter

38   *Arches of the Years,* Halliday Sutherland

39   *The Isle of Lewis and Harris,* Arthur Geddes

40   *I Crossed the Minch,* Louis MacNeice

41   *The Sea Fisheries of Scotland,* James R. Coull

42   *The History of Unilever,* Vol 1, Charles Wilson

43   ibid

44   ibid

45   *Highland Memories,* Colin MacDonald

46   *The Lewis Land Struggle,* Joni Buchanan

47   ibid

48   *Arches of the Years,* Halliday Sutherland

49   *Twenty Years of Hebridean Memories,* Emily Macdonald

50   *Land for the People?,* Ewen A. Cameron

51   *Transactions of the Gaelic Society of Inverness,* 1923

52   *Lord Leverhulme,* W.P. Jolly

53   *Transactions of the Gaelic Society of Inverness,* 1923

54   *Around the Peat-fire,* Calum Smith

55   *Metagama,* Jim Wilkie

56   *Men of Stress,* Dr Harley Williams

57   *Lord of the Isles,* Nigel Nicolson

58   ibid

59   *Highland Memories,* Colin Macdonald

60   *Hebridean Journey,* Halliday Sutherland

61   *Fit For Heroes?,* Leah Leneman

62   *I Crossed the Minch,* Louis MacNeice

BIBLIOGRAPHY

Buchanan, Joni, *The Lewis Land Struggle* (1996)

Cameron, A.D., *Go Listen to the Crofters* (1986)

Cameron, Ewen A., *Land for the People?* (1996)

Cooper, Derek, *The Road to Mingulay* (1985)

Coull, James R., *The Sea Fisheries of Scotland* (1996)

Darling, Frank Fraser, *West Highland Survey* (1955)

Domhnallach, Tormod Calum, *Call na h-Iolaire* (1978)

Gaelic Society of Inverness, *Proceedings, 1923* (1927)

Geddes, Arthur, *The Isle of Lewis and Harris* (1955)

Grant, James Shaw, *Stornoway and The Lews* (1985)

Harman, Mary, *An Isle Called Hirte* (1997)

Hunter, James, *The Making of the Crofting Community* (1976)

Jolly, W.P., *Lord Leverhulme* (1976)

Leneman, Leah, *Fit For Heroes?* (1989)

Leverhulme, 2nd Viscount, *Lord Leverhulme* (1927)

MacDonald, Colin, *Highland Journey* (1943)

MacDonald, Colin, *Highland Memories* (1949)

Macdonald, Donald, *Lewis, A History of the Island* (1978)

Macdonald, Donald, *Tales and Traditions of the Lews* (1967)

Macdonald, Emily, *Twenty Years of Hebridean Memories* (1939)

MacGregor, Alasdair Alpin, *The Western Isles* (1949)

MacKenzie, W.C., *History of the Outer Hebrides* (1903)

MacKenzie, W.C., *The Book of the Lews* (1919)

MacLeod, James Lachlan, *The Second Disruption* (2000)

MacNeice, Louis, *I Crossed The Minch* (1938)

MacPhail, I.M.M., *The Crofters' War* (1989)

Milne, Sir David, *The Scottish Office* (1957)

Morris, Edward (ed.), *The Making of the Lady Lever Art Gallery* (1992)

Nicolson, Nigel, *Lord of the Isles* (1960)

Pakenham, Thomas, *The Scramble for Africa* (1991)

Smith, Calum, *Around the Peat-fire* (2001)

Sutherland, Halliday, *Hebridean Journey* (1939)

Sutherland, Halliday, *The Arches of the Years* (1933)

Thomas, John, *The Skye Railway* (1977)

Watson, Angus, *My Life* (1937)

Wilkie, Jim, *Metagama* (1987)

Williams, Harley, *Men of Stress* (1948)

Wilson, Charles, *The History of Unilever*, Volume 1 (1954)

The author would also like to acknowledge the help given by the archives of various periodicals. William Grant's *Stornoway Gazette* arrived in Lewis shortly before Lord Leverhulme, and was an enthusiastic chronicler of his activities. The *West Highland Free Press* appeared a little later, but has been anxious to recover lost ground.

The *Invergordon Times*, *The Scotsman*, *The Manchester Guardian* and *The Glasgow Herald* also offered useful and various insights into postbellum Lewis.

INDEX